OCTOGENARIAN ODYSSEY

TRADING THE SOFA FOR A BICYCLE SEAT

Robert D. Fletcher

Author's Tranquility Press
ATLANTA, GEORGIA

The photos in this book were taken by: Kim Voogsgeed, Kyle Walker, Wayne Grover,
Janet Guthrie, Panagiota Georgakopoulou and Robert Fletcher.

Robert D. Fletcher/Author's Tranquility Press
3800 Camp Creek Pkwy SW Bldg. 1400-116 #1255
Atlanta, GA 30331, USA
www.authorstranquilitypress.com

Publisher's Note: This is non-fiction.

Ordering Information:
Quantity sales. Special discounts are available on quantity purchases by corporations,
associations, and others. For details, contact the "Special Sales Department" at the address above.

Octogenarian Odyssey/Robert D. Fletcher
eBook: 978-1-961908-15-4
Paperback: 978-1-961908-14-7
Hardback: 978-1-961908-13-0

"As we grow older, we experience an increasing number of major life changes, including career transitions and retirement, children leaving home, the loss of loved ones, physical and health challenges...

Robert D. Fletcher *depicts to readers because choosing to be active physically is the KEY to aging successfully and being resilient. He shares his story of high performance and vitality while living a life boosting longevity into his retirement.*

*Bob Fletcher has written this **must read** record-breaking Octodyssey and inspires all of us to be physically active daily and remembering age is only just a number!"*

Donna L. McLean MN ANP PhD
Alberta Health Services, Edmonton, Alberta Canada

_____

"Bob Fletcher has written a must-read chronicle for everyone who's ever had a dream and put off the doing of it for 'someday' ...Read this book and be inspired by an ordinary guy living his dream every day, not someday."

Cindy Schwedler
Two-time Woman Masters World Champion in Cyclocross

_____

"Mr. Fletcher is proof that your age is just a number on your driver's license and that an adventure is always waiting for you to say yes to."

Lori-Ann Muenzer
Canada's 1st Olympic Cycling Gold Medalist

_____

"Bob Fletcher's book will inspire readers to 'go for it', especially those reaching age milestones with implied societal limitations. He's an ongoing inspiration to his friends to tackle new pursuits and get out of our comfort zones. When walking the Camino together 10 years ago, Bob's goal was a 'triple-crown' annually (i.e., three new activities/year). He's achieved as much and more!"

June MacGregor
President, Edmonton Bicycle and Touring Club.

"Robert Fletcher is a self-described ordinary guy, but he has an extraordinary quality. He thinks of a challenge, then does it! This book describes not only his extraordinary journey of cycling through 9 countries, 14, 000 km, and setting a Guinness Record at the age of 80 in the process, but also his amazing life and mindset! You may not want to take up long distance cycling after reading this, but I guarantee you'll be inspired to think of your own extraordinary journey. No matter what you choose to do, Robert Fletcher will be encouraging you the entire way."

Greg Pommen
Author of 'Lessons of our Legends'

"Robert's book is a true treasure trove of captivating stories. His unwavering perseverance serves as an uplifting inspiration, reminding us that age is no barrier to achieving our dreams. Through his remarkable journey, he motivates us to keep pushing forward, embracing challenges, and setting new goals. This book beautifully illustrates how life's twists and turns can make it all the more fascinating. Moreover, Robert's story demonstrates the transformative power of

immense pain, showing us how it can be harnessed into an
incredible source of strength. As he breaks a world record, he
becomes a shining example of human resilience and
determination."

Elizabeth Williams
Ambassador of Canada to Costa Rica, Honduras and
Nicaragua

DEDICATION

I dedicate this book to my friend, John Burdett. John is a lifelong cyclist, having cycled in many countries, and is an avid antique bicycle collector. Though he loves antique bikes, he also rides an e-bike as I did on this journey. We met way back when we both belonged to the same cycling club and now, we're both members of The Royal Academy of Octogenarian Cyclists. However, most importantly, John believed in me and supported me throughout my Octogenarian Odyssey. Thank you, John, for your support and encouragement.

***

I also dedicate my ride, and this book, to all the seniors out there. It's time to get up off the couch and find what makes you happy. Live life to the fullest without fear and self-doubt.

***

Lastly, this book is dedicated to Matt. Matt and his wife, Ariane, were fellow long-distance cycling enthusiasts. The two joined us at the starting line in North Pole, Alaska. They rode with us for about the first thirty kilometers or so, and Matt signed the official statement for the Guinness Book of World Records. I only knew him for a few hours, but I instantly liked him, and I could tell the two were a happy young couple.

Unfortunately, we lost Matt during my Octogenarian Odyssey. He was hit by a passenger truck while riding his bike to work. This was something he had done for over twenty years. His will to live was so strong, he recovered faster than doctors predicted and was due to come home or move to a rehabilitation facility in just weeks—and was even climbing stairs with assistance—when a pulmonary embolism took him from us. Matt survived thirty-seven days before passing.

Ariane has vowed to honor Matt by fighting for safer biking in Alaska.

Oddly when we talk about the dangers of long-distance cycling in foreign countries, we generally only discuss cartels and bears and hurricanes when the real danger is the vehicles, we share the road with. The trucks and cars whiz by us. It's incredibly dangerous riding in thick traffic in the cities, with most drivers in a hurry, not paying attention, or distracted. So many times, have I thought, "My back wheel is in front of your front car tire, so back off, mate." Matt's passing was a loud reminder that I too could go at any time from a driver texting or not seeing me because my taillight wasn't fully charged. Cycling is freeing, cathartic, and safe, but you must take responsibility for your safety and that of others.

Should anyone have any doubts about whether you should get up off that comfy couch, take this lesson to heart and use it as the motivation you need. Life is short. How much time do you have left to do the things you've always wanted to do?

Canada
United States
Los Angeles
Mexico
Mexico City
Cuba
6H5
Col

Contents

FOREWORD

Pedaling to the edge of the map! Some explorers set their compass toward the horizon. The edge of the earth pulls them with some kind of mystical calling. They don't know what's out there, and yet, every cell in their body tells them to move. toward the edge of the planet.

Charles Lindbergh flew toward it. Amelia Earhart winged her way across the sky toward it. John Muir walked toward it. Tori Murden McClure rowed across the Atlantic Ocean toward it.

What is "it"? At the age of eighty and after decades of adventuring around this planet, Robert D. Fletcher rode his e-bicycle from Alaska to Panama, some 13,500 km. That's grinding up mountain passes. That's sweating through heat, cold, and rainstorms. Something inside him needed to express his guts, gumption, and creativity. He'd already climbed Kilimanjaro at 19,340 feet. He'd visited a hundred countries. He'd hiked the Caminos de Santiago. He'd pedaled from Quebec City, Canada, to New Orleans, America. And he'd accomplished so much, much more than that! There is something extremely uncommon about this man, though he would tell you that isn't so.

For all those accolades and so many more I don't even know about, I consider Robert D. Fletcher an uncommon person in this world. The vignette below describes his exemplary life path.

***

Dean Alfange (1899–1989) expresses best the character of an uncommon person:

I do not choose to be a common man [or woman]. It is my right to be uncommon—if I can. I seek opportunity—not security. I do not wish to be a kept citizen, humbled and dulled by having the state look after me. I want to take calculated risks, to dream and to build, to fail and to succeed. I refuse to barter incentive for a dole. I prefer the challenges of life to the guaranteed existence, the thrill of fulfillment to the stale calm of utopia. I will not trade freedom for beneficence nor my dignity for a handout. I will never cower before any master nor bend to any threat. It is my heritage to stand erect, proud, and unafraid; to think and act for myself, enjoy the benefit of my creations, and to face the world boldly and say, 'This I have done.'

So, what is this thing called "adventure" that Robert D. Fletcher seeks? Can one person define it? Does a woman see it differently than a man? Does a backpacker, canoeist, mountaineering skier, or surfer see it in different terms? That's for everyone to decide.

For long-distance touring cyclists, the spirit of adventure that Robert D. Fletcher seeks might be summed up in these words:

If the roar of a wave crashes beyond your campsite, you might call that an adventure. When coyotes howl outside your tent, that may be an adventure. While you're sweating like a horse on a climb over a 12,000-foot pass, that may be an adventure. When a howling headwind presses your lips against your teeth, you may be facing a mighty adventure. If you're pushing through a raging rainstorm, you may be drenched in adventure. But that's not what truly makes an adventure. It's your willingness to struggle through it, to present yourself at the doorstep of nature. That creates the experience. No greater joy can come from life than to live inside the moment of an adventure. It may be a momentary high, a stranger that changes your life, an animal that delights you or frightens you, a struggle where you triumphed—or even failed—yet you braved the challenge. But it's those moments that present you with uncommon experiences that give your life eternal expectation. That's adventure! —FHW

What you will read in this book will take you on an adventure. His story encompasses animals, people, places, events, countries, cultures, and living a spectacular life. Mr. Fletcher's prose may encourage you, excite you, and even inspire you. Whatever your mode of exploration, this book will engage you and courage you to journey toward your own adventures. Live them well! Set your destination toward the edge of the map, all the way to eighty and beyond!

Six-continent bicycle traveler,

Frosty Wooldridge

Golden, CO
Population/Immigration/Environmental Specialist
Speaker at colleges, civic clubs, high schools, and conferences
Facebook: Frosty Wooldridge
Facebook Adventure Page: How to Live a Life of Adventure: The Art of Exploring the World
www.HowToLiveALifeOfAdventure.com/www.frostywooldridge.com
Adventure book: How to Live a Life of Adventure: The Art of Exploring the World

Me and Frosty

ACKNOWLEDGMENTS

Before moving into the thick of my story, I want to take a moment to extend my heartfelt thanks to my phenomenal support team, without whom the Octogenarian Odyssey would not have been possible. Through the memorable days and the hard, through the freezing cold and the searing heat, through the wind and the rain and the mud and the muck, they were there. They kept the van running, they bought the food and cooked the food, and they found us places to lay our heads. Most of all, they got me to Panama safe and sound and in one piece.

When the weather was so miserable, I'd start questioning why I was continuing my journey, they'd make me laugh or point out a unique sight—like a moose or an elaborately decorated Tuk-Tuk, that would bring me back again. They kept me motivated and shared my love of life. Those guys live life to the fullest and are living, breathing examples of my philosophy and message. So, thank you, Kim Voorsgeerd, Yiota Georgakopoulou, Kyle Walker, and Johana Pineda. You made the odyssey what it was.

I also want to thank my cycling partner, Wayne Grover, for sticking with me nearly the whole long, long way. It was a hard ride sometimes, but he soldiered through it, motivating me to push through it when I needed it most. Thank you, Wayne, for being the official day-to-day photographer and recorder for our daily Facebook posts and for forcing me off my comfortable straight-and-narrow agenda at times so we could visit other towns and see new and unplanned sights. You even put your life on the line at times, all to see my journey through with me. You've been an incredible riding partner over the years, and I look forward to our next adventure.

And I could never forget the importance of my wife, Gloria, who graciously understands my need to explore the world, supports me through it all, and always says, "Sure, you go follow your dreams." Thank you, my dear Gloria.

Nor can I neglect to mention the importance of the support of my daughter, Janet, her husband, Peter, and my granddaughter, Annika. For years, they've been encouraging me to get off the sofa and carry out my adventures. It's tremendously motivating to know that those I love the most understand my message and my need to explore.

This book would not have been possible without the outstanding work done by Ms. Bobbi Beatty of Silver Scroll Services. She took all my material and transformed it into this book. Thank you so much Bobbi.

Finally, I want to share my gratitude for those folks who donated to the Panamanian children's bike fund. We changed many children's lives with those bikes, and I hope we set a positive example that they'll keep with them throughout their lives and on their own journeys. Thank you also to all my other sponsors and donors and folks who believed in me and encouraged me to go for it and to all my followers on Facebook and Instagram who followed me on my odyssey and supported me with their likes and positive comments. It meant a lot to me.

INTRODUCTION

I am not an extraordinary man. I am not an anomaly. I am not at all unusual. I am just an ordinary man who has lived an ordinary life.

I am, however, a true believer in living life to the fullest.

"But" you say, "you hopped on a bike and cycled from Alaska to Panama, and you're eighty years old! Surely that makes you extraordinary."

And I say again to you: I am not extraordinary. I am living my life to the fullest.

But then you say, "I could never do that."

To you I say, "So don't. Do what you love instead. Do something you've always wanted to do, however big or small."

That is the whole reason I did this. That is the whole reason I spent months planning and preparing. That is the whole reason I spent thousands of dollars and thousands of hours researching and planning. That is the whole reason I threw caution to the wind and jumped on my electric bike in North Pole, Alaska.

Now before you ask, "Who are you to tell me how to live my life?" I'll introduce myself. My name is Robert. Of course, with a name like Robert, I'm always being asked what people should call me. It doesn't matter much to me, so you can call me whatever you feel like calling me, depending on who you are. Some folks call me Robert, some folks call me Bob. Some call me Dad, and some call me Grandpa. Others still call me Uncle Boobie and even Mr. Wonderful as my granddaughter's friend decided to. Call me what you will do as long as you keep reading.

To me, living life to the fullest means doing what I love: touring the world on my bicycle. I love nothing more than exploring new territory, experiencing all of what nature has to offer, and encountering new people and new cultures—except maybe for staying active.

For you, doing what you love might mean planting a new garden, learning pickle ball, or writing that book you've always said you were going to write. Perhaps it means buying an RV or hopping on a plane and traveling the world. Or maybe it means taking that dance class you meant to take ten years ago or finally getting on stage and singing your heart out. Whatever it is, whatever your age, get off the couch and go do it. Why spend your life reading or watching stories about other people doing all the things you've always wanted to do?

As I sat on my own couch—for a short while—thinking about what it was I wanted to do for my upcoming eightieth birthday, I reflected on all the wonderful trips I'd taken with my wife, Beth, during our forty-eight spectacular years together and all the tours I'd undertaken since her death. We traveled the world together, her and I, sometimes on a bike, sometimes on foot because that was her preference. After I lost her, I eventually continued touring the world on my bike solo to honor her memory.

So, by the time I found myself sitting on that dreaded couch and trying to think of a birthday celebration that wasn't just the usual cake and presents and such, I'd already toured through Europe on a bike and ridden 10,400 km from Anchorage, Alaska, to Mexico City, Mexico, in 2015. I'd already become the second oldest person—at seventy-two—in that month to climb Mount Kilimanjaro, I'd already organized and led golf tours in Australia, and I'd already walked the entire 800 km of the French Camino de Santiago. I'd even run five marathons, completed three Olympic-sized triathlons, and bike-packed through southern England and France. What else was left to do? I didn't have a bucket list, per se, but I knew there was so much more to see and learn and do. I thought about exploring the countries of West Africa and riding a horse the length of the Portuguese Camino de Santiago since I'd already walked and cycled two of the other Caminos and the only other recognized way to achieve that is on horseback. Then I thought about doing something on the Amazon, but with COVID-19 to consider and the fact that I might have to eat monkeys and snakes, I quickly forgot about that idea. Yet my eightieth birthday was looming, and boy did I want to do something memorable, something with meaning. I wanted to do something to—literally—write home about.

Then, as I was sitting on that aforementioned loathsome couch, Ewan McGregor, and Charley Boorman's last TV series, *Long Way Up*, came on TV. It's a show about the trip the actors take on their electric motorcycles from the bottom of South America to Los Angeles, California. And that's when I knew.

I thought riding an e-bike from Fairbanks to Panama City would not only be a suitable feat, but also something that could test me. Riding an e-bike would require a little less exertion, thus my only concession to my age, and it would be both a new route and the longest trip I'd ever taken. And then I had another thought. Why not see if I couldn't make this trip really momentous and have my name live on? So, I contacted the Guinness Book of World Records, and lo and behold, they were interested. No one had as yet ridden as far as I planned to ride on an e-bike. And let me just say that while others might call this an "attempt" to break the world record, to me, this was no attempt. This was a fact. And while I learned later that there was a fellow named Gusto Stibranyi out there, riding long distance at seventy-two, it didn't appear he was trying to break any records. He was just riding, camping, and enjoying himself. Kudos to him though. He takes the first-to-do-it title, but I get to keep the oldest title.

But there was even more to my plan than that. This trip wasn't just about me and what I could achieve. I was tired of looking at my peers and watching them just fade away into nothingness. So, the true purpose of this trip materialized: to show a younger generation that life isn't over at sixty-five and to show those already older that they have so many options with which to fill those days no longer filled with work and kids and responsibilities. If I could convince just one senior citizen to get off the couch and get active or try something new, my trip would have been justified and my goal fulfilled. Creating a new world record is just icing on the cake.

And don't tell me you're too old to try something new or get physical now. I'm eighty years old and cycled from North Pole, Alaska, to Panama City, Panama, with a support team of just four people: Wayne Grover, my daily cycling partner; Yiota Georgakopoulou from Greece; Kyle Walker from the US; and my sister-in-law, Johana Pineda, originally from Colombia, who joined us at the US/Mexican border for the southern leg of the journey. Kim Voogsgeerd from Denmark supported us on the northern leg through the US and Canada. I'll admit, though, that I didn't undertake your typical bikepacking journey with all that sleeping on the side of the road or under a bridge or in a campground. I didn't rely on the hospitality of others night by night as many bike packers that belong to a fantastic group called Warm Showers do. They're a group of cyclists who offer other bike packers a roof; a bed; a meal; and as the name suggests, a hot shower for the night.

Again, I'm not extraordinary. I'm not in abnormally fantastic shape. It's just what I love to do and I'm not about to let fear or stereotypes get in my way.

Let me share my theme song with you. It's by Toby Keith and based on Clint Eastwood's answer when he was asked about how he can stay so busy as he ages. The song is called, *Don't Let the Old Man In,* and these are the lyrics:

Don't let the old man in.

I wanna leave this alone.

Can't leave it up to him.

He's knocking on my door.

And I knew all of my life

That someday it would end.

Get up and go outside.

Don't let the old man in.

CHORUS:

Many moons I have lived.

My body's weathered and worn.

Ask yourself how would you be

If you didn't know the day you were born?

Try to love on your wife

And stay close to your friends.

Toast each sundown with wine.

Don't let the old man in.

Many moons I have lived.

My body's weathered and worn.

Ask yourself how would you be

If you didn't know the day you were born?

When he rides up on his horse,

And you feel that cold bitter wind,

Look out your window and smile.

Don't let the old man in.

Look out your window and smile.

Don't let the old man in.

I like to change the chorus bit to, "Ask yourself how *old* would you be if you didn't know the day you were born." I remember my favorite TDA Global Cycling—a fine adventure-cycling company out of Toronto—guide, Emily, saying, "Bob is like a teenager but far more mature." And she would know because that trip took us from Agra, India, to the very bottom tip of the subcontinent. It took two months and covered 4,200 km. So, I take that as a compliment. Most days on the bike, I don't feel old at all.

In fact, the older you are, the more important my message is. Get off the couch! Being retired doesn't mean sitting on a couch in a corner and growing layer of dust and mold until you die. This is your opportunity! There is so much to life, and you have so much yet to experience. Start small. Walk around the block. Walk to the store instead of driving. Take a course in something. Pick up the phone and invite someone to experience something with you.

And if you're not yet retired—and spending your days wishing you were—what are you waiting for? Life is just going to keep ticking away, so why not fill those spare hours, or even minutes, with something you've always said you'd do when you retired? Why wait? Life is short. Learn a new instrument, volunteer, train for a marathon. Fill your life with life!

That said, come with me on my journey from Alaska to Panama. Share my experiences with me, meet some of the wonderful people I met on the way, and see the world through my eyes. Maybe my story will inspire you, spark an idea, or show you the world through a different lens.

PROLOGUE

As I sit here at my computer, staring at the blank screen and reflecting on the last five months of my journey, I find I'm of two minds. You'd think that after cycling through North and Central America and successfully breaking a world record, I'd be feeling melancholy or nostalgic, or maybe I'd be feeling ecstatic and on top of the world. But no. None of those emotions fit.

Instead, half of me asks, "Is that all there is?" Crossing the finish line in Panama City didn't feel extraordinary or life changing. It didn't feel like I'd just won a race or a lottery. It just was. As a matter of fact, now that I examine that feeling a little deeper, I realize that that's how I should feel. When I finished cycling for five months on an e-bike through nine countries and breaking a world record, when I stopped pedaling in Panama City, that wasn't the end of the journey. It wasn't the end of the line. It wasn't the end of the adventure. It was just a break. I pushed the pause button.

And that's why just days after I reached my goal and cycled 14,274 km, I started planning what will become Octogenarian Odyssey Part 2—and Part 3. I felt underwhelmed by the end of this journey because it *wasn't* the end of this journey. It was just a break to plan my next steps and accommodate Mother Nature. If it weren't for the fact that the next part of my journey will take me across South America, I'm sure I'd leave sooner than I'm planning to, but the last thing I want to put me or my team through is a trek through the mountains in the winter.

Perhaps I also felt rather less excited than one would think simply because there was just so much to do afterward, so much work to do and so many problems to solve. Not only did I have to fill in all the holes from this journey, but I also had to start planning part two. And I'd learned a lot about myself and working with a support team on this leg.

That's not to say we neglected to celebrate reaching the end of this leg. When Wayne, Kyle, and I rode into the park in the historic old center of Panama City—our prearranged meeting place—we had a few high-fives while we waited for the rest of the team to show up. Then we sat and took a much-needed rest with a couple cold beers while we waited. Eventually the car pulled in and Yiota, Johana jumped out. Wayne's wife was so happy to see Wayne. Not long after, Gloria, my wife, and her mother arrived, and there was a bunch of excitement and carrying on and such. Then we took a lot of photos with our e-bikes raised above our heads, and I guess we did make a commotion because we caught the attention of some police officers. They wanted to know what was happening, so we talked with them for quite a while as we seemed to do with the police the whole way, as you'll soon see.

But despite the thrill of reuniting with loved ones and rehashing our adventures, there was nothing more, no feeling of exhilaration or elation or even of winning. I think my brain had already moved on to planning my South American leg. Perhaps my subconscious was already cycling from Cartagena to Bogotá, then on to Ecuador, Peru, Bolivia, and the salt flats before hitting Chile and the high mountain deserts and riding on to Patagonia and finally the tip of Argentina.

And then of course there were the loose ends to tie up with this leg, and some of those loose ends were pretty big issues that needed to be dealt with. My biggest problem was what to do with the car my support team had driven. It turned out that I'd made a mistake at the Costa Rican border so with the law's surroundings bringing a car into the country, I was facing possibly paying $8,000 in taxes just to bring it back into Costa Rica coming home. I was certainly puzzling through how I was going to get around that.

I also knew I had to jump through all the Guinness Book of World Records hoops. It sounds easy to just break a record and say, "I did it. I'm done," and it's a done deal. I'm afraid it isn't that easy. There is a lot of paperwork to fill out and statements that must be sworn by witnesses, and of course you need proof. Suffice it to say trying to prove you broke a world record is akin to doing your taxes.

All that said, don't get me wrong. That's not to say this adventure didn't change me in some integral ways. More than anything, it changed my perception of the world and taught me a few things about myself.

When it comes to how it changed me, I must be honest and say it became clear to me that I really enjoy attention. I rode down the highways and side streets with a sign on the back of my e-bike that read, "Alaska to Panama." That sign elicited many honks and cheers and waves, and while I loved that attention and waved back, it really annoyed Wayne. I loved it when people would pull over and chat with us for a bit, ask us about our adventure, take some pictures, and sometimes even give us water or beer or snacks. Wayne would just shake his head and keep riding, but I loved the kindness and generosity of people in these Central American countries. There was just something truly energizing about the few minutes it took to stop, shake some hands, learn about the people and their culture, and listen to their stories. It really motivated me to keep going.

I even found I enjoyed all the interviews I gave. I had such a great time talking to reporters and bloggers and YouTubers. I took pleasure in telling the world about long-distance cycling and e-bikes and the wonderful people I'd met. I reveled in knowing that the more I told my story, the greater the possibility that I was hopefully motivating more people to start living their lives more fully, especially seniors. The more times I told my story, the more motivated I was to motivate others and to keep going. At the same time, I also discovered through my journey that I now had another message I wanted to share with the world, beyond motivating seniors to get up off the couch, and that too excited me.

I found I needed to tell my compadres in North America just how erroneous the media's portrayal of the people, the cultures, the countries in Central America were. I found more kindness, compassion, and empathy in the people in these countries than I did anywhere through my ride in North America. The cities were cleaner—in some places—and more modern than I'd been led to believe by the media and American politicians.

I can proudly call myself a world traveler, and as such, I've seen much of the world. Yet I was still taken aback by the modernness, orderliness, and organization of the countries in Central America. Back home in North America we're led to believe that they're all backward and dirt poor, and don't get wrong, that does exist in places. But for the most part, these people are just like you and me: they live in middle-class houses, they go to school and work, and the governments are generally stable, and its people average middle-class folk, if not even prosperous. And above all, for the most part, they're happy. And they're respectful. And they're so, so kind and generous.

So, there I finally was, standing in a park in Panama City. After a year of planning and more ups and downs than I had foreseen, that was it. That was the end of it. Five months and five days, 14,274 km. The heavens didn't open up and angels didn't sing, no marching band played a celebratory tune, and I felt no need to jump up and down with excitement. I just was.

Yet I knew deep down I was a changed man. I had completed long-distance rides many times before, I had climbed mountains and run marathons. I had visited new countries and met new people, learned about their cultures. But this time felt different. Not only was I not quite done this journey yet, but I had changed the lives of others along the way this time. I hadn't been just riding for me. I had raised money throughout this journey and used it to buy new bicycles for schoolchildren in Panama who were either very poor or had long, long journeys to get to school. From messages and comments, I received on Facebook and Instagram, I also knew I had achieved my goal of motivating people, motivating seniors.

And much of that prompted me to write this book. Maybe I can reach even more people this way. My purpose isn't to get everyone cycling around the world. It's not for everyone. But maybe the story of my journey, which wasn't always easy or pleasant, will light a fire in a few more people. Maybe I can even entertain you while I'm at it.

So come with me on my journey. Take an adventure that may help you discover that it's not so scary to do that thing you always wanted to do but thought you couldn't, or you'd wait for later to do. It all starts with that first step. So, let's begin with my first step: coming up with the idea.

THE ODYSSEY'S
True Beginning

My journey started long before I started pedaling in North Pole, Alaska. It started long before I thought of breaking a world record for long-distance cycling on an e-bike. It started the day I turned my catamaran upside down. After I had righted it, I did not have the energy to pull myself aboard. I wrapped the halyard around my wrist so the boat wouldn't float away and hung there till I had enough strength to pull myself back into the boat. When I returned to shore, I put on my runners and ran—or waddled—about a kilometer.

And I've never looked back. That episode led to a running career and significant weight loss. Not that there weren't speed bumps along the way. I am only human after all.

I remember struggling to leave my comfort zone and register for a ten-kilometer race. As I finally stood at the starting line, I was so nervous. I kept asking myself if it was too late to back out, what if I made a fool of myself, what made me think I was a runner? But I stood my ground, whether from fear, courage, or indecision, I'll never know. But I ran that race. And you know what? It all turned out just fine. I survived leaving my comfort zone, and racing became my new comfort zone. In the end, I continued running over the next few decades, including five marathons.

As I enrolled in more adventures, I seldom thought about my comfort zone until the adventure started getting closer, like the time I enrolled with Alaskan guides to climb Mount Kilimanjaro in 2014. I had friends that had climbed it, so I thought I could do it too. I was seventy-two years old.

Well, the week before heading to the Kilimanjaro airport, I was sitting on a beach in Zanzibar enjoying the company of a beautiful woman from Tanzania. I was in paradise. So, I got to thinking about why I was going to leave paradise to go climb a mountain. I had only climbed one other mountain, and that was Mount Fuji many years before. All my fears and doubts raced through my mind. My lady friend, Liz, tried to talk me out of going. However, something inside me prevailed, and I left that idyllic setting, my little place of paradise, and flew to Moshi.

There I started the climb. It wasn't until the final night that I really started to worry. I sat there starting at the summit, and all kinds of doubts flooded my brain. Why was I so stupid as to try this?

What if I didn't make it? What if I died? How do I get out of here? Fear set in then because I didn't want to leave my comfort zone.

Well, I did it. Don't ask me what made me go through with it, but it was great. I was the second oldest person to make the summit that month. The first was a German man a year older than me. Looking back, I now think of it as a great adventure, and I am so glad I did it. That adventure led me to visit many countries in East Africa, meet incredible people, find romance, and view the migration of animals on the Serengeti plains.

So glad I got off the sofa, fought back my fears, and left my comfort zone.

I have to admit something. I was never that kid that excelled in school. I was never that teenager that captained all the sports teams, and I was never that guy that sailed through college and landed that dream job right after graduation. I certainly was never that guy always achieving greatness and amassing awards and accomplishments.

My childhood was average. I was average. My life was average. I had nothing to complain about, but my life was just as ordinary as everyone else's. My family was middle-class, if maybe a little upper middle-class, my parents were hard-working professionals, I have a brother and a sister, and I spent my time playing sports, namely football, baseball, and hockey. I remember listening to ball games, Friday-night fights, and sports events on the radio as I lay in bed at night. When I was young, Gordie Howe was my hero—and the Detroit Red Wings—though I went to all the Edmonton Eskimos games. By the time I got to high school, I'd discovered golf, and Gary Player and Arnold Palmer became my new heroes.

We took family vacations to our summer cottage in Grand Bend, Ontario, when I was really young, maybe seven or eight. I loved going down to the beach to collect pop bottles or wander or swim or jump off the pier. Later, after we moved to Edmonton, our summer vacations took us to the Shuswap in BC, where I went fishing near Salmon Arm when I was nine or ten, maybe eleven, in a rowboat. I'd row most of the day and try to catch something, and sometimes I even did.

My biggest constant throughout my life though will come as no surprise. I always had a bike. I mean as a kid, it was a great way to get around. It meant freedom—and adventure. When I was eight, I'd ride it through the new construction in the mud, getting the bike clogged up with mud. At six, I crashed it into a fence. I guess that didn't stop me!

Nothing spectacular happened when I was a child, nothing traumatic or fantastic, so I'm not trying to run from something or work stuff out by achieving the milestones I do now. My parents didn't often fight, they didn't separate or divorce. I might not have been close with my siblings because we were just very different, but we didn't have any insurmountable issues either. I wasn't bullied in school, and I had friends enough. Like I said, my childhood was incredibly ordinary.

Eventually, we moved from Ontario to Alberta, but it wasn't life-changing for me. I adjusted, I earned decent grades because my parents insisted, I studied hard, and I kept playing sports. However, moving to Alberta would prove to be the foundation of my future. While attending high school in Edmonton, I met the love of my life and future wife, Elizabeth Wilson.

As I neared the end of high school, I rebelled for a while and started acting up in class, so I didn't get enough credits to graduate. I ended up having to go back to high school for a fourth year, but that was okay with me because it meant I got to play football for one more year and help manage the basketball team. As it turns out, that rebelling would land me in Mr. Rudomsky's chemistry classes in my fourth year because I kept skipping all my study periods. And because I was sitting in on the younger-year classes, I always sat in the back. Elizabeth sat in front of me, and that red hair of hers caught my eye.

She was struggling with chemistry, and thankfully, I happened to be good at it—liked it even. So, I started to help her with her homework, and that led to a date, which led to lots of dates, which eventually led to fifty-five years together, forty-eight of those married. Funnily, in the early days of dating, she would have to drive us because she was six months older and had her license. It wasn't until six months later that I would get mine.

I eventually made it to university, likely because being with Beth helped ground me. I thought I would be a science major, but I ended up hating the labs and learned to play bridge instead. As a result, I ended up flunking out after the first year and taking a job at the Bank of Montreal in Tofield, Alberta. That lasted a year before I transferred to Hamilton for a year and Toronto for another year before I requested a transfer back home to Edmonton. Turns out I didn't much like banking. Plus, I was starving to death on that salary, so I decided to give university one more shot. This time I went as an education and math major, and that try worked out.

Beth didn't accompany me through my time working for BMO, but we kept in touch. I guess I asked for a transfer back home because I was missing her. And who knows, maybe she's why I finally succeeded in university. All I know is we tied the knot in a traditional little ceremony in Edmonton on a beautiful day, December 18, her in a stunning white dress, me in a suit and tie, and the bridesmaids all in orange. We celebrated with a small, short reception—alcohol-free—then jetted off for a short skiing honeymoon in Banff.

Through the course of our, generally strife-free, marriage, we adopted a baby boy, Cameron, and later had a baby girl, Janet. I remember the day we got Cam. He was maybe a month old. When I held him in my arm, he fit in the space between my elbow and the palm of my hand. I couldn't believe he was so small and couldn't believe we finally had him, this perfect, tiny little baby. It was an emotional and powerful thing I guess, all this love for such a small little boy. As he grew, he became an incredibly creative, artistic sort.

Then Janet came, and she turned out to be a perfect daughter who excelled in all sorts of things: music, biking, parachuting, climbing, and becoming a divemaster. She has a good job, she's very personable, and she was always good at school. It's strange to think that fate had a plan for her because she was entirely unexpected given my low sperm count. It was a joy for Beth and I to experience creating our own child together. Back in those days they didn't let fathers in to witness the birth, but I got to see Janet's birth because Beth was a nurse and worked for the doctor. Though even though I hadn't taken a course or anything, the doctor said, "Come on, Bob, let's go up." I was pretty thrilled to get to be there.

After some twists and turns and various teaching and education jobs, I eventually ended up teaching junior-high math. Though I'd gotten into education truly by accident because I'd thought it would be the easiest faculty to succeed in, once I did my first student-teaching day, I was hooked. I found I loved it. Maybe it was because I was teaching math, not the higher math but the challenging math just before taking that leap, or maybe it was because it was like acting. I could stand at the front of the class and act like a teacher. All I know is that through thirty years of teaching, I didn't regret going to work for a single day.

From there, I gravitated to becoming a school principal, even getting a chance to take part in a school-principal exchange program in Australia. Then I got the opportunity to open a new school, and as its principal, talk with the architects and help decide on things like the layout, the furniture, and the computers.

However, as much as I loved what I did, adventure was always in my blood. I retired at fifty-five so Beth and I could travel the world. We'd begun our marriage that way before starting our careers, so it was fitting to finish that way. We packed up and traveled around the world in 1968, leaving in the summer and taking the train to Vancouver before sailing on a cruise ship to Australia. Then we spent about a year and a half there making some money before moving on to travel through Indonesia, Singapore, Malaysia, and Thailand. After that, we flew to India then up to Nepal. We bused through there, caught a bus that took us back through India, then up through northern India to Pakistan, Afghanistan, Iran, Turkey, and finally to Europe. When we got to London, UK, we bought a camping van and drove it all around the United Kingdom then all through Europe before selling it at the end of August 1970. It was sadly time to head home to Edmonton to start teaching at Wellington Junior High.

But I loved my job, I loved my wife, and I loved my life. And we didn't stop traveling just because we were grownups with careers. We still had our adventures like the bikepacking trip we took through southern England and France in 1972 for about seven weeks. It's just that I decided to retire early because there was so much more I wanted to do with my life, so much more to experience.

Through my teaching years, the running that I'd taken up led me to open a running store with a few partners in Edmonton. That lasted three or four years before we shut down. After retirement, Beth and I wintered in different warm locations around the world—Cancun, Manzanillo, and Bucerias in Mexico, and California—until inflation started rising. That's when I thought, *"well, maybe I could do something with my love of golf,"* so I started a golf touring company for golf in Australia, B&B Travel. That's B&B for Bob and Beth not Broke and Busted or anything like that. I only found out later that my friends and family liked to call it B&B Oops Travel.

Anyway, that was a country that hadn't really been explored in that way yet, though golf tours were common in other parts of the world. Those were great times. Beth and I would visit new places—golf courses, resorts, and things—to scout out affordable but enjoyable locations for our tours. We would organize the tours and book the groups and lead them on the tours. We even made a little money at it. So, we expanded into New Zealand and even looked at expanding to Argentina and Uruguay, but there was no interest. I turned my attention to Ireland then, but no one wanted to golf there either. We did get a couple bites when we started offering tours to Costa del Sol, Spain, but that didn't last long. Our last potential target was Vietnam, though that didn't pan out either. Eventually, the business fizzled, simply because Beth got sick then and it got too hard to continue. We enjoyed the most memorable eight years touring the world, scouting out and offering golf tours. I'd do it all again if I was a younger man!

When that adventure ended, until the ravages of dementia took her from me at seventy-one, I did what I could to keep life normal as we went through the course of the disease, continuing to travel and experience what the world had to offer while we could still do that together. But as the course of the disease progressed as it's wont to do, we eventually went home to Edmonton. Then her health worsened further, and I had to accept she needed more care than I could give alone. It became time to take her to the hospital.

During those darkest days of my life, I slept by her bedside almost every night for two weeks. One fateful night, I decided to go home and shower. I'd grab some sleep in a bed and head back before the sun was even up.

I think about that decision all the time now. Before I could get back to her, my phone rang. My best friend, the love of my life, my wife of forty-eight years, my companion of fifty-five years, the other half of me, was gone. She had succumbed to Alzheimer's, and I hadn't been there. That was 2013, a bad luck year.

I remember coming home from the hospital after saying my goodbyes and blindly taking care of the official stuff and feeling sorry for myself. It had dawned on me that life as I knew it was over. Beth and I had been companions in everything; we'd golfed together, skied together, traveled together, biked together, hiked together. In fact, it had been her idea to do the around-the-world trip in '68. That was the kind of person she was.

After she was gone, I was directionless. I was lonely. I wasn't quite sure what to do with myself and my life if anything at all. For a while, every day was the same: wake up, ride my bike for a while, sit on the couch, watch TV, eat a Hungry Man dinner, down a bottle of wine, and pass out on the couch. I did manage a couple club rides, but that was it. Then one day, I'm not sure I know what precipitated it, but I came out of the fog. I realized this path was no good; I needed purpose. I needed to pull myself up with my bootstraps and do something because I was on a slippery slope.

So, a friend set up a profile for me on a dating site, and from there I tried coffee dating. That's when I realized there was still more life to live and the possibility of new love. I enjoyed a few brief relationships after that, and that's when I decided to go cycle the Dalmatian Island in Croatia—because my wife had always wanted to go there. Then I walked the Camino de Santiago because my wife was a walker. Beth loved to go walking. She loved going on hikes in the mountains, and wherever we traveled, we did a lot of walking. So, I decided I'd take on the Camino de Santiago and dedicate my certificate to her. Then I thought Africa was the next best candidate. At that time, it was just about the only place I hadn't been. And that takes us right to that story of my climbing Mount Kilimanjaro. Beth loved the book, Kilimanjaro, so I dedicated that certificate to her too. I still needed to explore some other countries though, so I cycled in Tucson, Arizona, then through India.

Let me tell you, India was an eye-opener. That was my first real long-distance ride, covering roughly 4,400 km in just two months. We started at the Taj Mahal and rode all the way to the bottom of the country. That journey taught me just what long-distance cycling was really all about. Take my dust-up with the water buffaloes for example.

One day when I was riding with my tour group, we were on some back roads going through a small village when we came upon a local farmer with a relatively large herd of water buffaloes up ahead. Of course, the water buffaloes are like cattle in India: they use them only for leather and meat because it's against their religion to eat cows. Well, those water buffaloes pretty well covered the road, so as I was riding along, I was trying to decide the best way to go around them. So, I—being from North America—thought, *"well, they're coming toward me, and I'm riding on the right side of the road. I'll just stay on the right, and they'll pass to my left."* Well, I guess water buffaloes in India are accustomed to cars and traffic and things riding on the left as you'd see in Australia or England because they stayed on the left, and I stayed on the right. We were heading right for each other. As we got closer, I realized they weren't going to move, so I had to move. But where? Left with no other choice, I rode to the right—straight for the ditch. Now that ditch wasn't a big ditch or anything, nothing to be afraid of really. It just had some mud in it that looked like it was from last night's rain or something. But as I got closer, I noticed the mud was quite soft and it had a sort of green-blue slime growing on it.

Well, my front tire went into that mud and sank to the axle because the mud was deep. The bike stopped abruptly. I fell over sideways to the right, but I was still clipped into the pedals. So, there I was, in the middle of this goo that almost covered me from the top of my head to the bottom of my feet and over the center of my chest, and I was trying to get out of my clip-ons, but I couldn't get any leverage to get my shoes unhooked. In my futile quest to achieve this, I was thrashing around like a seal on the beach.

Suddenly I realized there was a large group of people gathered around me. In India, it's not unusual to always be surrounded by many people, but in my case, even schoolchildren were all huddled around me, laughing at this guy in a fancy Lycra outfit and a bike helmet thrashing around in this ooze. Fortunately, one fellow dressed in a suit and tie and nice shoes was kind enough to wade into the mud. He grabbed my feet and unclipped my shoes so I could stand up. The crowd stopped hooting and hollering then and became incredibly sorry for me. I looked down at myself and I looked like a piano keyboard, all white and black: black with mud down one side of me and white on the other side. Half of me looked like a swamp monster, there was so much mud on me.

But the people of India are wonderful. They took me to a house still under construction nearby and hooked up a hose. They sprayed water all over me while they got a big push broom and tried to scrub off as much mud as they could. They did their best to clean the thick layer of mud off me. By the time they were done, I thought I wasn't looking too bad—but I guess that's only what I thought.

I thanked them all profusely and went back to my bike and hopped back on. Just then, along came a couple of fellow cyclists in my group: Joe and Marta. Marta took one look at me and shouted, "Bob, what the hell happened to you? Look at you! You're so muddy!"

Of course, I replied, "Shut up, Martha. I'm fine. I just got cleaned up. I'm perfectly clean."

Well didn't she just burst out laughing? She laughed so hard she couldn't ride her bike. She had to get off, and Joe hollered, "Did you get a video? Did somebody get a video of that? I got to see it." Those two just died laughing. I took my cue, got on my bike, and got away from there as fast as I could.

That night, I spent a long time in the shower, showering with my clothes on trying to get the rest of the muck and mud off—and the stink. That ditch had obviously been a community greywater catchment, or maybe even somewhere someone's toilet water drained into. Either way, that story of "How Bob Met the Water Buffaloes" taught me a lot about the realities of long-distance cycling. On a positive note, I decided that after diving in that cesspool I would likely gain some immunity to anything else that came my way in the future. As it turned out, I never got sick in India, other than one hour one night from eating some bad food, and I rarely get sick in any other country to this day. And I contribute that to having a swim in a cesspool in a little town in northern India.

Too bad that same principle didn't apply to near-death experiences. I seem to be prone to those.

My first experience also happened in India. I still find it interesting that I didn't give up long-distance cycling after India. But I guess it's just because I never give up.

Anyway, that day, I was cycling high in the Western Ghats Mountains. It's a beautiful area in western India, full of tea plantations and lots of flowers. It was rated one of the top one hundred most beautiful places globally by *National*

Geographic. I was heading down that mountain, the wind whistling in my ears and tearing my eyes. I like to descend fast because I'm a slow climber and a slow rider. One way I can make up some ground and catch up to the people in front of me is to descend rapidly. I do it so often that over the years, I've picked up small prizes for such awards as downhill destroyer, fastest descent, and such. With that last one, I reached eighty kilometers per hour.

So, I was descending—and fast. The road was quiet, there wasn't much traffic, and I wasn't too worried about my speed because in India everybody honks their horns. If they're going around a corner, you can hear the car honk. So, while I raced down those mountains, I thought it would be relatively safe for me to take my line and cut the corners where I had to at that speed. I knew there were a few hairpins turns coming up, so I'd be riding on the other side of the road. I assumed that any oncoming cars would honk before they came around the corner. Well, that didn't happen.

I rounded one corner on the wrong side of the road, and there in front of me was an Indian driver and his family in a Jeep, and I was staring him right in the eyeballs as I came at them head on. All this happened in a few seconds. I thought, *oh, oh, I need to be on the wide side, and if I go back to my side of the road, that's probably where he's going to try to go to avoid me, so I will stay where I am.* Well, lo and behold, he stayed where he was. That left me having to decide either get hit and become a bug on the windshield or try to get out of there safely. I slammed on my back brake and went into a ninety-degree skid shot across the front of his front bumper, missing him by just thirty centimeters or so. That worked fine, except then I was heading for the ditch, and the ditch drop-off was two or three meters so that wasn't an option. Once again, I had to hit the back brake and make a ninety-degree left turn. I shot between him and the ditch, whizzing down that mountain without pause. I mean it. I don't think I breathed or blinked. There was no time to think, no time for anything but an instant, visceral reaction. I have no idea why

I decided to use the back brake and go into skids, but something told me to do that, and it worked out well; I didn't get a single scratch or scrape.

Not long after my India adventure, I was cycling through Germany and nearly encountered death a second time. It was one of those peaceful, beautiful days, and I was riding on a scenic, tranquil country road. Up ahead, I saw a John Deere tractor, and in behind it, a small white Volkswagen that kept peeking out from behind to see if it was okay to pass. I was keeping my eye on the car and not really watching the road as it was well paved and was slightly downhill, so it was a serene, cruising type of day.

All of a sudden, I heard a big bang, and I was thrown up onto the handlebars. Fortunately, my grip was strong enough that I didn't go over the handlebars and I stayed upright. But because the road had turned right at that moment, I was now on a gravel section headed for disaster. Straight ahead was a big hay rack with its prongs sticking out. People say when they're faced with death that they see their life flash before their eyes. Not me. I thought, *oh my God, I'm going to be shish kebab. This is going to hurt a lot.*

What could I do? Well, I could hit the ground and skate across the gravel on my side with my feet up in the air and let the bike hit the hay rack first. That would save me from being shish kebab, but it would give me some horrible road rash. Just then, I saw a small opening, slightly larger than the width of my handlebars, between the hay rack and the fence posts beside it. It took only a fraction of a second to decide that was my only option. I was going to go through that opening and miss the hay rack, but I would have to be incredibly careful. I couldn't afford to go off the center line, otherwise my handlebar would hit, and I'd be thrown forward.

In the same second, I decided I was going through that gap, I saw what sat just behind the hay rack and the fence: a huge pile of metal barrels, tractor parts, and such. And I wasn't going to have time to stop after I went through the hole. *Oh, well,* I thought, *I gotta give it a try.* So, I shot through the opening.

The very moment I hit that opening; I applied both brakes as hard as I could. I came to a stop just a foot short of the scrap-metal pile. My heart was thumping in my chest, and I was breathing hard. *Wow,* I thought, *was I lucky.* That could have been a disaster. What the hell had happened?

A little shakily, I got off my bike and calmed myself down a bit. Then I walked back onto the road and found a tree limb that had fallen onto the road in the shadows. So, in that moment when I'd been watching the tractor and the car behind it and I hadn't been watching the road, I'd hit this branch that was probably twelve, no, maybe more like twenty-four centimeters in diameter. That's what threw me off course and onto the handlebars. Then I went and checked my skid marks, and they were right in the middle of the opening, in perfectly the right spot. I took a picture of the scene and recorded it for prosperity before continuing with my ride. That day, I learned to always keep one eye on the road. You never know what's going to be lurking that could cause danger and collision or upset.

By now you must be shaking your head and saying, "And still he puts himself in danger after two near-death experiences on that bike. You'd think he'd hang up his helmet."

Well, that's where you're wrong. I had three brushes with death.

Though I did learn to be a little more cautious, I didn't quit cycling. I didn't give up on long-distance rides because that's not how I operate. And things did go smoothly for years after that.

Since that first trip around the world with Beth, I've traveled around world four times and visited 112 countries. One day on my travels, a thought came to me. I really could use a home base, but I didn't want it to be somewhere cold and dark like Edmonton. So, I started investigating. I considered Cape Town, Port Elizabeth in South Africa, and Lake Victoria in Uganda. But life had its own plan for me.

I took on another long-distance cycle challenge again. This one from Alaska to Mexico City. After I finished, I spent some time exploring a few cities in Central America because I had no return plane ticket, so I was wondering what I was going to do. I'd chosen Central America because I hadn't been there yet and wanted to check some of those countries off my list of places to visit. So, I jumped on a plane and took off. I toured Panama for about a week, then went to Costa Rica and El Salvador, though I missed Honduras on that trip, then moved on to Guatemala. One reason I'd decided to check out San Jose, Costa Rica, was because lots of friends were starting a ride from San Jose to Belize then, a tough ride of six to seven weeks with lots of climbing and back roads, so I thought I'd go see them.

And lo and behold, I met my second wife, Gloria. We met quite by chance when I stopped into the National Theater of Costa Rica in central San Jose with one of my friends. Well, after we'd finished our coffees, my friend went to the washroom and a lady came in and sat down at a table near me. For some reason, I felt compelled to go over and talk to her, though I spoke hardly a lick of Spanish.

For a while, I debated whether I should talk to her because I was going to be leaving at 4:00 a.m. the next day, but in the end, I thought, *Ah, what the hell.* That's worked well for me throughout my life, thinking the worst that can happen is they say no. So, I approached her and asked her if she spoke English, but she said no, she did not. Yet she was so happy and smiled a lot, so I ended up talking to her anyway, however haltingly.

When my friend came back, he saw us and said, "Oh, you look busy. I'll come back in an hour. I have some stuff to do anyway." Gloria did order lunch that day, but never did eat it. She ended up taking it away because we talked so long, though I don't know how because I spoke not much Spanish and she spoke no English, but somehow, we talked. Eventually, we wandered outside and chatted on the corner till her friend came to pick her up to go shopping. It was a wonderfully enjoyable hour, and I even got her number!

When I got back to Canada, I contacted her on WhatsApp, and we continued our chats as best we could. After a time, I told her I was leaving for Australia for a long ride, but I was going to do Peru and Machu Pichu on the way. Then I asked her if she would like to go with me, and she said yes. So, a few months later I went back to San Jose around New Years 2016, and we flew down to Machu Pichu. While we were there, she asked if we could make a stop in her hometown of Medellin, Colombia, so we did. However, we set a little surprise up. Gloria's sister, Johana, set things up so that her mother and stepfather thought it was just me needing a place to stay for the night while on my ride. When Gloria and I got to Medellin, her brother picked us up at the airport and took us to his mother's house. I went in first and they welcomed me warmly. Suddenly, there was a knock at the door. Gloria entered and her mother let out a huge scream. It was such a total surprise. It was a happy, beautiful moment as tears fell from Gloria's eyes and her mother's eyes, and everyone else beamed.

After that visit, I flew to South Africa for a cycling tour, then continued to Melbourne, Australia, for a month-long bike ride to the Gold Coast in Queensland. But it wasn't long before one thing led to another, and I moved to Costa Rica. Gloria even had a lovely daughter named Julie, so now I'm lucky enough to have a third child, though she's grown now. My daughter, Janet, calls them my southern family. And Gloria and I have been together a good six and a half years now.

Would you believe that Costa Rica is where I met up with death yet again? It would prove to be my closest call of them all.

It all happened not far from where I live. Whenever I'm home, I ride daily, always switching up my routes. I have one route that takes me up to a volcano. There's about twenty kilometers of climbing if I go all the way to the national park; it's not a difficult climb, just a little long. I ride through a couple valleys and follow a river part of the way. It's quite scenic with the mountains in the background. I'd ridden this road maybe a hundred times and never experienced any problems. That fateful day was a hot, sunny day with a nice clear sky. On that day, instead of going all the way, I only went about halfway up to a small town there, then turned around and started my descent. Like I said, I've ridden that road regularly. I knew there were speed bumps. They're even brightly painted yellow. They'd never ever been a concern; however, on that day, after I'd ridden over the first speed bump and was heading for the next one—at a decent rate mind you, nothing extraordinary, maybe thirty kilometers an hour—I came across a car parked in my lane. There was a lot of activity around it, so I was concerned about people opening the doors and maybe a child running out in front of me. In that particular moment, I chose to move to the other lane— the oncoming-traffic lane.

Just as I did that, I felt something was wrong. Very wrong.

The next thing I remember is waking up in the ditch with a whole crowd around me and a bunch of cars parked nearby. What happened, I still have no idea. But I turned around and looked up at the road and saw the yellow speed bump. That was what had caused me to crash. After thinking about the crash for a long time, I realized that when I'd moved to change lanes, I'd ridden over that speed bump and its slippery yellow paint with my slick, twenty-three millimeter, no-tread tires, and they hadn't been able to get any traction. They'd slid out from underneath me, making me fall to the pavement like a sack of potatoes. I landed on my hip and shoulder, and my head was fuzzy.

That fluky accident gave me a concussion, three broken ribs on my right side, and a fractured right hip. Thankfully I at least had enough sense to give people my wife's phone number, and she got a neighbor to come and get me. There wasn't much pain then either, but maybe that was the shock. Once I got home, the neighbor's wife looked me over because she was a doctor, and she insisted that I had to go to the hospital because I had knocked myself out and bruised my shoulder.

Though I thought maybe it was a waste of time, I went to the hospital. There, the pain really started setting in. That was a lot of pain. The doctors took some x-rays of my ribs and my hip, did an MRI of my head, and suggested I spend the night in the hospital, but I insisted I was going to go home and rest there. By the time I got back home, I was in tremendous pain, so I took some painkillers before taking a closer look at my helmet. I discovered later it was smashed into three big pieces.

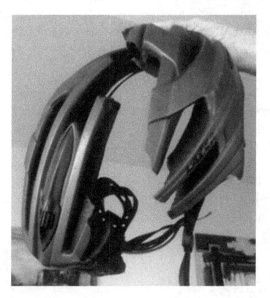

Without this helmet my skull would have looked like this.

I sure must thank my helmet because if I had not had it on that day, I wouldn't be telling this story. I've always ridden with a helmet, and it saved my life for sure that time. My head must have bounced off the road at least twice to do the damage it did to that helmet.

Over the next few days, the pain kept getting worse. I just did not seem to be recovering, so I decided to go back to Edmonton to get another opinion. And imagine that, when I did get back to Edmonton and went for x-rays, they discovered that my hip was indeed broken. It turns out the doctors in Costa Rica had missed that in their x-rays, although I don't blame them as I was in a lot of pain and couldn't get into the positions, they needed me to.

So, as I recovered, I analyzed everything about that day, and the lesson I learned is never ride without a helmet on. You never know when you're going to crash, whether it's a speed bump or loose gravel or a car turning in front of you and forcing you into the ditch, things can happen very quickly. And if you don't have that helmet on, you're really in trouble if your head hits the pavement.

In any case, accidents, or no accidents, I love it in Costa Rica, and I know I'm not done with my adventures yet. I need to stay away from long stretches on the couch, so I don't just wither away. There's nothing I love more than discovering what's around the next bend and surrounding myself with the camaraderie of like-minded people. I love meeting new people and listening to their stories and learning about their culture. I've never wanted to be a tourist, but I've always wanted to be a traveler. Long-distance cycling gives me all that. There's only about 5,000 of us that I know of in the world, and it's a tightly knit group. However, we always welcome more! Little is mentioned of the long-distance cyclists in the world, about the distance they cover and their experiences. Few know of what you experience when you go that distance on a bike: the heat and the sweat, the rain and wind and cold, the dirt and dust and grime, the spills and the road rash and the close calls with vehicles. At the same time, few know of the smells of the forest or the jungle or the ocean, the sounds of the birds that delineate a geographical area, or the crazy sunsets and sunrises, crashing waves on the coastlines, the flora and fauna you get to see up close and at a much slower speed than in a car.

Heck, once upon a time I thought I was a hotshot long-distance cyclist—until I met a lot of other riders that is. Then I'd ask them about their rides, and they'd respond with rides they'd completed that were so much longer, so much more thrilling than what I'd done, and I was humbled. Now, they've become lifelong friends, and it's both amazing and comforting each time I come across them here and there on the road as I ride, wherever I happen to be.

On a different note, think about this: A CBC article from April 27, 2022, says,

A closer look shows that the number of Canadians aged 85 and older rose almost 12 per cent from the time of the last census, while Canadians aged over 100 roses by more than 15 per cent. Over the next 30 years, the number of persons aged 85 and older could triple from 861,000 to 2.7 million... Statistics Canada population projections indicate that by 2051, almost one-quarter of the population could be aged 65 and older, adding up to almost 12 million people.

That's an awful lot of senior citizens and a lot of retired folks. Society may have this stereotype of senior citizens sitting in old folks' homes doing puzzles or watching TV or sitting in their rocking chairs in their living rooms watching Netflix or old movies, maybe knitting, or reading, but we need to shatter that. People are living longer than ever—and living better longer. We spend our entire lives working, raising our families, taking care of our responsibilities, and always saying we'll do this or that someday. When is someday? For those that are retired, or nearing retirement, someday is now! Sure, it sounds scary to go outside your comfort zone, but didn't you always say you were going to do that thing, whatever it is? Maybe it's hiking, maybe it's taking a world cruise, maybe it's auditioning for the community play.

As you get older, you need to be active, to get out of your comfort zone and have a purpose. Find something that motivates you to get up and move. Trying new things keeps the brain and body active and leads to a longer, better life. Don't become part of the 20 percent of seniors that are depressed and abusing substances to self-medicate. Retirement isn't the end of your life, it's just the beginning of a new chapter, a chapter about freedom and overcoming fear, about doing all those things you thought you might want to do. Exercise, think, ease out of your comfort zone for the sake of your mental and physical health. Remember, anyone can do it. I'm just an average guy, always have been. I'm just the same as everyone else. The only difference is I've decided to push my boundaries, especially when something scares me. Our lives are but a blink in the history of the world, so I'm going to fill my blink with as many experiences as I can.

I have a confession though: my Octogenarian Odyssey, cycling from Alaska to Panama, might seem like it's out of my comfort zone, but it's in my comfort zone, at least ever since I biked from Alaska to Mexico City. The part that was outside my comfort zone was the planning, finding financing and sponsors, writing this book, and dealing with all the fine details along the way.

So, take your bike out of storage or get a new one and even just ride around the block. Quit Netflix and Amazon Prime and plan an activity. Get someone to join you and try something new, whether it's walking, biking, traveling, or anything. Age is just a number. Start small and slowly get bigger but surround yourself with people. I believe I've kept young by associating with cyclists and surrounding myself with younger people.

So though planning a journey, my longest adventure yet, was way out of my comfort zone, I buckled down. I reminded myself that my career as an administrator trained me to be a good planner. I've used that training to plan numerous bike tours of varying distances and group sizes. Plus, it's just this kind of planning and thinking and analyzing I need to keep my brain young. Between that and my daily cycling, my mind is active, and my body is in shape, and that keeps the old man out. And I'm never letting him in.

To take that first step to make this adventure happen, I reminded myself of just that. Everything else would fall into place from there. My first step was to find a cycling partner. Wayne Grover, then sixty-nine, agreed to accompany me the whole way, but his plan was to ride a regular bike, not an e-bike. Either way, I was thrilled to have the company of someone I'd ridden with before and someone I considered a close friend.

Then I had to plan the route I'd likely take. During my ride from Alaska to Mexico City, I'd already cycled down through Alberta, Montana, Wyoming, Utah, and Arizona then down the Baja, so I knew I wanted to find a different route this time so I could keep things fresh. Meeting new people and learning about new cultures, discovering the unknown around the next bend is integral for me. Therefore, I ended up plotting a route that took me through the interior of Alaska, Yukon, and British Columbia before heading west and cycling down the coast of Washington, Oregon, and California. Once I hit Mexico, I would brave the Sonoran Desert before heading east to eventually cycle through the rest of Mexico, then Guatemala, El Salvador, Honduras, Nicaragua, and Costa Rica before finally arriving in Panama.

As I planned my journey, I had to acknowledge I would turn eighty while I was away. I still didn't want the traditional party and gifts and cake and such, but I knew it would be nice to see my loved ones. So there appeared my first speed bump. I had to figure out where I would be on my birthday, plan a party, and make sure I showed up on time. That's easier said than done with long-distance cycling. Anything can get in the way of your timing: bike repairs, illness, road construction, you name it. But, I determined, I could stay on schedule. This wasn't my first rodeo. Ah, but isn't hindsight 20/20? Meeting that deadline ended being one of the hardest things about my odyssey, as you'll discover later.

The next step was twofold: I had to decide which e-bike to ride, but I was also going to need funding. This would be an expensive trip, and even the bike would be expensive. I'm not rich by any means, so I had to find a way to reduce my costs. Sponsors were the answer. After doing some research on the best e-bikes for long-distance cycling, I reached out to EVELO. Once I'd told them my story and my plan and agreed to shout their name and praises to the world—which I have no problem doing because the bikes didn't let us down despite some hiccups—they gave me a couple bikes and spare parts for free. That was an incredible expense not coming out of my pocket.

Choosing an EVELO bike didn't take much thought given my specific needs. Not only did I need something sturdy enough to make the entire 14,000 km journey, but I needed a bike that looked like a bike, and with the Guinness Book of World Record requirements, I needed an e-bike that allowed me to power it with my pedaling. I didn't want a folding bike or a fat-tire bike or one that looked like a military-type bike. Nor did I want a step-through bike or a trike. Also on my list of must-haves was a mid-drive motor, solid components, a 48V battery with good amps so I could get plenty of power, and a 500W or more mid-drive motor. So, when EVELO said the Atlas bike included all that, and that was the one they would provide, I knew I'd hit the jackpot. It looked and sounded like a good bike, the EVELO Atlas!

The EVELO Atlas electric bike that carried me from Alaska to Panama

So that was one sponsor on board and the most integral part of my journey acquired. Little did I know that was all to the be easiest part of the planning. Looking back, the thing that surprises me most about this odyssey is that it got off the ground in the first place.

TRAGEDY

I was exactly five months and one day away from beginning my journey. My earlier difficulties had all been ironed out and all the pieces were falling into place. Suddenly from out of nowhere, I was dealt a blow that left me reeling.

My son had had a major heart attack and doctors had put a stent in his artery. They'd put him in an induced coma to cool his brain after all the swelling. It didn't look good.

The days after that passed in a haze, so I don't remember much besides the worrying and the planning and the fear.

And then I got the news I dreaded most. My Cameron, my little boy that I'd cradled in my arms as I wondered at the miracle of him, was gone.

One-minute life is moving along swimmingly, the next it's like someone has taken the ant farm that is your life and given it a good shake. When the ground settles, you just can't tell which way is up. Why is life so unfair? Why is everything so random?

What a difference a day makes. The day before, I'd been sitting in a nice restaurant celebrating my good fortune of having an excellent company like Airbnb join me as a sponsor for my adventure. After a few drinks, some good food, and perfect company, I retired for a short sleep. Then I rose early to check my phone, hoping to see if someone else had preordered a book. There I found a message from my son's wife informing me that Cameron, my 49-year-old son, had suffered a massive heart attack and was in the ICU in an induced coma with his brain being cooled to try and prevent further brain damage. They had already found a clogged artery, opened it, and placed a stent in the vessel.

25

I could not think of Airbnb then but only of Cameron's wife and two daughters, aged fifteen and thirteen. What were they to do? How would they cope? Would Cam recover and be able to live a quality life?

I couldn't let the pain in yet though. There were things to plan, things that needed doing. I needed to get a PCR test for COVID-19; I needed to book a flight; I needed to call the rest of the family.

Once that was all done, though, once the sun had set and the world was dark and quiet, the thoughts came, and with them the questions. Why Cam? Why had I lost my wife to Alzheimer's nine years earlier? Why was I the one still living when they had led healthier lifestyles? I'd planned my finances to take care of them after I died. Why was I still here and they weren't? Life is random, I decided. This all proved it. I'd never believed in God, and that was just more proof He surely couldn't exist. The thoughts and questions just wouldn't stop coming, wouldn't stop racing through my mind. Was I still here because I exercise and make up for my diet of hamburgers, chips, steak, potatoes, pastries, ice cream, candies, beer, and wine? Or was it just the luck of the draw?

In a sort of fog, I finally found myself sitting in a plane flying to Vancouver to try and offer some assistance, again thinking what a difference a day makes. As I sat there in that plane, I reflected on my own near misses, the accidents I'd survived while riding my bike, and wondered why I'd survived. I'd been hit by a truck and only gotten a sore shoulder out of it. I'd flown over the handlebars another time, breaking three ribs and my elbow, and knocking myself out. I'd crashed on my road bike and damaged three more ribs, fractured my hip, and knocked myself out once again. Yet I'd survived all these accidents and a few additional minor ones only to recover and become even stronger. Heck, a broken hip for most people at my age was usually akin to a death sentence. So how could my continued life be explained while Cameron and Beth hadn't been as fortunate? How did that make any sense? *Don't give me that shit that God works in mysterious ways*, I thought. *Life is random, dammit!*

Of course, I went from there to question some of my choices. Should I have been off cycling through Spain instead of being home? Should I have spent more time with my family instead over the years? Should I cancel the upcoming cycling tour I'd organized in Costa Rica? And what of my Octogenarian Odyssey? Maybe this was a sign that I was supposed to hang up my hat.

In the fog of my grief, I glanced around the plane, not really seeing the people or the attendants, or anything else really. Airplane seats being what they are, I switched positions yet again to try and get comfortable and went to cross my right leg over my left. I'm sure the poor lady beside wondered if I was all right as I froze mid-move.

When I remembered to breathe again, I finished the maneuver I'd begun but leaned down and rubbed my right calf as though I could feel the tattoo hidden beneath my pants leg.

I thought back to when I'd gotten it. It had taken me quite a while to decide that I was going to even though I'd thought about getting a tattoo for a long time. I'd originally thought I'd get one like my son, Cameron, had, but he'd said I should get something meaningful to me. So, I took some time and came up with a tattoo I felt had a lot of meaning: it was a Canadian flag riding a bicycle. As a sidenote, I've got many compliments on it. People have even stopped me and told me they're from Canada too.

Nevertheless, it wasn't a quick or easy decision. More than twice, I'd started off to a tattoo parlor in Edmonton to try and get it done. And on both occasions, I'd chickened out, turned around, and gone home again. It wasn't until I was on a solo bike ride in southern Ontario and had stopped in a beach town called Grand Bend that I wandered over to a local pub on their main street that was showing the World Cup finals on TV. That was the year Germany won, so I had two or three pints of beer while I watched the football game. When I came out, I went for a walk down the street, and wouldn't you know it, there was a tattoo shop not far from the pub I'd just visited. So, I wandered in, and the artist showed me a design based on my mental image. I didn't mind it, so I said, "Well, that's okay. How much?"

"$200," he said.

So, I decided okay, let's do this. As soon as I said that I started to worry it might hurt, but it felt like nothing more than an electric toothbrush rubbing on my skin. In fact, I actually fell asleep while he did the tattoo, and when he was finished, he had to wake me up.

Later, when it was safe to uncover it, I took a picture of it and posted it on Facebook. Of course, my daughter's reaction was not good. She said, "WTF, Dad? What are you doing? You've always told me never to get piercings, never to get tattoos, and now you've gone and done that. How come the double standard?"

And then there was my son's response. He said, "Way to go, Dad!" He even suggested I should get a sleeve on my arm or leg or wherever with all the sports I'd played over the years.

And that memory did it for me. It straightened my spine and gave me the sign I hadn't even known I'd been looking for. I never gave up, and Cam wouldn't have wanted me to. He'd always supported my adventures and achievements.

In that moment, I let go of my guilt, my questions, and my self-doubt and determined to keep moving forward. And that meant solidifying the plans for my Octogenarian Odyssey ... *after* I finished the cycling tour of Costa Rica in less than two weeks with the group I'd organized.

While I still grieved for my son, I kept moving forward. I did what I could for my grandkids and daughter-in-law, I finalized my Costa Rica ride, and pushed on with planning my odyssey. The pain was still lodged deep in my heart and soul, but I couldn't dwell on it, or I'd end up in the same dark place I was in after I lost Beth. I still had what was left of my slice of life to live, and Cam would have been happy that I was living it. If you take nothing else from my story, take just this: You don't need to be extraordinary. I'm not extraordinary. I just love life. We all get just one pizza slice to pile the toppings onto before it's gone, and I'm going to make sure mine is deluxe.

So, once I got home from helping my family, I still had to line up a support team, some form of transport, whether that meant a van or a car and a tent trailer or something else, I had to plan accommodations for each night of the adventure, and most importantly, I needed more sponsors. At damn near eighty, I wasn't going to make this trip bare bones. This was to be a different sort of cycling adventure, so a certain degree of comfort was a requirement on my anticipated 153-day odyssey.

Thankfully, I remembered that good fortune had struck again. I'd reached out to Airbnb before Cam died to ask them to also sponsor my incredible journey, and they'd agreed to fund 50 to 60 rentals over the entire adventure. What a weight off my shoulders that was. That was another huge cost reduced, plus it meant I and my support team could rest in some degree of comfort whenever and wherever an Airbnb was available.

When I lined up a production crew to do a documentary about my journey, I was walking on air. They were going to double as my support team and were even originally going to provide a school bus outfitted with bunk beds and a kitchen. We could camp most nights and cook our meals. Then I managed to line up Swagman Bicycle Racks and McCrady/Rourke Advisory, BMO Nesbitt Burns, as sponsors.

Never had things gone this well before. The stars must be shining on me in my later years!

Or so I thought.

Of course, my string of good luck couldn't continue. Somehow, in one fell swoop, my production crew, transportation, and support crew disappeared, dropped out of the adventure, just when I thought I had it all lined up. The production crew had failed to secure the grant funding they'd anticipated, leaving me without the school bus and with just three folks still on the team: the director, his girlfriend—who was a paramedic—and a cameraman. This meant I would have to spend some money. So, I paid them $7,500 CDN, and they bought a vehicle.

Thankfully, the director and his father were carpenters and welders and were going to redesign the truck to hold two rooftop tents, convert the cab seats to a bed, and make a sleeping area on deck. They planned to add storage boxes, some foldouts for cooking, and an awning for shade. It was even supposed to have a fridge, some solar panels, and some camp chairs—all donated—by the time all was said and done, at least according to my director. He was hoping for more donations though. But whatever the truck had or didn't have, at the very least, this vehicle was going to be unique and attention getting.

Then one day, I was suddenly left frantically searching for a new support crew and transportation.

Here's what happened. Not long after I'd secured my sponsors and was moving forward with the truck adaptations, for whatever reason, I was again doing some research into how to get a truck across the border into Mexico. I'd come across all kinds of things that said the truck I'd bought was too large because the limit for a temporary import permit was 3,500 kgs and our truck was probably well over that. I think I panicked a little bit because I saw a disaster waiting for us when we got to the Tijuana/San Diego border and were refused entry, so I got hold of my film director. I told him about all my brainstorming about different scenarios that might work, that could help solve the problem and keep the journey alive. But he got quite upset and replied with, "What's the matter? Why don't you trust me? I know what I'm doing. That's just a small, minor problem. We can handle that."

I said, "No, this is a major problem, you know, and we need to talk about it." Unfortunately, instead of trying to work out the problem, he just gave up.

He said, "Well then, you don't trust me. I'm going to give you back the money for the truck." So, he refunded my money, and suddenly I didn't have a truck or a support team. That wasn't a good situation, but again, I never gave up. I got on it.

After I thought it through, I decided I didn't need a professional director really. Just the right people and the right tools, which I already had in Yiota—and later Kyle—and his cameras and drones. So, I refocused, then hustled and found some vehicles in Edmonton I thought might do the trick, but that didn't pan out. But my friends, Dave, and Barb, had heard of my problem and put me in touch with someone selling something I was rather sure would work. So, I ran the pros and cons around in my mind and decided the Dodge Grand Caravan I'd come upon would do nicely. It had a large storage compartment in the back, and it was large enough to accommodate three to four people, and our gear, plus we had a roof rack and a bike rack we could attach courtesy of Swagman Racks. One person could even sleep in a van if necessary. The only problem with this option, which is precisely why I'd had to mull it over, was that it was in Canada, and I was in Costa Rica, and buying a vehicle in another country isn't exactly easy.

I spoke with the car dealer anyway, and the sales manager took my deposit and assured me that the vehicle was mine. Then the next day he texted me to say it had been sold to someone else! That left me fighting to get my deposit back. But remember, I never quit! I put my head down and kept searching. Finally, I happened upon a private deal for the same type of vehicle, and it worked out.

The team and our trusty Dodge Caravan as the adventure begins.

So that solved the problem of a vehicle, but now I needed drivers and a support team. I posted an ad on the Pan-American Facebook group and lined up interviews. As I wrote out the ad, I realized I was really going to need someone who could speak Spanish on the team since I don't speak Spanish. I've tried, but languages just don't seem to work in my brain. Numbers yes, words, not so much. It's much like the time I tried to learn how to salsa. Despite my best efforts, that is the one thing I can say I failed at. So, while I can remember a few Spanish words and phrases—even if maybe I butcher them— I cannot remember a single salsa step. You don't want to see me try.

Anyway, I also needed people who were okay with camping it in the northern sections where we weren't likely to find a hotel or motel or Airbnb, and I needed people who were happy earning just the $25/day I was offering, plus expenses of course. This amount might sound like a pittance, but it's actually pretty standard in the long-distance cycling world. You do also get to experience new cultures and landscapes after all, plus your lodgings and food and such are covered. Surprisingly, or not so surprisingly, I ended up with lots of choices, making me start to think I was going to make out better finding a support team the second time around. But in the end, my top candidates started disappearing. It really was the lack of substantial income that had them turning me down, I think, however standard the pay rate was.

But no matter. Into my life popped two wonderful young ladies with backgrounds in long journeys like mine: Yiota Georgakopoulou, who would accompany us on the whole trip, and Kim Voogsgeerd, who would support us for the northern leg. Kim was a great photographer and video creator, and they would both be cooking and driving. I chose them because though they were young, they felt that tug of adventure, plus Yiota had driven around all of Australia and Kim from Seattle to Argentina. Also, I found it telling that they never brought up the money issue. All they talked about was the adventure, the opportunity, and my message. They too wanted to help show seniors, and young people, that getting off the couch and experiencing life is more important than anything else in life. Eventually, I got some more good news: my sister-in-law, Johana, agreed to come on board for the southern leg. Given she was from Colombia and now lived in Costa Rica, she spoke Spanish and English. What a lifesaver!

By now, less than three months out from the Octogenarian Odyssey, my brain just wouldn't stop whirling. There were just too many things to worry about, too many things going wrong, too many things that could yet go wrong. With no truck and camper, we were going to need tents for the northern leg in Alaska and Yukon where we weren't likely to find hotels or motels or Airbnb's. So that meant a lot more things to pack and somehow fit in and on a Dodge Caravan.

Would the bikes be held up by the supply-chain crisis? The pandemic had done me no favors thus far between finding supplies, masking on planes, and requiring PCR tests for COVID-19 at borders.

Would the van and camper be ready? Would the support team show up? What was the best way to register the van to avoid problems at the border? I wondered if maybe I should ask TDA Global Cycling, a first-class cycling tour outfit in Toronto, how they do it. What had I forgotten? Would the crew and Wayne be able to get along? What if someone gets fed up and leaves? Would I amass sufficient interesting material for this book? Should I record medical data each day in case someone might want to do an article on long-distance biking and its effect on an 80-year-old's body given a dear nurse friend of mine, Donna, had sent a letter requesting sponsorship in return for being the subject of a research project?

Did I have enough time in Edmonton to get a new passport since it was currently full, even though it had four years remaining? Should I fly to Edmonton during the trip to renew my health insurance? Fly from where? Puerto Vallarta? The thoughts went on and on, the questions kept coming, and the worry kept growing. I was definitely way out of my comfort zone.

Beyond all that, a film crew was still due to fly in from Mexico to shoot a two-minute video for a fundraising campaign my previous director had arranged—the results of which I never did see. On a sidenote, I later encountered Ryan, who'd spent the day shooting the video, on the highway south of Prince George, BC, and we chatted about his visit and how he was following my journey on Facebook. Anyway, I also had to renew my driver's license since at eighty you have to take a mental-fitness test and get a certificate from a doctor confirming you're still fit to drive, and I had to buy the plane tickets to Alaska. I even still had to buy the tickets for Gloria and Julie to meet me in Newport, Oregon, for my birthday. On that note, I worried daily that Wayne and the team and I would get there in time for the party we'd put together, to meet all the people flying in to join us. At least I'd built in three extra days just in case we hit bad weather or something. Still, the worries were enough to drive me crazy. My Octogenarian Odyssey was going to kick off on July 4, 2022, and I wasn't flying to Edmonton, where I'd undertake the final arrangements for the odyssey, until June 10. That gave me just twenty days to finalize every last detail, including getting to my son's wake on June 26.

And even more questions pummeled me in the middle of the night. Would I finish it in the expected 153 days? Would I be able to fulfill my expected average of 116 km a day? Would circumstances prevent it in some way? Would our bikes fail us?

By the time May rolled around, just two months away from my anticipated starting date of July 4, I was stressed. The closer I got to the journey's start, the more problems there were to iron out and the more details appeared that needed my attention. Like they say, the first 80 percent of the work is only 20 percent of the total work.

And then along came June. I still had to visit the dentist and doctor, shop for all the necessary items we'd need for the first leg of the odyssey, and drive to Vancouver to pick up the bikes. Then EVELO decided they wanted me to pick up the bikes in Seattle. That was definitely going to be a no-go. Customs would be a pain, and they'd had a year to get the bikes up to Canada. I had no choice but to insist that I pick them up in Vancouver on June 22.

And just as I thought I was working my way through the issues, the problems that continually popped up like a game of Whack-A-Mole, the other shoe fell.

While I was in Edmonton for my granddaughter's graduation, I tested positive for COVID-19. Not that I felt all that sick, but I did have mild symptoms like a head cold, and I had to isolate, which meant no work was getting done. I really didn't have time to get sick because I had to be better and out of isolation in time to get to my son's wake, a memorial for a friend, and my niece's wedding, right after which I'd have to head to Vancouver to pick up the bikes and put them in the van so Yiota and Kim could transport them to Fairbanks, Alaska.

However, I did have the peace of mind of knowing that between camping, friends' houses, and Airbnb, most of our accommodations were likely covered, circumstances depending of course, and I'd sent out a couple of letters seeking some supplies for camping and Gatorade and such. A contact of mine was even working on setting up something special for when we arrived in Panama City, maybe a police escort, maybe a nice restaurant to celebrate at. We had even decided to change our starting point to North Pole, Alaska—with Santa starting off with us—rather than Fairbanks, Alaska, and had kicked off a fundraising campaign to bring toys to children in Panama City thanks to a suggestion from Corinne Leistikow and Nina Tartakoff. That felt like something special, a way I could give back after all the good fortune I'd had in my life, despite the rough times.

And along with the worries was the excitement at the attention the media was showing to my adventure and its purpose of getting seniors, and people in general, up off the couch and doing something important to them, something they love. I had interviews lined up with Global and CBC and local newspapers. I even had podcasts scheduled before and during my journey! My greatest wish was that I could share my message with many, many people and raise enough money to purchase plenty of toys for the Panamanian children.

Then it was time for me to hit the road, driving from Edmonton to Vancouver via Penticton and then back again. This trip was going to total roughly three thousand kilometers. I might as well have driven to Alaska given it's three thousand kilometers from Edmonton to Fairbanks, Alaska. But I had to do it, go out to Vancouver to get the two electric bikes, a lot of clothing, spare parts, tires, tubes, brake pads, spare motors, a few more lights and other supplies. On the way to Vancouver, I'd stop in Penticton and swing by Swagman's main office to pick up the road-bike rack they'd donated for the roof of my van, a hitch rack for the two electric bikes, and a rooftop cargo box.

So, off on my pre-journey journey I went. Wouldn't you know it, when I got to Penticton, one of the racks wasn't available, so I had to continue to Vancouver and pick the rack up in Penticton on the way back. There's always something!

But I got some help installing all the racks and some great tips and stuff from Swagman, who overall had been great. So, all in all, I guess it wasn't all that big a hurdle to make a stop on the way back since I'd planned on going through Penticton anyway.

When I returned to Edmonton, I took a little time to fit in on a small ride so I could try out the new e-bikes. Turned out I was quite happy with just that little ride I did on the new bike. It was going to be an excellent, comfortable bike ride for the next five, five and a half months.

However, it did occur to me that when people saw and read and heard about us, they were going to say, "Oh, what a luxurious biking journey!" with my support crew and vehicle and someone riding with me, not to mention my using the e-bike as opposed to a regular bike. Perhaps that might give them the impression my odyssey was easy. After a little thought though, I realized I knew better, and that's what mattered. I'd be pedaling the whole way, up hills and down, in traffic and out. And it wasn't like this was ever supposed to be one of the typical barebones bikepacking trips. At this point in my life, I like to enjoy at least a little comfort, and if that means a roof over my head, a hot shower, and good meal, then so be it. Let people talk. Cause it was sure going to look like a party when we set up camp up north with five camping chairs set out and everyone sitting around having a cold one. We'll make memories, I thought.

But what I expected people to say never materialized. From the moment I posted my plans on my Facebook groups until we reached the finish line, I received encouragement from hundreds of bikers, mainly seniors. Their responses were encouraging, and I expected many of them to come out to ride with me as I passed through their towns and cities. Many of them read like this:

"Wow! I'm going to use you as inspiration! Safe travels, and we look forward to hearing/seeing posts from time to time from you! And good luck. You're such an inspiration to us older riders."

"You are an inspiration to this 68-year-old 'youngster.' Ride on!"

"Oh wow!!! This guy is amazing!!!"

"You are an inspiration to all of us old geezers."

"You're a badass 👊."

"Best wishes on your amazing adventure. You truly are an inspiration. I plan to share your story with my cycling club friends."

"Robert Fletcher, thank you! I am 72 and you give me hope! I look forward to watching your journey."

"So cool, be safe. I want to do something like this someday. Take good notes!!"

"Absolutely amazing! This is pure inspiration for me to accomplish my goals."

"Wow, what an inspiration!! I am in awe of your energy and ambition. I look forward to following your journey 👊."

"You are a hero, Robert."

"Amazing. I'm 80 and still on the sofa mostly. But my e-bike gets me out for a daily 10-mile ride. Will follow you along on your trip."

Me and Wayne, longtime riding partners, experiencing all life has to offer.

While I love seeing that I'm inspiring people and hopefully improving their lives in some way, the reverse is also true. Their messages fill me with such energy, motivation, and inspiration that it keeps me full up with happiness. Every day that I see these messages is a good day, however difficult the planning gets or how bad a day it might seem to be at first. And when I received this email on June 27, days sure before I left for Alaska, from the Canadian ambassador to Costa Rica, I was floored—and humbled:

Dear Robert,

Mucha mierda, mensaje de despedida! Good luck, send-off message!

I so wish I could join your send-off celebration! I am honored that you have asked me to share a few words as you get ready to spend A LOT of quality time on your bicycle seat!

While we have not yet met in person, I am very inspired by your story and who you are as a person, taking on new challenges, your sense of adventure and curiosity, your openness to not only new places but also new people.

I remember when Sean Rourke told me about you last fall, how you had moved from Edmonton to Costa Rica and work as a bike guide (I thought, cool), your plan to cycle from Alaska to Panama City (wow!) to celebrate your 80th (WHAATTT, who is this guy??) Until that last detail, I had you pegged as a thirty–something with wanderlust! Learning about your career as an educator, the challenges, and adventures you have undertaken, you are breaking all stereotypes and biases and an excellent ambassador for making the most of time, opportunities, and abilities!

I, like many others, will be tracking your adventure across North and Central America. I hope that the highs of each day, the people you meet, the words of encouragement, and positive energy we are all channeling your way help carry you through the tough climbs, inclement weather, and scary wildlife encounters! Remember to register yourself in the "Registration for Canadians Abroad" [database] so that my consular colleagues can contact, assist, and protect you and your co-travelers in case of emergency.

Wishing you all the best, Robert, on part two of your Octogenarian Odyssey! Looking forward to hosting a belated 80th/Guinness World Record celebration for you when you return to Costa Rica!

Pura Vida!

Elizabeth Williams
Ambassador of Canada to Costa Rica, Honduras and Nicaragua

With all those positive messages and goodwill in my back pocket, I was excited to get started. For good or ill, it was time to hop on a plane and jet to Alaska to be there by the first of July for Wayne's birthday. I laughed when reporters asked about who I was riding with. I told them I was riding with a youngster because Wayne was only going to be sixty-nine when we started. He's such a great guy to ride with though, and a really good friend. We've ridden together a few times, so I was happy he'd agreed to ride with me on my odyssey.

Anyway, by then, I was more than glad to start peddling and relieve some of the stress I'd been buried under for the previous six months. I couldn't wait to see what new experiences and people and sights I came across!

So come and join me as I cycle through the incredible scenic wilderness of Alaska, Yukon, and British Columbia. Follow me along the spectacular Pacific coast of the US and through the colorful countries of Central America. You will see beautiful landscapes, experience new cultures, and meet and experience the lives of the people as I ride my bike through their towns and villages. Watch me overcome difficult times and problems at the borders and enjoy the food, the language, the people, and the music.

This odyssey will take 157 days, more or less, take me through nine countries, and cover about 13,500 km. Many of my friends warned me about the dangers that might be lying ahead. Bears in the far north, forest fires, extreme heat in the Mexican desert, drug cartels, vehicles, and the high humidity of the southern jungles. I always just thanked them for their concern and reminded them that I've completed many month-long rides, climbed mountains, and walked across Spain. Fear wasn't about to stop me from living, from following my dreams. Nor was I one to hop on a plane and whiz to some enormous all-inclusive on a beach and miss everything and everyone in between there and home.

As someone once said, I would not be buying things; I would be making memories.

ADVENTURE and ADVERSITY

It was about time. Day one of the Octogenarian Odyssey was about to kick off. All the apprehension had melted away and excitement had replaced it as I stood there beside my sparkling new EVELO Atlas e-bike in North Pole, Alaska, with my riding partner, Wayne Grover, my support team of Yiota Georgakopoulou and Kim Voogsgeerd, and Santa. As I looked around at my team and the supporters and curious folks that had gathered around me, I marveled that I'd gotten to this point. I think I do at least a little bit at the start of every journey where I'm doing the planning.

After all the ups and downs of the last six months, we all finally arrived safely in Fairbanks, Alaska, and got to greet the friendly airport moose to start things off. In fact, things went better than originally planned because Wayne and I were able to catch an earlier flight out of Anchorage, allowing us to get to Fairbanks three hours early! We didn't have any issues to speak of with the flights or timings, and wonder of wonders, there were no more COVID-19 test requirements to deal with anymore at the Canadian/US border for fully vaccinated folks. Talk about great timing.

Kim picked us up at the airport because I'd met her in Edmonton a week earlier and given her the van. From there, we headed to a nice restaurant on the river called Pike's Landing to celebrate Wayne's sixty nineth birthday. This place has had the honor of being either the start or finish lines or a marker for the Iron Dog Gold Rush Classic, the longest snowmobile race in the world, since its inception in 1984. It's even been the starting line for the Iditarod sled dog race a couple times. This was a fantastic setting for the beginning of my own odyssey.

It was a good chance for Wayne and I to get to know Kim and vice versa. We sat relaxing, and maybe imbibing a little, in the twenty-eight-degree heat and the cloying forest-fire smoke, taking in the folks enjoying the long weekend on their jet boats, water skis, kayaks, and skidoos on the river as it sparkled in the late afternoon sun. Turns out in the winter, Pike's Landing is an ice bridge you can drive over. In the summer though, you can try your hand at hitting golf balls over the river—if you don't knock out any boaters!

Kim and I at Pike's Landing.

Later in the evening we met a chap who was also celebrating a birthday on the same day as Wayne, and we had a nice chat. He was from Oregon and he and a friend were riding through Alaska and Yukon on their way to Alberta. Once there, he was going to spend some time checking out Olds, the town he'd been born in. What are the odds of running into someone with not only the same birthday as you but also with ties to your home province? Turns out he also played in the NFL for Seattle and a few other teams for a while. And he was turning seventy-four.

So, it turned out to be a wonderful evening with some great company and an even more spectacular view. We brought out a cake for Wayne, and the whole restaurant sang Happy Birthday to him—and the fellow from Oregon. We still had a lot to do the next day though—like buying tire liners and a tailgate tent for the van—as it was to be our last day before we began our adventure. So, we called it a night before it got too late and made our way to Corinne Leistikow's empty house, just twenty-three kilometers outside Fairbanks, that they had graciously offered to let us use for three nights. She and her husband were away in Washington participating in a bike race, so we had the space to ourselves.

**

The next day we discovered just how lucky we were to have been given use of a house because to organize all our stuff for the trip, we had to spread it all out before we could pack it all into the van. And of course, this was where the hiccups began. While we were organizing everything and deciding on procedures and sleeping spaces during the trip, it became apparent we weren't all on the same page.

Kim and Yiota wanted to sleep in tents, so they didn't have to unload the car every night, but I thought it was important for someone to always sleep in the van because of all the gear we were toting, even if it meant we had to put all our supplies in a tent each night. I understood where they were coming from though; four people made for a lot of stuff: three bikes, spare parts, camping equipment, the big Swagman racks on the roof, food, and all the incidentals. That's a lot of extra work every night, but at the same time, that's what I was paying them for. Well, that and cooking, shopping, and driving. In the end, those logistics worked out. I decided I'd sleep in the van, and they could sleep in the tent trailer. Simple.

But then things became not so simple. Before we took off for the North Pole and the first day of our odyssey, we had to deal with some more frustration. We had to put the bikes together and somehow, I still don't know how, I turned on the bike when I wasn't supposed to and caused a spark that caused a fire in the battery. On top of that, it turned out we were missing some spacers on the handlebars, we were going to need new ones. The frustration was building inside me. I didn't know how I was going to pull this off, if we would leave in time, or if we would even get going at all!

But wonder of wonders, I managed to arrange to pick the spacers up in Fairbanks, Alaska, so we took some downtime to wander the streets of downtown Fairbanks, chatting with a few people, visiting some historic sites, and taking some photos. It's a beautiful town of about 32,000 people, and it's one of those rare places that seamlessly combines a wild, natural feel with modern, urban amenities. Here, we got to experience incredible art displays, historic buildings, and abundant wildlife. Not to be missed was the site of the Yukon Quest—a thousand-mile international dog sled race from Fairbanks, Alaska, to Whitehorse, Yukon—with its sod roof, the Ice Museum housed in an old 1940s movie theater, and the clock tower. All this plus the Fairbanks Downtown Hostel, the courthouse, and the most magnificent graffiti-art wall— was all downtown. Of course, to top it all off, we stopped at Beaver Sports to fix my faulty e-bike headset.

About the only thing we didn't get to see was the northern lights, or aurora borealis. It was just too early in the year yet. We did, however, get to experience once again the wondrous but confusing twenty-four-hour day. As lovely as it is to have sunshine all day, it's a little tough on the brain and the internal clock.

But as we all know, all good things must end, and in this case, we had to move on to bigger and better things. So, after a nice relaxing dinner, we went back to Corinne's house to get a good night's sleep—as best we could with the sun still up anyway—in preparation for the big day. It was going to be early morning because we still had to pack everything in the van and the camper and make sure we cleaned the house behind us.

***

The next day dawned sunny and dry, but with the smoke obscuring the sun, it felt cloudy and dreary. But no matter, I was filled with excitement and energy. I am always at the beginning of a journey. If I really dwell on that, I think I might even have to say I enjoy the beginning more than the end, however difficult a journey may turn out to be.

After a hearty breakfast and a cup of coffee, we went to face our first hurdle: packing everything, including the bikes, in the van and camper. Now that's a bigger challenge than any good old-fashioned game of Tetris. Somehow, not only did we have to get all our bikes, supplies, and incidentals stuffed in, there were four of us to fit in that one Dodge Caravan.

A few hours later, we'd somehow managed to pack everything up, do our laundry, and clean the house, and we were on the road. Though driving down the quiet highway should have been peaceful as I watched the pines and poplars whiz by, I was still fraught with worry. Given how long it had taken us to pack up, had I bought too much stuff? Had we all perhaps personally brought way too much? Maybe I'd bought the wrong vehicle/tent trailer setup since we couldn't put the bike rack on top of the tent trailer. Though Wayne's Road bike fit fine on the rack atop the van, having to put all the bikes and gear in the van had been an almost impossible feat. Heck, one member had so much stuff—three bags! —it just took up so much room!

Not long after we'd left, we came across a park with a lookout on the Trans-Alaska pipeline, so we pulled over to look and stretch our legs. I decided then to shake off my worries and melancholy and just appreciate the moment. I was impressed reading about the pipeline as it stood dwarfing us. At the time the pipeline was built, the billions of dollars it had taken to do so had made it the most expensive project in the world, and in history! The whole thing totals eight hundred miles of pipeline built above ground to avoid messing with the permafrost.

It's hard to mope and worry when you're in one of the most spectacular natural vistas in the world. My mood improved from there, and I focused on just absorbing the scenery while I had this rare opportunity to sit in the van. The spruce and birch and poplar trees were interrupted only by the pink fireweed that stretched for miles, and that was punctuated occasionally with bright blue wild iris.

And suddenly, before I was quite ready, I think, we were in North Pole, Alaska, just a small town twenty-three kilometers south of Fairbanks, with its candy-striped North Pole monument, towering Santa Claus, and Santa Claus House. To my delight, three local riders had decided to join us aways, and a friendly fellow named Austin took us to see the North-Pole pole, which turned out to be a pole that had originally been dropped on the real north pole to celebrate a geological thing, later found in a junkyard, and placed in North Pole.

After we officially kicked off the odyssey, we all rode out to check out the famed Santa Claus House that sold all things Christmas. I'd been hoping I could convince Santa to officially start our journey, but I should have known he would be far too busy.

Me with Santa and Mrs. Claus.

But while I was there, I bought some postcards for book pre-purchasers that I would personally write something in and sign that night before dropping them in the mailbox in Tok, Alaska. Of course, we also met Santa and had a long chat about us helping him out and buying Christmas presents for kids in Panama with donations that we'd hand out at the end of the journey. Wouldn't you know it, Santa was so impressed, he made me an honorary elf and filmed a video for us that we could use to help get more donations for presents. Our last stop was to visit Santa's reindeer in their pen and to take a picture of the world's largest Santa.

And then there I was, standing beside my EVELO e-bike with Wayne beside me, about to embark on a journey to break a world record. A group of well-wishers surrounded us and added to the buzz of excitement in the air, along with the ever-present smoke.

The Guinness Book of World Records required witnesses to sign a statement testifying that they did indeed watch me start my journey pedaling on an e-bike in North Pole, Alaska, so I asked some of the cyclists from the local cycling club that were joining us for a little while to do so for me before we got started.

Then with all the official junk out of the way, we could finally start riding. Two folks from the North Pole biking club, Matt and Ariane, a happy younger couple, guided us down the highway for about thirty kilometers, and I reveled in every one of those first minutes back on my bike, the wind on my face and in my hair, the sun on my skin—what I could feel of it through the smoke—the conversation.

With all the time that had already passed earlier in the day with the drive from Fairbanks and our sightseeing, it wasn't long before we pulled in for lunch at Knotty (Naughty) Restaurant. We later learned it had been named after all the deformed trees people carve animals into; there was even a giant mosquito! It was rather fitting since I got eaten alive later that night. Anyway, we had a fabulous lunch before setting out again. We were still only halfway through our planned distance for the day after all. We picked up the river flowing high and fast from the mountains and followed it as it ran all muddy beside us. It was a relief to not ride in rain, which was good for us, bad for the fires, so we rode until the sun was a big orange ball in the sky.

From left: Wayne, Ariane, Matt, and Me

After the peaceful, successful start to our day and our journey, you know it was inevitable that we'd hit a speed bump. And we did when the girls, Kim and Yiota drove ahead to start setting up at the campground I'd planned to stay at for the night. To my surprise, they drove back not much later, only to tell me that that campground was full. Luckily, we had just passed a private campground called "C" Lazy Moose RV Park. So, we turned around, put up the tents and trailer, and settled in for the night. It was a nice warm night, but because the first campground had been full, we'd had to stop sixteen kilometers short, which meant we'd have to bike 103 km tomorrow to a place with cabins and a small roadhouse. On a positive note, I was comfy in the camper that night. It had good ventilation, and I only needed a light sleeping bag when it cooled off late into the night. As tired as I was though, it was still a little tough to fall asleep with the sun in a sort of permanent twilight phase.

***

The next day, our first full day on the road, started off cool, with no wind and the orange sun trying to beat its way through the thick smoke. It was supposed to get hot again though, and it occurred to me that it felt odd to have this kind of heat here at the beginning of my journey. I had expected it in Mexico and Central America, but though I know Alaska can get warm in the summer too, somehow, I hadn't quite expected it to be quite that hot. I supposed that was just more evidence of climate change.

Anyway, I got up first. After a few peaceful moments with just me and nature, the team started stirring. That's when we came upon our next speed bump. Wayne seemed to have felt the thirty-degree, no-wind heat the day before. He'd spent the night in the tent, so it was likely we'd have to rotate weekly between the tents and tent trailer so he could cool off too. In fact, he was feeling so rough on our second day that he declared he wanted to stay in a cabin the next night for an extra $90, but I really preferred to keep camping given the expenses on the trip. I understood where he was coming from though. I mean, heat will do anyone in, so I ended up going ahead and renting a cabin that night. However, it was both to help Wayne and because I'd already planned to stay at a nice place at the end of that day's route; I'd just originally planned on camping, not getting a cabin. A little voice inside me hoped Wayne wouldn't always be making demands. He even suggested everyone put in another $1,000 each so we could all stay in hotels every night. I wasn't thrilled with that idea at all. The girls loved camping, and I loved camping, so there didn't seem to be much reason to put all that money out. And the girls seemed quite suited for camping every night; they certainly weren't princesses. Besides, I had a lot of expenses, and the trip was just starting. Thank goodness that idea never got off the ground.

Well, once Wayne was feeling better and the girls had the camp all packed up, we headed out for our first full day of riding at around 8:30 a.m. It was a little cool still, but there was no wind, so if it weren't for the smoke hindering our breathing, it would have been a perfect day for riding.

We spent the day cycling alongside the Tanana River. It was an enormous river, about a mile across, and it was flowing high and fast, stirring up all the mud and muck and making it look brown and dirty despite it being cleaner than most rivers. I was sure the smoke obscuring the sun wasn't helping any. With no real sunshine to speak of, there was no light to sparkle on the water. That's not to say it still wasn't incredibly beautiful as it snaked around sandbars and islands carpeted with trees.

When we stopped at a little turnout at the top of a climb, I learned that this river had been the site of a 1902 gold rush. That gold rush had attracted somewhere around 1,500 miners, who over five years, took away $10 million worth of gold. It benefited many communities, even all the way up to Fairbanks, whose merchants prospered from selling the necessary mining equipment until the rush petered out around 1916.

From left: Wayne above the Tanana River, moose in a pond.

As we rode along the mostly flat highway, suddenly, my attention was caught by one of the most awe-inspiring dangers no one had warned me about, though I should have thought of it: a moose. Not that we bothered him, nor did he even seem to care about us though, we'd stopped to get a closer look. He was just hanging out in a pond, likely cooling off from the unusual heat, maybe even trying to find some relief from the thick smoke from the nearby forest fires that clung to the air.

After that, apart from being attacked by mosquitos each time we stopped—and black flies and horse flies—well and missing the shining sun thanks to the forest-fire smoke, our first full day went rather smoothly. We didn't have any close calls, the highway was straight and clear and well-maintained, and the bikes held up well. In fact, we made such a good time there was plenty of time to stop and take photos in the turnouts at places like Delta Junction, which is what they call "The Northern Terminus of the Alcan Highway." Seven army regiments and forty-two contractors had worked simultaneously from Delta Junction South and Dawson Creek North to finish the highway during World War II.

I did indeed get us some cabins for the night, and they were clean and cozy. It certainly made Wayne happy, and I suspect

Yiota and Kim didn't mind either. I'll admit I didn't mind sleeping somewhere cozier than the van too.

***

The next day was much like the previous, and I was so caught up in the adventure and the beauty around me that I spent the time just enjoying it instead of taking mental notes. I didn't even stop to see if I had cell service. What I did notice, though not until the next day when we'd reached Tok, Alaska, and our first rest day, was that Airbnb had written up a fantastic article about my Octogenarian Odyssey called, "Living anywhere at any age: One retiree's 'Octogenarian Odyssey.'" Tell me that wasn't thrilling! It was quite a treat to see my name and story published, but the most important part to me was the quote they included: "Life doesn't have to stop just because you're retired. Through my Octogenarian Odyssey, I want to show people of all ages how important it is to stay active, keep traveling, and live anywhere the world takes you." That was the exact message I wanted to spread around the world, and that article was a step in the right direction.

By the end of day four and after riding 340 km, we'd reached Tok, Alaska, and got to enjoy our first rest day. Even if we didn't really need a long rest yet, it seemed my e-bike did. For some reason, the batteries hadn't been syncing properly. That wasn't the end of the world since you can charge one battery while you're using the other and then switch them out, but it's lot easier, not to mention more accurate, to have them synced together.

The riding, though, was smooth sailing with lots of wildlife to entertain us, moose in particular. Funny, on this trip, we saw many moose—we even had one wander through our campground the previous night—and even bears, but on my last trip up here I saw neither of those. It did make me wonder why, but I couldn't decide if it was because we're encroaching even more on their habitat or if the quiet of the pandemic brought them out. But other than nature, we had the highway to ourselves, with long straight stretches and not many cars to bother us. We didn't have a boring moment riding that day; there was so much to see on the way from Sasquatch forms, Mukluk Land, and a giant beach chair to Moon Lake State Park, enormous banks of solar panels, and Tok Memorial Park.

That night, we stayed at the Alaskan Stoves Campground and Hostel. That was one unique campground. Not only could you rent existing trailers or RVs or just rent a spot as we did, but they offered hotel rooms that were exact replicas of Sam McGee's stove, which yes, comes from Robert W. Service's (1874–1958) poem, *The Cremation of Sam McGee*. For fifty bucks a night, you too can spend the night in Sam McGee's oven and imagine you're being cremated. If you make it through the night, you earn a certificate. It is well-appointed and comfortable, however. The campground itself was a wonderful place for a rest day. We had use of a quaint but nicely functional outdoor kitchen, hot showers, and laundry services.

Now that we were a few days in, it was becoming obvious that we had to give Yiota a little more help setting up camp. She was starting to seem stressed and overworked, so I determined the group needed to pitch in more by hauling the bags and things. I knew she liked to do things on her own, like if she saw me carry a bag she'd do it instead, but everyone can do it with a helping hand. There were still many, many miles left to go, and we couldn't afford to have her burn out or grow resentful.

Kim, I'd discovered by then, was a great photographer and got some amazing shots with her still camera. We had a drone too, catching some mind-blowing footage, but there's just something about a photo that catches a moment in time.

The mosquitoes, of course, were awful the whole time. They didn't affect me all that terribly other than being an annoyance, but Kim was covered in big, red, itchy bites. There was just no getting away from them in the wilds of Alaska despite using gallons of bug spray to try and mitigate. Worse than the mosquitos—I think anyway—were the black flies and horse flies. Those things are ruthless and determined, and it hurts like hell when they get you! And there's billions of them. The mornings aren't bad, but once you stop for lunch, they come in on you. So, then you jump back on your bike and pedal as fast as you can to try and lose them, but those crazy bugs will keep up! They'll follow you for miles before they finally give up.

Anyway, a satisfying dinner after we'd pulled into the campground and gotten set up was just what we needed. We ate at Fast Eddy's, which is renowned throughout Alaska. It has enormous portions. Yiota ordered a medium pizza thinking it would have maybe six slices, but it was so big it could have been a large. I'd hate to see what the large and family size pizzas look like! She managed to eat four pieces though, but that still left enough for everyone to eat it all the next day. Either Kim or Wayne had lasagna with the salad bar—I can't remember which anymore—and I had a much-needed steak sandwich. It wasn't the best I'd ever had, but though it was tough, it was still good.

***

Happy hour at the Three Bears next door to our campground was the highlight of our rest day. I spent some time talking to the bartender and a fella at the bar who was headed to the Fairbanks army post for a two-year stint. Everyone was friendly and chatty, and that's always what motivates me. It's what I love best about long-distance cycling: meeting new people, finding new restaurants, and trying new food. I have a bit of a reputation for finding small, quaint restaurants where locals dine. It makes my mouth water just thinking about eating casados, pupusas, empanadas, tacos, arepas, tamales, patacones, and more on my ongoing trek.

I expected to cross into Canada the next afternoon, which would bring us closer to our first two-night stop in Whitehorse. Maybe with some down time everyone could rest, and the little dramas like with the sleeping arrangements would ease. A man could hope, right?

My other worry was still the bike and its battery-system problems, so I spent a good chunk of my break writing a long email to EVELO. I wondered if they hadn't put in an older second battery in the brand-new bike because there'd been some bugs in the electrical system—though by the time I'd finished my journey, I'd realized I might have damaged the set up when I'd put the bikes together because it was only the backup battery that would never work right. But at the time, it seemed one battery would get about 113 km, then I had to fiddle around and replace it with the second one to get any farther. The problem was I didn't want to have to carry around the backup battery on my back panier. It would be much nicer to have the system sync and work as it should so when the range meter said how far I had left before having to stop and recharge, I knew it meant both batteries, not just one.

And of course, then we noticed another issue. Funny how there's always issues, things you never would have thought of. Maybe that's half the fun of an odyssey: the challenge of overcoming unforeseen obstacles. So, Yiota and Kim noticed that they'd gotten the wrong form for the Guinness Book of World Records filled out back at the starting line in North Pole, Alaska. *Oh, jeez*, I thought when they told me. *What a great way to start the journey.* But I decided it was neither here nor there. I wasn't truly doing this just to break the world record. I assured them that we could just start from Tok, Alaska, instead and get a couple people to fill out the right form here.

But lo and behold, the universe gave me a break. I was on Facebook and Instagram later that day and came across someone who said they were the mom of the young couple,

Matt, and Ariane, who'd signed the original form. So, I sent her the correct one, she got the two to sign it, and she sent it back to me. The rub was that Ariane had noticed the form said it had to be signed by someone important like a doctor or lawyer or something.

So, I took another look at the form, and it just said it *should* be signed by someone like that, not that it *must* be. My response to Matt and Ariane then was that there's nothing saying we must obey. And besides, who says a bike rider or plumber or someone else isn't as important as a doctor or lawyer? That was kind of garbage, and we wouldn't take that. If Guinness accepted it, they accepted it. If not, it wouldn't be the end of the world.

And so, our first rest day came to an end. We had a lovely rest, learned a few things about the history of Tok and the people, and chatted with some fantastic folks. I was even feeling confident that we'd ironed out some of our issues, and that we'd get along even better now, especially after a good night's sleep.

***

After we finished packing things up that morning, we hopped back on our bikes again, Wayne and I; the girls followed in the van. An air of excitement buzzed in the air, and the ride was a pleasant one besides the bugs and the odd traffic, but the weather stayed in our favor—for a while.

As soon as I gave thanks for the weather we'd had thus far into the journey, we crossed what must have been the weather border. As crazy as it sounds, right about the time we crossed into Yukon, Canada, the weather took a turn. It was almost like it was trying to discourage us from continuing, trying to make us turn back because we weren't welcome there or something. The temperature dropped, the skies clouded over, and the rain—the so, so, so cold rain—gave us a beating.

Of course, also after crossing the border, we lost cell service somewhere around Beaver Creek, the most westerly community in Canada, and went the next four days without, so this was part of the odyssey that was just miserable. As any long-distance cyclist knows, they can't all be great days. Some days can be downright dark and dirty, and you question why you keep doing this to yourself. Nevertheless, Wayne and I kept pushing through despite freezing temperatures, putting plastic bags on our feet and shoulders to keep them dry and warm, and sometimes even having to take shelter anywhere we could. Every time we'd have to stop and find shelter though really slowed us down, so when we got going again, we'd have to boogie to catch up to Kim and Yiota in the support van. Some days we even came up short on our kilometers, and that was incredibly stressful given I had to be in Newport, Oregon, on time.

On the other side of that coin, with the rotten weather and no cell service, is that at a time like this on a ride like this, you're completely alone with nature. It's entirely humbling to look around you as you ride and not only see but feel the power of nature: the stately mountains rising in the distance, the pines towering into the sky, and birds soaring above from tree to tree. In the backwoods like this, your music is the song of the birds and breath of the trees as they sway in the wind, the patter of the raindrops hitting the pavement and your helmet. You can forget about the cold and the wet for a while when you immerse yourself in the wonder of it all. You just don't get that when you travel through in a vehicle. You miss all the little things, all the important things that make you glad to just be alive to experience both the beauty and the hardship.

The incredibleness of nature

Even those times at camp at night when the disagreements and the drama reached a head and got to be too much, when Wayne felt the girls weren't respecting him, and the girls felt the same way about him, when the arguments about the sleeping arrangements popped up, and the rain kept pouring down and trying to put out the campfire, there were still so many positives.

***

So, after all those days in the rain and wind, our total distance ridden was a little over four hundred kilometers. It got cold once, around six degrees Celsius, but at least I got a warm room and a shower one night.

Eventually, after stops in Beaver Creek, Destruction Bay, and Haines Junction, we made it to Whitehorse, where we stayed with a Facebook friend. Well, we were supposed to stay with them, but in the time, it took us to get here, they'd had to pivot to attend a wedding in Calgary. However, their father and daughter were happy to host us in an RV in the driveway for a couple nights. And to say we appreciated their hospitality after the weather we'd come through was an understatement. Everyone we'd met on the road was kind, generous, and really interested in what we were doing. That sign I'd put on the back of my bike, "Alaska to Panama," really worked!

While we were in Whitehorse, I gave a couple interviews, one on TV that didn't go as well as I would have hoped, and another for the Whitehorse Star. Morris Prokop, the sports editor, wrote a fantastic piece about my Octogenarian Odyssey, calling my journey, "epic."

Then Wayne wanted to look around old town, so we went down to the river and took some photos before stopping in at the Visitor's Center. We spent a good half hour learning about bears from a lovely instructor too. I learned some new, helpful information given how much time we spent out in the open in nature, such as to direct the bear spray at your feet before moving it in a circular fashion upward because bears keep their heads down. I hope I never need that information!

Old town Whitehorse, Yukon

***

Well, we ended up leaving Whitehorse late, not until noon, because the battery in the car wouldn't start—which was an omen of things to come—but once we got going, I fell into enjoying the rolling hills and the three moose we came across just off the road. We stopped and looked at them and they looked back at us. That is true peace. The air was even warming up, and the sun was trying to peek out from behind the clouds!

After we pedaled down the highway on that peaceful day, it was easy for me to think the next day would be serene and warmer too, but the only great part about the next day was when we came upon a fellow cyclist from Japan taking four or five years cycling the world and another from Vancouver riding all the way to the Arctic Circle. I love meeting new people. Ah, but Yiota did make a fantastic soup for dinner. I'm not sure what it was, but I think I remember there was egg and lemon in it. What I remember for sure is that it was exactly what I needed after a long, cold, hard day's ride with lots of climbing, and into headwinds at that. The weather had not been kind to us since Alaska, and it was putting everyone on edge.

JUST A SHORT INTERRUPTION

Now that you've read this far into my story, perhaps you'd like to be the first to know when book two comes out. Or perhaps you would like to see and hear a talk I gave to the Edmonton Bike and Touring Club; this will give you more information about what you have been reading. Or perhaps you'd like me to speak at your event or to your group. If so, just head to https://octoodyssey.com/subscribe-to-video/ and leave your email address and a comment if you like. I'll get in touch with you to arrange a speaking time and place and/or I'll reserve a copy of book two for you.

Thank you all for your support.

DELIGHTS and DRAMAS

Not far out of Whitehorse, I got to meet up with a longtime friend and former coworker, Peter, and his wife, Joanne, just outside Whitehorse. They prepared a lovely dinner of moose heart, bison burgers, and Yukon lobster—or Northern Pike. That was another positive about my odyssey. We always ate well, and all the food was spectacular. Whether we came across new restaurants or the girls were making chili con carne or Indian food or soup, the food was a definite high point. Maybe it was just the fresh air and exercise that made it all taste even better, but even if that was the case, it didn't matter to me. I always ate well, and I always ate my fill.

Once past Whitehorse, the warmer weather nature had momentarily teased us with disappeared and we pushed through more bad weather, climbing, and headwinds. How fortuitous that I'd stopped in Whitehorse and bought some long pants! The upside was that once we'd reached Carcross Corner, where the highway to Skagway, Alaska, meets the Alaskan Highway, all the trucks disappeared finally, and we had the highway to ourselves.

Well, despite the stupid weather that just wouldn't cooperate, we rode on, spending the night at a scenic campground beside Squenga Lake, surrounded by mountains. After a great supper of BBQ ribs and potatoes, we finally woke up the next morning to a sunny day and were in for a sunscreen kind of day. Not that I was complaining. It had been a long time since we'd seen the sun.

Unfortunately, there was still friction in camp, and it showed no signs of easing. Yiota and Kim were upset that Wayne didn't put things back after using them, and Wayne was upset that they never had things like water, hand wipes, or hand sanitizer out at lunch when he arrived. His point was it only takes a minute, so why wouldn't they do that?

But because the sun had shown up that morning, I tried to convince myself to worry about it later. That day was only going to be a short ride, only about 71 km before we'd reach our campsite on the river at Teslin. We were going to have to cross a huge steel bridge with lots of holes to get there, though. A bridge like can be scary for riding, at least on a road bike like Wayne was riding, but I was sure we'd be fine. They're a little more dangerous but not all that scary for me with my e-bike and its fatter tires. I just say the hell with it, go, and stay tight in my lane.

I looked around the campsite that morning and took in the sun shining on everyone. The car was running, the inverter was running, and the coffee was percolating, so I knew deep down it would be a good day. Besides, I had no idea what I could do about the friction. I'd already tried talking to both sides, but it was clear it was all still simmering under the surface.

In the end, we reached Teslin with no real issues, but it was still bloody cold at night. Then we continued to the Continental Divide as we neared the Yukon/British Columbia border. Along the way, we spent a night at the Baby Nugget RV Park in Nugget City, where Wayne was positive, we'd discovered the snowbirds' secret breeding grounds.

Baby Nugget RV Park

Adding my name to the list in Nugget City

I loved that campground as soon as I saw the Wolf it Down restaurant but decided it was an incredible place when we learned it kept a list of all the cyclists heading north and south through the area on a big billboard. I learned it was a great way to keep track of where your friends, or just other cyclists, were on their journeys. I signed my name on it, and as I did, I noticed with interest that there were about fourteen folks headed for Argentina in June 2022. I made a mental note to look them up and check out their routes when I started preparing for part two of the Octogenarian Odyssey.

After yet another cold day, dinner that night was noodle soup and burgers, then we huddled in the tent trailer with the heater going, all warm and cozy.

***

The next day, the battery in the support vehicle quit again, so I told Kim and Yiota to take it in to Watson Lake to buy a new battery and some groceries. I didn't think much of it until it started getting late and they still hadn't returned, so then I started worrying. Had they had car problems? Had they been in an accident or encountered bad people? Then I moved onto worrying about where Wayne and I would spend the night if they didn't come back by then—or at all. Thankfully, we'd joined our good friends, Colleen, and Bernice, by then, so I wondered briefly if we could all sleep in their tent for one night before ruling that out. So, then I thought maybe Colleen and Bernice could take Wayne and I to a hotel, leaving the bikes at the campground and hoping the girls would show up with the trailer by the next day to pick us and everything else up. I just couldn't figure out the most ideal option, likely because I was concerned about Yiota and Kim.

Well, it turned out I was overthinking it. The guy at the store just sold the car batteries, he didn't install them, so Yiota and Kim had had to go to a mechanic to get it put in and didn't get back to us until later that night. So of course, there was $250 for a new battery and installation. The old battery had been maybe nine years old, but I was still mad because I'd taken the van to Canadian Tire in Canada before leaving and shelled out $1,000 to make sure the van was road worthy and good to go. Not once did they say anything about the battery needing replacing. Heck, they didn't even test it.

***

Well, we had another short distance to pedal the next day, and for a time I reveled in the smells of the forest as the sun kept me comfortable. Then after a delightful lunch of chicken masala leftovers, we had to face the mountain range on our way south. As Wayne, Colleen, Bernice, and I amused ourselves with a game of leapfrog, we heard about other cyclists through the grapevine, in other words, people we met whenever we stopped at rest stops or stores. Finally, we crossed into British Columbia on our way to Boya Lake. Of course, that's when horrible headwinds overtook us, and with just fifty kilometers to go, it started to drizzle. Before we knew it, the rain started coming down hard the last twenty kilometers, soaking Wayne, and I from head to toe. Unfortunately, I'd been wearing just sandals and old socks, so I got drenched fast. By the time we finally reached Boya Lake, we just wanted to get warm. At least Colleen and Bernice camped in the site right beside us, so with two fires to finally warm us, it at least ended up being another one of those nights that make for good memories.

***

Thank goodness the next day dawned warm and sunny, making the blues and greens of the lake sparkle in the brightness of it all. Even the wind had finally settled down, enough so the water of the lake was clear as glass.

Beautiful Boya Lake

Beautiful Boya Lake

When the sun graced us with its presence that morning, I finally got to drink my morning coffee as I basked in its warmth. As Colleen and Kim changed for a quick swim, I decided then that maybe we were finally out of the coldest, wettest part of the journey, so I put on less layers that day. I was hoping I wasn't tempting fate.

Colleen was gracious enough to start our day off strong by making French toast with fruit salad and yogurt for breakfast. That was a superb way to start our daily trek. And things happily went well from there. Though we did face a headwind and some rolling hills for a while, most of the day was good riding. We even came across a moose with two calves, two foxes—one with lunch in its mouth— and a bear that day.

It was about time we'd finally had a good day. It had been getting harder and harder to keep our spirits up the farther away we got from Alaska. Perhaps that was contributing to the tension in camp too. For my part, I figured I had to weigh everything. Though the weather had been miserable for a long time, there was no cell service or internet, and the world around us had been desolate, that also made for little traffic. Most days we came across only a few trucks and campers, sometimes some motorcycles. It made for much safer and more relaxed riding. Though I'll admit it was tough to be prepared with no internet or cell service, at least as far as the weather was concerned. The only way we could find out what kind of weather was in store for us ahead was by asking folks coming in the opposite direction. One time, we met a group of thirteen bike packers who'd started in Montana and were heading for Alaska on a two-month trip. That encounter helped me better appreciate my situation. I didn't envy them camping in parking spots by the river off the highway in the nonstop rain.

Later in the day, after leaving Boya Lake, we stopped in Jade City and talked to some locals about how they mine the jade in the hills, transport it down to town, and ship it to China before it comes back as expensive carved items sold in the Jade City shop. I wasn't worried about the time this stop took because I'd planned this stop from the beginning. We did have time to make up however, so we still didn't dally long.

Sawmill Point Recreational Campsite on the northeastern shore of Dease Lake was our home that night. It wasn't anything special, but it had picnic tables and toilets, so I wasn't going to complain. Besides, the scenery was something else, with all the pines and deciduous trees surrounding the lake and the mountains above that in the distance. Those mountains though, created quite a steep incline on the access road to the campground, so we had to pedal hard to get in. And the mosquitos there! That was one of the worst places for them on the whole journey; there were millions of mosquitos milling around. Between the six of us, I'm sure we went through a dozen bottles of bug spray that night. And after I'd retired in the van for the night, hiding from more pouring rain, I must have spent a good ten or fifteen minutes sitting in bed trying to kill as many as I could. Sure, they weren't as big and mean as horse flies and their bites didn't really bother me, but man, that buzzing in my ear all night drove me nuts!

***

Once again, the sun came out again after Mother Nature had handed us a more terrible than usual day the day before, allowing me a beautiful morning to eat my raspberry muffin and drink my coffee with the sun on my face again. My tranquil moment was not to last, however.

Shortly afterward, the drama came to a head. Wayne declared he was making eggs and bacon for breakfast, and I was pretty sure it wasn't just because he wanted them but because he was making a point. He said Kim and Yiota should be making supper and breakfast and doing the dishes, and he made that last point pretty clear when I automatically got up to clean up after I'd finished my breakfast and he told me to sit down. Well, we had words after that, but we worked it out as we rode through what of course transformed into another grueling day in the wind and rain. I thought maybe that would be the end of it, but even though I'd spoken with the girls before leaving that morning, they still decided they wanted to have a meeting that night.

You'd think that would work things out, but it didn't really. The only thing we got out of it was that the girls would make breakfast and we'd help with the clean-up, and of course that set Wayne off again. He thought I walked on eggshells around the girls, and I thought we should just all respect each other and help where we could. But to be fair, maybe I did treat them with a little extra care. I mean, at the very least, I really needed Yiota to go all the way to Panama with us and not fly home once we hit Vancouver like Kim would. I wasn't sure what the answer was just then, but I refused to let it get to me. I was determined to just enjoy my ride as I always do, drinking in all the facets of nature and discovering what was around the next bend.

That night, we halted a bit early in Dease Lake, which gave us an opportunity to do normal, everyday things like banking, laundry, and shopping. There was even—hallelujah—free Wi-Fi at the college between 8 a.m. and 5 p.m., so we got a chance to catch up on emails and social media, but most importantly, talk to our families back home. Bernice even rounded up a couple big salmon for us after talking to a bunch of locals, so we enjoyed a fantastic meal later that night ... though Yiota and Kim didn't join us. They decided to eat in the tent trailer. Wayne did, however, fortuitously find a new use for that aforementioned hand sanitizer. Turns out it makes a great fire starter! Before the pandemic, I never would have thought to carry oodles of hand sanitizer, but I was sure glad we had!

***

When we pulled out of Dease Lake around 9:30 the next morning, we were still blessed with some sun and blue skies, though it was only 11°C. Colleen, who may not have been an experienced cyclist but was a great one nonetheless, led the way, and Wayne assumed the rear. But that was only because we were tackling a four-hundred-meter climb and he was riding an ordinary road bike, not an e-bike like me.

As we left town, we crossed the Arctic-Pacific Watershed Divide, and not long after, I thought I saw a moose up ahead again. But no, it turned out it was just a lady out running in the middle of nowhere. My mistake was clear when she told us to have a nice day with what sounded like a French accent!

Well, because we'd cut off early the previous day, that meant we had a lot farther to go that day and the next day, and lots of climbing, but we did it. I had to get us back on schedule somehow. There was an eightieth birthday party waiting for me still, and I couldn't reschedule that. So, we put our heads down and rode through the low, threatening clouds and the cold and kept on pedaling. Our eyes were open to the landscape surrounding us though. We may have had to push hard, but the views were absolutely stunning and not to be missed, particularly approaching Kinaskan Lake. Besides, what better way is there to get through the tougher times than with positivity and beauty?

Approaching Kinaskan Lake

And boy did the others have to keep their eyes wide open when we came to one of those metal-grill bridges, the kind where you can look down and see the river through the metal bridge deck. We also got the pleasure of breathing in lungs full of dust as we trudged down a gravel road and semi-trucks flew past us. I'm not sure which could have been worse, breathing in the dust in the sunshine or journeying down that gravel road in the pouring rain as the trucks rolled by and threw mud and water all over us. On a more peculiar note, we also discovered a beaver dam along the way whose occupant was not only patriotic but also looked as though he had cable with the satellite dish and Canadian flag adorning his dam.

***

As two long days passed with only brief pitstops to sleep for the night, Wayne and I rode like men far younger than we were to reach our next rest day at the halfway point between Dease Lake and Smithers. Then just as we neared it like a couple of work horses heading back to the barn, we were thwarted. I'd planned for us to stay at the more upscale Bell 2 Lodge and had been looking forward to it—and to eating at the fine restaurant there. But it turned out a mining company had booked the whole campground and hotel for the entire summer, so we were left with no choice but to resort to bush camping at a little turnout with picnic tables about two kilometers down the road.

Between the drama, the weather, and the circumstances, the stress was growing exponentially, and we were all hoping for things to get better. I was no longer sure if Yiota was going to stay, and the girls were spending all their time after dinner in their tent watching movies. They'd originally said they wanted to be part of a team, but I wasn't seeing that just yet.

The bottom line was, I guess, that we'd hopefully hit the deepest valley of the journey, worked through the adjustment phase, and things could only improve from then on. My hope was that the farther south we got, the better the weather got, and the better the accommodation got, the better our relations would get.

Always wishful thinking I am. But I'll get back to that in a bit.

***

After our disappointment with Bell 2 Lodge, we continued with our previously scheduled itinerary. That made our next stop and a rest day at Meziadin Lake Provincial Park. We were still smack in the middle of the mountains, so our days were full of climbs and descents, the latter of which are always my favorite part. I love taking them as fast as I can, and they help me catch up to Wayne, but here there'd been so much rain I had to reign it in a bit. I also couldn't help but remember my broken hip and ribs.

Of course, the weather continued to be gloomy and cold. Of course, tempers continued to be short and tensions high. Of course, we continued to fight the steepness of the mountains. However, we did meet up with an interesting crew adventuring in an old Mercedes expedition-type truck in the park. One would imagine it would look something more like an army sort of vehicle given the backcountry we were traveling through, but nope. The bright pink and green it was painted really lightened the mood, and the hundred or so bumper stickers plastered all over it gave us no choice but to smile for a while. Even better was supper that night: fresh-caught salmon from the neighboring river accompanied by the extra-special roe we discovered when we cleaned it. So, though it was dreary and almost freezing outside and we were quite sick of it, we did enjoy some wonderful company and filled our bellies.

***

The most uplifting touring vehicle I've ever seen.

On our rest day, we piled in the car and visited Stewart, British Columbia, for a bit of tourist time. Hopefully it would give us some downtime to relax and remember how to get along again. On the way, we had the good fortune of driving by Bear Glacier. Glaciers are always breathtaking, and this one was no exception with its baby-blue ice and marshmallow-white snow, the earthy-brown mountain peeking out beneath it pockmarked with the verdant green of the foliage. All this encompassed by the vast lake below and the cottony, low-hanging clouds above.

Once we'd managed to tear our eyes away from the sight, on we pushed on to Stewart. Its historic buildings welcomed us and captured our imaginations: the HighTide Gallery, the Silverado Café and Pizza Parlor, the Bitter Creek Bar and Lounge, the Toastworks, the Marmot Bay Trading Co., the Ripley Creek Inn, John A. MacDonald House, and of course, Stewart House. Each one looked as though someone had reached in, pulled it out of an old western movie, and plopped it right down in Stewart. Yes, we certainly had to stop and drink it all in and even walk the boardwalk in the estuary at the end of the Portland Canal, a ninety-kilometer-long fjord on the Alaska Panhandle border and the longest fjord in Canada.

Then Wayne and I stopped for a lunch of soup and sandwich at a cute little deli called Temptations Bakery and Deli, the interior of which was covered top to bottom in the names of visitors to Stewart.

Afterward, we came across this little poster before continuing to Hyder, Alaska, to get "Hyderized" at the Glacier Inn:

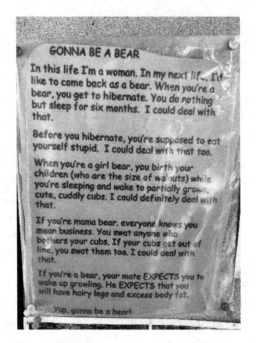

GONNA BE A BEAR

In this life I'm a woman. In my next life, I'd like to come back as a bear. When you're a bear, you get to hibernate. You do nothing but sleep for six months. I could deal with that.

Before you hibernate, you're supposed to eat yourself stupid. I could deal with that too.

When you're a girl bear, you birth your children (who are the size of walnuts) while you're sleeping and wake to partially grown, cute, cuddly cubs. I could definitely deal with that.

If you're mama bear, everyone knows you mean business. You swat anyone who bothers your cubs. If your cubs get out of line, you swat them too. I could deal with that.

If you're a bear, your mate EXPECTS you to wake up growling. He EXPECTS that you will have hairy legs and excess body fat.

Yup, gonna be a bear!

I'm sure men and women alike can relate.

That gave us all a much-needed chuckle and put us in the right frame of mind for some Hyderizing. For those who don't know, getting Hyderized means downing a shot of the town's 150-proof alcohol. It's so strong, it must be served with a glass of water for safety! All six of us downed a shot... and we're all still alive! After spending some time wandering around Hyder, appreciating its history and scenery—which was much like Stewart's—and watching bears, we turned back around and headed back to Lake Meziadin to take care of some necessary chores before we had to hit the road again.

***

Our time in Hyder and Stewart finally marked the end of the cold, gloomy weather, and the sun came out again the next day to start the next leg of our journey and our last day on Highway 37. It wasn't without its own delightful surprises as we got to stop and watch a few salmon at the beginning of salmon-run season. I have to say it was incredible to be able to enjoy a nice warm day and the sun shining on me as I rode.

Next up was Kitwanga after a long, 155-kilometer day. Wonder of wonders, the sun was still shining, and the sky was still clear by the time we got there! We also got the added bonus of discovering the site of an old Native mound—once an old fortress from the 1700s—and the multitudinous totem poles. But the very best part of the day, and likely the best part of the trip yet, was when we reached the bridge over the Skeena River connecting the Cassiar Highway to the Yellowhead Highway ... and finally got cell service!

On that day, nature gave us only a little tailwind, and the roads were great. It was one of those rare perfect riding days. This day had gone so well with so many positive signs, I was sure we were coming out of that tense relationship valley we'd been stuck in thus far on our journey.

I should have just stopped thinking that. Every time I did, things blew up.

Yiota and Kim had apparently had a powwow and decided they were going to exit the journey in Prince George, just three days from then. I didn't know if it was the weather or Wayne's behavior toward them, but I gulped and went through my options. I had brought a few emergency phone numbers with me just in case, so I went through them that night. The first option was a kind soul who just needed a day to see if they could rearrange some things, the second was two young men who'd said they were happy to help out, and the third was someone who would take the bus to Prince George and drive the van as far as Vancouver. That last one really wasn't a viable option given I'd still need someone to drive the rest of the way to Panama, or at least until my sister-in-law joined us.

So, I decided on the first option but figured I'd call them the next day. It had a been a long, exhausting day, and we were due to make Smithers, British Columbia, the next day.

At least we were on schedule, it was supposed to be another hot day with no wind, and we only had 114 km to ride. Without the girls, Wayne and I would have to make some adjustments to make do with just three people, like staying in more Airbnb's and hotels and eating in more restaurants to make things easier and so the new addition wouldn't have to always put up and take down camp themselves.

***

After a rough, worry-filled night, the next day, Smithers, British Columbia, was our target, and again the sun was our friend. We rode through more picture-perfect scenery— rolling hills, lush greenery, little towns—and the sky stayed clear. Temperatures rose and so did my spirits.

So, after maybe 114 km of trouble-free riding, we reached Smithers. After settling in and freshening up, Bernice, Colleen, Wayne, and I visited a wonderful, quaint restaurant. It was modern, well-kept, and had great food. In fact, it was much closer to the restaurants we're used to seeing and enjoying in bigger cities. I enjoyed myself so much, I decided to just ignore the relationship drama for one night and get a good night's sleep... which I did.

Our next big stop was in Prince George, where we'd get another two-day break. Before we got there though, we were going to have to earn it with about 330 kilometers to ride in two days. At least the weather remained on our side as we passed through Houston, scaled Six-Mile Summit with an elevation of 2,756 meters, edged by Decker Lake, and popped into Burns Lake where we stayed the night. Colleen and Bernice were still with us too, so that kind of took the edge off the drama between Wayne and the girls. Our night at Burns Lake was to be the last night they'd accompany us, however, and we celebrated with Saskatoon-berry ice cream and the Saskatoon berries Colleen had collected while avoiding a couple bears who also loved the berries. Both Bernice and Colleen had been great help and great company, so I would sorely miss them, as would Wayne, I was sure.

On a journey like this, I'm always most taken with the little things, things most people never hear about or see, not the big tourist-trap places or commercial outfits. Not far out of Burns Lake the next day, I was reminded of this very fact when we came upon a little hamlet called Tintagel. The name may or may not ring a bell, but if it does, that could be because there is a town in the UK by the same name. If you've been out this way, you'll perhaps be acquainted with its mighty claim to fame. If not, let me tell you the tale. Named in 1913 after the town of the same name in Cornwall, UK, this BC hamlet is home to a cairn, the center stone of which was once part of the wall of a Norman castle, Tintagel Castle. In case you don't think that's a big deal, then you should know that that particular castle was the reputed home of King Arthur, Knight of the Round Table.

Finally, we made it to Prince George, the spruce capital of the world so we learned, and it looked like the weather was going to continue to be favorable. Here was the summer we'd been missing! Anyway, nestled in a valley at the confluence of the Fraser and Nechako Rivers, Prince George is also known as the capital of northern British Columbia. It's not an overly large town by many standards, but it is cozy and cute, however smelly it may be given its pulp mill, the driving industry in town.

It really felt like a weight had been lifted when we arrived. It wasn't just because of the weather I don't think, but also because we could rest, take care of things we'd put by the wayside, and get back on schedule. I'd been saying we were on schedule, but that was only because I'd originally scheduled three days here but had deleted one to get us back on track.

One of those things we'd shoved under the rug until we got to Prince George was all the drama among the team. I'd called my friend, Mike, earlier in Burns Lake and explained my issue. Being the good friend he is, he'd offered to jump on a plane and come drive for me until we reached Vancouver. So once settled in Prince George, I bucked up and addressed the problem straight out. I gave Kim and Yiota a choice: they could go then, or they could stay and press on at least to Vancouver, but if they stayed, things would have to change. They'd have to give a little extra effort and a little extra cheeriness. They needed to be part of the team as they'd initially said they'd wanted to be.

Well, I don't know if they'd thought they had me over a barrel and I would be stuck in Prince George without them, but their first response was a question. Who would drive for me if they left? When I said Mike would, well that took some wind out of their sails. When they didn't say anything after that, I told them they'd be silly not to go on because Kim would lose the $500 bonus, I'd promised her to get us to Vancouver. The same went for the bonus I'd promised Yiota so she could go see her boyfriend in Louisiana. They countered by asking to be paid more, and I flatly refused. I also said they weren't going to take the van to Alberta to see the mountains on our rest day as had been their original plan.

Well, after I adopted my firmer stance, they went off and discussed things with their families, then finally came back and said they'd continue to Vancouver. In response, I relented and let them take the van to Alberta, but I reiterated that this BS had to stop. I reminded them that Wayne and I could get to Panama without them. Then I ended the discussion by saying, "Let's just get this thing to Vancouver, and we can say our goodbyes."

Well, glory be, that little tete a tete seemed to do the job. The girls' demeanor changed for the better and their work improved. So, with Mike and another guy, Keenan, on-call to fly into Prince George from Vancouver to temporarily help if needed, it looked like this festering problem had finally been solved. Unfortunately, though, I was still waiting to see if Johana, my sister-in-law, was going to be able to get a visa to meet us in the US. If she couldn't, we'd have to wait to meet her in Tijuana, and I didn't have anyone lined up to help drive and set up camp while we were in the US. But that was just about the only real worry I had left, so I was sure feeling lighter. I could finally take some time to reflect on my journey thus far. That and give an interview to the Prince George Post!

When we hit Prince George, we'd reached 2,700 total kilometers traveled. It felt so good riding all day, and I felt strong. Sure, I had an awfully sore butt some days and some of those climbs were a challenge, but all in all, it felt great. One of the girls, I can't remember rightly which one, commented that I was losing weight, so I knew I was burning lots of calories, likely a little more than I'd meant to having to survive all that cold, wet weather.

On that note, the weather had finally been on our side the last few days, and that had allowed me to enjoy the mountainous, untamed wilderness around me. We encountered wildlife in some form every day, whether it was bears or moose or foxes or fish, sometimes deer. The birds calling and singing made every new place feel familiar, and when there was no traffic, the air smelled fresh and clean with an undertone of pine and wildflowers. And when there was traffic, the sensations were the opposite: dieselly and dusty with the odd rotten-egg or acrid burning smell thrown in. Sometimes as we rode, Wayne and I would chat about this or that, only disturbed periodically by my phone ringing. Whenever that happened, I'd pull off and let Wayne go ahead, but my e-bike always helped me catch up fast. I like to go fast on flat stretches, and it was no different on this ride, so it took no effort to catch up. But every time we came to a hill, Wayne would always say he takes the stairs and Bob takes the elevator. I thought that was a clever way of illustrating that my EVELO e-bike enabled me to just give a twist of my wrist, then change the gears using the gadget on my handlebar. Then the transmission would give me varying levels of assistance when I came to a hill, depending on how hard I found I was working. Most times, I only put it in power level one or two though. Still, I guess he was right. He takes the stairs, and I take the elevator!

There'd been lots of traffic on Highway 16, which I'd taken as a sign of healthy economic activity in the area, what with all the tourism, construction, large pipeline projects, and big gold mines being built. We'd also met an interesting lady back on the Cassiar Highway, or Highway 37, who was heading north. We stopped to talk, and when she found out where I was going, she said, "Hey, you're that guy I read about on Facebook, the eighty-year-old guy going to Panama."

I shrugged and just said, "Yeah, that's me." I gotta say, though, I loved the recognition.

Then as we were pulling into Prince George, we chatted with a guy who said, "You're getting your exercise!"

"Yeah, yeah," I said.

To which he replied, "Hey, I saw you on guys on television!"

I thought those meetings were pretty cool. It thrilled me that word was getting out because that meant I had a greater chance of motivating more people, particularly seniors, to get up off the couch and do something new, to keep busy and not waste away. The more people that heard about my message to trade the sofa for the bicycle seat, the more purpose this journey had. Plus, more awareness could lead to more funds raised for the kids in Panama.

Another positive was that we hadn't had any major mechanical issues to that point in the odyssey, besides the car-battery issue, but I did have to take the bike in to the service department of a local store while I was in Prince George. A curious clanking noise was coming from the rear hub where the transmission was, and I didn't want it to become an issue when we were in the middle of nowhere. They agreed, yes, there was a noise, but they didn't think it would cause a major problem.

While we didn't have any major issues, I did experience a minor one. I'd gotten a flat bike tire the night before we got to Prince George. Fortunately, I'd been close to the support van and had been able to ride to it. There, we decided to pump up the tire and see how far I could get since there was only thirty kilometers to go. So, I strapped the pump to the bike and set off. I made it a whole fifteen kilometers before I had to stop and pump it up again. The last pump got me to camp though, where I decided to inject a can of the van's tire sealant into the bike tube; luckily, I always carry a couple valve adapters. I gave the tube a good squirt, inflated the tire to the required pressure, and crossed my fingers. It did the trick. The tire retained its pressure. Good thing too because that was the first time, I'd ever injected sealant into a tube. And what was left in the can was enough to get me at least three more applications, maybe more.

So, with that memory fresh in my mind, Wayne and I sat down on one of our rest days in Prince George to watch some YouTube videos to learn how to take the back tire and CVT hub from the second e-bike, which hadn't been ridden yet, and install it on my bike. And wouldn't you know it, we did it. What did we used to do without YouTube? Anyway, I thought then that with luck, this fix would maybe get me at least to Seattle where EVELO was based. Then I could either get someone to look at it or give me some advice.

Later, as I sat relaxing with a cold one in Prince George on our last day, I decided that overall, I was happy with this particular biking experience so far: the exercise, my conditioning and shape, and the scenery and wilderness of the Yukon and the Cassiar Highway. I'd originally gone into it thinking it would be just another mountain-type road, but it had turned out to be so much more than that. Highway 16 had been another story though. It hadn't been as pleasant an experience. There'd been too much traffic—noise from semis makes for incredibly unpleasant riding—and the weather had been hot, not that it had bothered me. Six years living in Costa Rica had likely made me immune to the heat.

***

Well, once our rest days were over, we were ready to travel our last six hundred kilometers down Highway 97 to reach Vancouver. First though, we rode through Quesnel, which turned out to be an awfully busy little town with an attractive downtown that we took a little tour through. We had a lovely ride too, passing by lots of lakes. No shortage of water there!

Next came Williams Lake after a ride of about 128 km with lots of hills. Wayne and I powered through that one in steady rain and cool temperatures once again. As much as I love long-distance cycling, shivering while you ride and having all your clothes soaked through and getting your fingers all wrinkly is the most miserable part of it. Besides maybe those damn horse flies that'll take a chunk out of you. And yet it's all part and parcel of the experience, and as tough as it is, there's just something alluring and addictive about it all. Maybe it's feeling the freedom while you're suffering or maybe it's the excitement of adventure and the unknown that makes me do it again and again, much like that Pauper in Paradise song by Frozen Ghost. Mostly though, I think it just makes me feel alive. It reminds me that I still live and breathe and experience.

Anyway, I digress. Because it was such a cold and rainy day, I got Wayne and I a room at a hotel that night. Kim and Yiota spent the night in a nearby campground with the tent trailer. We all met up for a good, hearty dinner at Denny's later to celebrate our three-thousand-kilometer milestone, and it turned out to be a lively night. Then I felt like I finally had the team spirit I'd been after. We took photos, some of Wayne and I wearing our EVELO clothes for the sponsors to use and had quite a fiesta!

From left: Wayne, me, Yiota, and Kim celebrating our 3, 000 km milestone!

The next day promised to also be rainy and cold during our trek to 100–Mile House, so I had Yiota and Kim book Airbnb accommodation ahead of time, but it only rained a bit in the end. The weather wasn't bad at all when we arrived, but it was easy to tell they were all happy to stay in a house for the night. The girls and I chose to go out to eat that night, but Wayne decided to stay in and munch on some sandwiches.

Dinner was tasty and relaxed, and we even came upon the world's largest cross-country skis while we were here. Then we headed back to our accommodations to get some rest. We had to get on the road on time again the next day because I still had to get to that birthday party of mine in Newport, Oregon. Boy I was tired that night.

Suddenly, at exactly 11:38 p.m., I woke Wayne demanding to know why I'd deleted his CV from the website. I replied, "I didn't. Trust me."

But Wayne didn't have any of it. He said, "Well, it's not here. It's not here!"

So, there I was, that late at night and startled wide awake and having to figure out what his problem was. I heaved myself out of bed and over to the computer, but I couldn't find anywhere I would have published it, let alone deleted it.

**

The next morning, tension filled the air as we started off for the day, and Wayne was quiet. Finally, he stopped me on a hill and said we needed to settle this thing. I shook my head and asked, "What thing?"

It turned out he hadn't let the issue go. It must really have been eating at him, so he said, "Why you deleted my bio. People want to know about me too."

I promised him I hadn't deleted anything, that I wouldn't do that. Well, that set off a shouting match. Wayne got even angrier with me, and I swore I hadn't deleted anything.

He said, "Well, I'm part of this team and it should be posted!"

Wayne continued venting for a while until something finally dawned on me. When he paused, I asked, "Wait, are you talking about the posting on *E-bike Odyssey*?"

He cocked his head at that and answered, "Oh, how many of those things do you have? No wonder I can't find anything." Then he hopped on his bike and rode off on me.

So, before I got going again, I took my phone out and looked up my *E-bike Odyssey* blog and found that yes, of course Wayne's bio was there. And that's what I'd been trying to find earlier, but when I couldn't find it, Wayne had just automatically accused me of deleting things.

By the time I caught up to Wayne at the next rest stop where the girls had a snack waiting for us, I was fuming mad. So, I went over to him, showed him my phone, and said,

"Here's what you're looking for, Wayne, *E-bike Odyssey.*" Then I walked away.

After a few minutes, Wayne finally followed and said, "I guess I made a mistake."

I didn't think that was a great apology, but being the man I am, I let it go like water off a duck's back in the interest of the distance we still had yet to travel. An argument over something as small as that just wasn't worth it. Looking back now as I write, this was the lowest point of the odyssey. Teamwork, positivity, and optimism all rose day by day after that day.

After that, we continued in better spirits. I got another flat tire and did a patch job, though. Wayne was impressed when I fixed it without pulling the tire off to patch it, but I only hoped it would hold. We rode on to 70 Mile House, with its incongruous general store that also housed an M&M Meats, before reaching 59 Mile House and the village of Clinton, originally known as the 47 Mile House and The Junction given its location at the joining of the Douglas-Lillooet Road and Yale-Cariboo Road after they were completed in 1861 and 1863 respectively. Clinton was another quirky little town oozing with history and charm with its Palace Hotel and Clinton Emporium, a flea market that also boasted the Emporium's Happy Days coffee shop. There, you could find anything from windows to washtubs to an old, rickety, two-person, horse-pulled buggy.

That day ended on a much nicer, more peaceful note. We spent the night at a beautiful place called Marble Canyon Provincial Park Campground. It didn't have any facilities, but the beauty of the lake against the mountains and the waterfall racing down the rocks into the lake was worth it. Facilities or not, the campground was still full. And after patching a hole in my air mattress, I ended the night by chowing down some satisfying hamburgers.

The beautiful Marble Canyon

Then we hit our hardest day of the trek yet. We only had a hundred kilometers to go, but 1,560 meters of that would be climbing as we pushed back through the mountains again, and that usually puts it closer to two hundred kilometers of riding. Wayne would have a tough time for sure but he's an amazingly strong rider. I'd be fine, though I knew I'd use lots of battery power on our way to Whistler, British Columbia!

But we were edging ever closer to Vancouver, just two more days. We went through Lillooet—where we came across what Wayne thought might be the most northerly vineyard and encountered another bear—spent the night in Duffy Lake, and headed for Pemberton, just outside Whistler, the next day. To my surprise, I discovered Pemberton and Whistler also have a pretty hopping summer scene too. There is so much more to do there than just skiing, such as tubing, kayaking, or paddle boarding down the river; cycling; or attending the Pemberton Barn Dance if you get bored.

However, thanks to a very long and very steep downhill, the girls burned out the brakes on the van and had to spend a night in Pemberton so they could get new front brakes the next day. Wayne and I rode on to Whistler, so we didn't even see them until we reached Horseshoe Bay just outside of Vancouver. And yes, Yiota and Kim had most of the supplies with them, so the next day I had to stop and charge my battery at a kind stranger's house just so I could make it to Vancouver.

But, after enjoying the quiet and comfort of sharing an Airbnb with just Wayne in Whistler, we took to the Sea to Sky Highway, and I hoped more than anything that there wouldn't be any more drama. Even mechanical issues are better than tension and conflict. I knew that was just the way of it with teams and families, but it really eats away at the enjoyment of the trip. Heck, that day in 100-mile House, I'd even come really close to telling Wayne that this wasn't going to work and that maybe he should go home when we got to Vancouver. Thankfully, I'd held my tongue because we'd been able to patch things up. We were back to being best buds. Good thing too, because when we left Vancouver, we'd be hitting another big milestone: crossing into the US. That would mark the beginning of the second leg of our odyssey.

THE SECOND LEG

Well, after more than 3,000 km biked, four weeks of mostly cold, wet weather endured, and numerous tensions overcome, we finished the first leg of my Octogenarian Odyssey and began the second. We successfully crossed the border into the United States, and thankfully, had no issues. I was thrilled that they had finally done away with the required COVID-19 testing. It was eerie reading this inscription on the side of the Peace Arch though: "May These Gates Never Be Closed." My whole life, and it was likely the same for many others, I'd always assumed there would never be a reason for the Canada/US border to be closed. We'd never lived through such a time and couldn't comprehend or imagine a time it ever would be. Yet they did just that on March 18, 2020.

All it took was concerns over the spread of a global pandemic like COVID-19 for us to isolate ourselves, for us all to close ourselves off from our nearest neighbors and closest friends. Granted, it was understandable given it was a novel virus that was killing people, and we didn't know much about it. It was just disappointing the way both countries retreated into themselves and forgot that so much more can be achieved together. That was a dark, difficult time for a lot of folks, and it's going to take a long time to reach the place of unity we used to occupy, if we ever really get back to that place. One of my greatest wishes is that we, as North Americans, can put away those suspicions and distrust that filled us during the pandemic and learn to work openly together again, to be the brothers we used to be.

Wayne at the Peace Arch at the White Rock- Blaine border crossing

But to get back on track, I suppose I shouldn't say we had no issues at all at the border. To be more specific, Wayne and I had no issues because we easily crossed into the US on the bicycle path, which had no line-up. The same couldn't be said for Yiota though, who was driving the van and pulling the tent trailer.

She spent three hours in line waiting to cross and had to wait another hour while the border guards searched the vehicle for contraband. The silver lining was they gave her no problems, found nothing of course, and were quite friendly.

Kim flew home yesterday from Vancouver, leaving us all a little melancholy. Her leaving was a bit sad because she had been having a lot of fun, drama, or no drama. Now it's only poor Yiota setting up and taking down for a week until a promising young man named Kyle will show up to take Kim's place and take care of the drone footage. Until then, I'm doing the best I can to accommodate Yiota by staying in Airbnb's and eating in restaurants whenever possible. As sad as it was to lose Kim, that means the drama should be over now. Hopefully it stays that way.

As the first leg came to an end and the second began, I began to ruminate on my journey so far. It occurred to me that another theme was making itself known, beyond my overarching theme of getting seniors active and removing the stigma attached to senior citizens. As I pedaled through the first leg, which I was by now calling the northern wilderness section, I couldn't help but recall all the friendly people we'd met along the way so far. Some fine people had let us stay in their homes, chatted with us, made us lunch, filled our water bottles, and asked questions about my journey. If you were to read a newspaper these days, you'd think the world was going to hell in a handbasket. But that hadn't been my experience thus far with all the people we'd met. Everyone we'd come across had been so friendly and helpful, even to strangers. I'd gotten lots of honks so far thanks to the sign on the back of my bike, "Alaska to Panama." One fella even pulled up in a car the other day as we were entering Vancouver and rolled down the back window to shout, "Way to go, fellow! Let me buy you a hamburger!" as he waved two five-dollar bills in his hand.

I chuckled at that and waved and said, "No, thanks very much. That's okay. I don't need that, but thanks for the encouragement!" The strange thing is that's pretty typical of a day. Of course, it's also my favorite part of this trip, and of long-distance cycling period. I love to stop and talk to as many people as I can and learn their stories. Another guy a couple days later wanted to know more about riding e-bikes. He had one leg amputated below the knee and was curious to know if an e-bike could work for him.

Though mine is a little different because it has no throttle, I said, "Oh yeah, you could ride one. Just get one with a throttle and you can ride it like a motor bike. Then with your leg as it is, you can learn to work the pedals slowly." Of course, with mine if I don't pedal, I'll fall off, but this guy was really interested in getting some more information to work with. It's pretty incredible how common it is to be quizzed about e-bikes. I must have been doing some good marketing for EVELO on my odyssey.

One big reason I've always traveled so much is because I want to see as many places as possible and meet as many people as possible. I want to experience their culture in their backyard. Traveling is so important in understanding other people, getting rid of stereotypes, and preventing people from being racist and xenophobic and bigoted. I mean if you travel, you can't be those I don't think. How can you? Once you're armed with knowledge and you really experience a people instead of passing judgment just based on what you've heard and not experienced, how is it possible to be racist?

Regardless, I'll get back to the story. We got to Richmond late in the afternoon a few days ago. I have to say, riding through Vancouver had been an experience. The roads had been packed with traffic, but at least there'd been lots of bike paths. Crossing Lions Gate Bridge had been memorable too. You could look down and see the ocean, a cruise liner heading out, and even Stanley Park. A day like that just reminds you that though it's nice to be in civilization some day, most of you wish you could be back in the wilderness when you're suddenly not. But it's good to get that reminder so when you are back in the middle of nowhere and you're wishing for a little civilization you remember that it's not all it's cracked up to be. The wilderness has little to no traffic, and it's so quiet in comparison. Even with the birds singing—or cawing and squawking—and the wind in your ears, it's still quite enough that at least you can hear your own thoughts. Riding some of those roads in civilization, especially in a major center like Vancouver, are just overly noisy, terrifically noisy.

Me about to cross the Alex Fraser Bridge in Vancouver, British Columbia

After arriving at another generous FB friend's home in Richmond, we'd had a couple rest days scheduled, so I'd taken the van to Langley for my son's memorial, held for his British Columbia friends. I'd met a few at his memorial in Edmonton a few weeks earlier, but I'd enjoyed the opportunity to meet a few more here. My daughter, Janet, her husband, and my granddaughter had driven in too, so we'd also gotten to enjoy a lovely family evening. With all my traveling, I know I don't get to see them enough and I miss them a lot, especially as my granddaughter grows up. It bothers me sometimes, but this pull just keeps pulling, and there's so much to discover and learn and experience and explore before my clock hits midnight.

But here I am deviating again. Back to it. So, I broke a shifter cable a little while back, so I'd taken the opportunity to get it fixed in Richmond. Plus, instead of me having to scoot into Seattle, Washington, the EVELO folks had met me at the hotel to carry out the 3000-mile checkup on the bikes, and they'd been kind enough to bring more spare parts. Then the bikes were in good shape and riding nicely. Everything appeared to be in shape to tackle the Pacific coast section. I guess it's obvious I've given the four sections names: the Northern Wilderness section, the Pacific coast section, the Mexican section, and the Central America section.

I have to say, weatherwise, we'd gotten really lucky after Quesnel. It had stayed continuously sunny and warm, so there'd been nothing to complain about there but nothing to write home about either, so I'll move on. I had learned during that stretch though, while enjoying a nice farewell dinner in Steveston with Kim, that an American couple, Flipper and Skipper, had broken the e-bike distance record with a tour of 11,500 kilometers. They did it in their own backyard however, while I was crossing borders and getting out of my comfort zone. While it was a bit of a shock, I was still confident I'd shatter that record. Besides, they're a fraction of my age!

Then, rested, refreshed, and repaired after our time in Vancouver, we'd set out again for an eighty-nine-kilometer ride headed south that morning. Unfortunately, my hopes for a quiet ride along the coast were dashed because it turned out we had to cross and then ride parallel to I5, or Interstate 5. The traffic volume and resulting noise were so high it was almost unbearable. And we had to cross it a good five or six times!

Nonetheless, we made it through the noise and arrived in Bellingham, Washington, for the night before continuing our way through Burlington and Arlington as we headed for Everett, Washington, the next day. Those hadn't been my original destinations, but I'd had to make some adjustments and rearrange the schedule because of the four-hour wait for the van to cross the border. It was too bad though because I'd been anticipating the opportunity to stay with some friends. Either way, at least my itinerary alterations weren't going to affect my meeting up with four, maybe five, cyclist friends who would ride with us into Newport, Oregon, or making it to my eightieth birthday party on time. I still had a week to get there, and if nothing else happened to slow things down or get in my way, I'd make it.

You'd think I'd be looking forward to the party itself and celebrating with my friends and family, but do you know what the biggest reason I was looking forward to this party on August 19 was? It was because then the weightiest element of stress would be off my shoulders. To say it was incredibly stressful knowing I had to get to Newport on time because everyone else was scheduled to get there then was an understatement. I had no choice but to get there on time, come Hell or high water. At least after the party, the schedule wouldn't matter so much. Who cared when we would get anywhere? The Guinness Book of World Records wouldn't matter. Arrival time wouldn't matter to anyone.

Anyway, while we were in Washington, Wayne took the opportunity to get his COVID-19 booster. He just dove into the first drugstore we came across. While we waited, I reflected on the change in his behavior toward Kim and Yiota after we'd left Prince George. He'd become more agreeable with them, to the point where I thought even, he was sorry to see Kim leave Vancouver. I'm not sure what caused the change, whether it was knowing she was going to leave soon, or knowing he'd been heard, or just getting to know them better, but I guess it just goes to show that no matter how long you know someone, you still don't always know everything about them. I'm glad he and I had patched things up though. He has always been a fantastic riding partner and a good friend, and this ride would have been far too lonely without him.

And if he hadn't been here, if I'd thrown caution to the wind and told him he should go in Prince George, I wouldn't have been able to tell him my oyster story later that day. I was reminded of it as rode down the Washington coast because they raise oysters there. We rode past lots of oyster bars and restaurants along the way, so it was like a ride I'd done in southern Ontario, along Lake Erie. I'd pulled into a restaurant for dinner and sat down; I was going through a wine and oysters and oyster bars kick at the time. When the waiter came to take my order, I asked him what kind of wine they had. He retorted, "Red and white."

So, I shook my head and asked for white. Then I went on to say, "I see you have oysters. Where are they from?"

"I don't know," the waiter said. "I'll have to ask the chef."

Off he went to ask, and when he came back, the waiter said, "The chef said they come from the ocean."

So, I didn't order any oysters.

As we cycled through Washington State, I found it interesting that like in the Canadian wilderness, rural Washington also had its share of quaint, historic little villages. Besides Burlington and Arlington, we also passed through Blaine, right on the Canada/US border, Custer with its cute county store, and Ferndale with its old grain mill. Then after we left Everett, we discovered Edmonds, on the outskirts of Seattle, where we got a beautiful view of Puget Sound and caught a ferry across to Kingston. There we came upon the historic Old Kingston Hotel, established way back in 1886. Next came Silverdale and Shelton as we made our way south, continuing along the west side of Puget Sound to avoid riding through Seattle proper. Then it was on to Victorville, where we felt like we were in the Wild Wild West again with its saloon-looking structures, stables that housed cars instead of horses, and white picket fences. Finally, as we traveled closer and closer to the Pacific coast—though we were due to head south toward Portland here—we rode through Elma, Washington, where we ate at Tuggs & Chuggs Tavern and camped the night at Elma RV Park. Its welcoming sign proclaimed that we were doubly welcome to stay.

This place was certainly calling to us.

Unfortunately, the weather started to turn there. While it wasn't the pouring cold rain of Yukon, it was foggy and drizzly, and that just makes for an uncomfortable ride. It does offer a different perspective of the world though, seeing it through fog. And on the upside, the sun did come out later in the day, allowing us to take in the phenomenal views along the highway: the rivers and creeks and inlets, the farms, and the imaginative gardens the inhabitants of the little out-of-the -way homes created. There were bald eagle carvings, horse-and-buggy silhouettes, log carts, and flowers of every color, shape, and size. Wayne said the gardens' creators must be retired.

In Centralia, Washington, we were greeted at a stoplight by a giant tin man made entirely of mufflers. Riding through town, we absorbed the incongruous atmosphere of old and new as we cycled past the modern Walter Science Center and Centralia College before coming to the old brick buildings on Centralia Square. As old as they were, they were well-maintained and clean and really very modern looking, especially with the lovely mural painted on the top floor of one. However, I later learned that I shouldn't have perhaps thought it was lovely as it represents an event sometimes referred to as the Centralia Massacre and sometimes referred to as the Wobbley War. The gist of it is that around 1919, Centralia's labor force was suppressed, and tensions came to a head between the American Legion and the Wobbleys, also known as the Industrial Workers of the World, on Armistice Day, November 11, 1919. By the time the dust had settled, five Legionnaires were dead, and a man deemed to be the Wobbleys' leader, Wesley Everett, was taken to jail, only to be stolen away and hung by a lynch mob over the Skookumchuck River. The mural remains controversial to this day.

Moving on, we then journeyed in the direction of Toledo, spending that night deep in the heart of Washington State in Lewis and Clark State Park, a beautiful park full of old-growth trees and nurse logs, all brought together by lush ferns and foliage in every shade of green. Even with amenities like fire circles, equestrian campsites, and an amphitheater, it still cost only $42/night. I say "only" because two nights earlier I'd paid $300 for two rooms at a Super 8. Once we'd crossed into the US, we'd had to work hard every day to find the most affordable yet doable options because the farther south we went, the more expensive it got. My hope was that once we got out of Newport, Oregon, maybe the prices would drop because then it would be the end of August, with tourist season letting up.

I slept in the van that night of course, and Wayne and Yiota still chose the beds in the tent trailer. Sleep was elusive though because of this enlarged prostate of mine. I've had it for a long time now, but it's just one of those things I must work around as a senior. Often when I'm riding, I must stop to pee. Wayne's familiar with it, so he just rides on, and I catch up. Besides, it doesn't take me long because I've become quite a master at peeing the way Tour de France cyclists do. They don't even get off their bikes. They just stand right there on the side of the road and urinate. Unfortunately, my prostate really acts up sometimes, and it was really starting to pester me again, so much so that I started bringing a big bottle in the van with me at night, so I didn't have to go in and out every hour on the hour. It's a pain in the you-know-where, but I deal with it. It's just one of those things we all must plan for and work around when we get older. We can't let it stop us or keep us on the couch. It just takes a plan.

***

Again, the next morning I was the first one up. I was almost always the first. And it always took a good two hours to hit the road because it was just such slow going with cooking, eating, cleaning, and packing back up again. That morning it was particularly hard to get up and moving because no sunlight could make it through the tree canopy, so it was hard to tell what time it was.

But though it took more time than I would have liked to get going every day, things were progressing nicely by then, and the bike was running well... Wayne and I helped Yiota a little more with packing up camp every morning, and despite the cost, I tried to get more Airbnb's and restaurants for her, so she was less stressed and a little happier. And it's funny how every day, no matter where we were, people were still friendly; they all just wanted to chat. One time, when Wayne and I stopped at a gas station with two kilometers to go to relax on a bench with a couple beers each, we ended up chatting with passersby for an hour. People just kept stopping and asking questions after seeing the sign on my bike. Those were the highlights of each day for me. Wayne wasn't quite as fond of being stopped chatting while he was riding, but I hoped every day would include chatting with new people even if that meant being stopped.

I even made time many days to do interviews while I rode. For me, it was incredibly important to get my message to as many people as possible and hopefully make a difference in someone's life. So that day too, just before Toledo, I did an interview with a radio show called "Traveling Guys" around

4:30 p.m. Some days I was lucky enough to make it to our stop for the night in time to comfortably do the interview, but other times, as I had a few days earlier, I had to do my interview while riding. Wayne, and people driving by, looked at me like I was some kind of crazy person talking to myself, but it got the job done.

We did get some disappointing news that day though. Five cycling friends were going to meet us the following day to ride with us to Newport, Oregon, but two, Rachel and Mike, had to bow out because their daughter was ill. I was a little dejected with the cancelation. I'd ridden with them in Costa Rica, Nicaragua, and Alberta, and I was really looking forward to spending time with them again. Mike was my friend who was going to fly in and come to the rescue back in Prince George when Kim and Yiota said they were going to leave. What a great guy.

But on a positive note, three other friends—Danielle, Donna, and Sandy—would meet up with us in Astoria the next day and ride with us to Newport. It would be so much fun to have some new energy. I was sure it would lift everyone's spirits and help add to the anticipation of the celebration in Newport. I knew I was really looking forward to seeing my family again too: my wife, Gloria, and her daughter, Julie, who were flying in from Costa Rica, and my daughter, Janet, and granddaughter, Annika, who were flying in from Canada.

Until then though, we started the day with a few glimpses of Mount St. Helens. To just look at it, even in real life rather than on TV, it's still hard to imagine that a volcano erupted in this part of the world. It happens all the time in other parts of the world, but not usually in North America. Then of course, we had to stop for coffee in Toledo, the gateway to Mount St. Helens, so they say. We even ended up getting our coffee from the hardware store—and some tasty, packaged pastries.

Mount St. Helens wasn't the only spectacular sight we got to view in this area. We also caught a clear view of Mount Rainier, near where we turned west toward the coast. Imagine our surprise as Wayne and I finished climbing a rather large incline, only to get to the top and be treated to the sight of Mount Rainier rising into the sky in the distance, the sky almost utterly blue around it. Only a few wispy white clouds framed it. Moments like that make a hard climb worth it.

Mount Rainier

Then it was back on the road again, and of course, we had to cross the I5 again. I took a little time out to give an intriguing bicycle trick park we happened upon a try before we dared it though. Not to worry, I came out of it without any bumps, bruises, or broken bones!

We continued following the Columbia River, which visibly widened as we went, toward the ocean and Cathlamet, where we took the ferry across to Oregon, leaving Washington State behind. We made camp that night beside a small marina full of sailboats and motorboats, and even an old fishing trawler. After wandering through town for a bit, taking in its intriguing old buildings dating back to 1860, we went out to dinner, though only Yiota and I ate inside because they didn't serve alcohol outside, and Wayne didn't like the ventilation with COVID and all.

***

Then we were back on the road again and aiming for Astoria, Oregon, to meet our three friends: Danielle, Donna, and Sandy on yet another blissfully bright, peaceful morning. First though, we rode through Clatsop State Forest and tackled Clatsop Crest, the summit of which was 200 meters. Once at the top though, the view was breathtaking. The Columbia River widened even more there, and it was punctuated by numerous islands, some large enough to be populated. This river's water was a bright blue like the sky, the grasslands, and trees around its varying shades of green.

A restaurant called The Logger Restaurant caught my eye that morning after we'd gotten through the Clatsop Forest, so I decided to stop for a midmorning snack. It was starting to look like riding through Oregon was going to involve a lot of climbing, and it was making me mighty peckish. So, we popped in and discovered they served my favorite: apple pie! But not with ice cream, with cheddar cheese. Oh, so good! Our previous team member, Kim Voorsgeerd still doesn't quite get it, but I love it.

Anyway, Wayne and I hopped back on our bikes again after our tasty snack, our eyes set on Astoria, our goal for that day. As we got closer, we discovered people living in floating houses on the river. I'm not making this up! These houses looked just like any other house, with two floors, a deck, and outdoor space. The only differences were that they had a boat instead of a car, and they had a river around their house, not a lawn. It seemed they were all connected by one large platform in places, and they shared a walking bridge to the bank. It was rather cute!

Then as we hit Astoria, the river became wide enough to accommodate container ships, given its proximity to the Pacific Ocean. We stopped and watched the ships go in and out of the port city for a while, a residential neighborhood at my back, before going to meet up with our friends. Those amazing ladies had just finished the 130 km L'etape Canada by Tour de France in Edmonton the morning before and had still taken the time and energy to meet up with me. Talk about loving what you do and being wonderful friends!

It was such a treat to meet up with friends that Wayne and I chose that day to stop and have a midday snack and beer with them before riding on to the ocean and finally our campground in Astoria, Oregon.

Reaching the Pacific Ocean in Seaside, Oregon

***

What a pleasure it was to ride along the coast after a slower than usual breakfast. With five of us riding together now, it was more like a party than a chore, even on the climbs. That day we would ride through Cannon Beach and Garibaldi on our way to Tillamook to spend the night in yet another gorgeous Airbnb. Though the prices of the Airbnb's we were coming across were starting to skyrocket to unbelievable highs, despite their sponsorship, that home was splendid, nonetheless. I sure hoped though that costs would change soon, or I'd be destitute.

Either way, we were treated to some breathtaking ocean views along the way, but we had to pay for them with all the climbing and descending we did. First, we'd be trudging up over a headland where we'd look down on the waves crashing on the shore, then we'd be racing down into a beach town to see those same crashing waves up close. We did the up-and-down routine so many times I lost count. There was one awfully memorable scary part we had to ride through though, that had nothing to do with waves or climbs or descents. It was a tunnel. It was long and dark, but the designers had obviously thought of cyclists because we had to push a button before entering that caused lights to flash, telling drivers there were cyclists in the tunnel. There was even a sign explaining this at the tunnel's opening, but if I didn't know any better, I'd say that just made drivers angry rather than aware. I guess the allure of the sign on my bike was nullified in the darkness of the tunnel. People had usually been so friendly until then.

That said, the ladies traveling with me certainly weren't used to the attention I drew thanks to that sign on my bike, "Alaska to Panama." Lots of people still honked as they went by, not a get-off-the-road-buddy sort of honk but a short beep, and though I waved at them, it still caught the ladies off guard. It took a while for Danielle to figure out why so many people were honking. I had to explain, "Oh no, that's quite common. I just wave so they can see me in their rearview mirror. I also stop and chat with them when they stop at viewpoints and such to ask questions about when we started, where we're going, and that sort of thing."

I even told her about the time one guy said, "My God, you know there's psychiatric help available in this country for you?" He and I had had a good laugh at that. He was a good-natured fellow, so we chatted about Canadians.

He said he'd never met a Canadian he didn't like, so I said, "Well, you haven't spoken to me yet."

Another time, a fellow said, "Gee, can I touch you?" That was so funny, it got me to thinking maybe I should start charging $5 for a kiss, $3 for a touch, and $1 for a photo. Maybe I could make a buck or two to refill my coffers after all those expenses. Then on the way to Astoria the previous day, I'd met a fellow bike traveler, Joe, who'd been towing a trailer behind his bike and had lots of panniers attached because he was camping all the way back home to California. I'd stopped talking to him, though Wayne had ridden on of course. Joe had been a teacher for twenty-five years and had just retired. He'd spent the last few years taking all sorts of long-distance bike trips, and he had all kinds of stickers on his bike to show it. And it turned out he wasn't alone on his travels. Would you believe that in the trailer was his dog? The trailer wasn't toting the camping gear I'd thought he would be. It had been hard to see the dog in his little cage, but whenever another dog came by, he'd bark up a storm.

Finally, the five of us made Tillamook in one piece after 111 kilometers of riding and 800 meters of climbing. And though that day was the penultimate day, my birthday, there was no time to stop and enjoy a rest day. We were due in Newport the next day to meet up with my family and friends, I still had a party to plan, and it was sometimes difficult to keep my three lady friends moving. Point in case, when they stopped for a morning coffee in Seaside and a winery across the street opened its doors, all three ran over. They sampled some wine and bought a bunch while I finished my coffee at the coffee shop. It took them a fair while to get going afterward, so I ended up saying the lunch stop would have to be shorter since they'd spent so long at the coffee/wine stop.

In the end, we made up time by having lunch on the side of road. Not that it wasn't a tasty lunch, with some excellent wraps made from the supper the ladies had been kind enough to make the previous night, which had consisted of pork chops, baked potatoes, vegetables, salad, and wine with blackberries and ice cream for dessert.

It had been such a beautiful riding day that day though, that it got me to thinking about the sensations I experienced while riding, like coming out of Alaska and Yukon and finally riding into the forests, smelling the pine trees. Then there was getting to Prince George, and besides the pulp-mill smell, there were the freshly cut hay fields, mown clover, and cut grass—or whatever else makes hay. On the other side of that coin was the big logging trucks whizzing by us a meter, a meter, and a half away, but you could smell the freshly cut cedar and other woods, combined of course with the exhaust of the trucks and cars. The exhaust was especially strong at stop lights when you were stopped right behind them.

Riding down the coast to Tillamook though, the air had been filled with the smell of seawater and blackberries. Donna said she could smell all the blackberries along the side of the road as she drove the support car for the girls. Because there were three of them, they would alternate having two on bikes and one driving their car each day.

Anyway, the weather had stayed hot as we'd made our way down the coast, but with the marine layer off the coast, we got lots of cool doses, especially in the late afternoon. One section was so cool I started putting on my jacket. I expected that marine layer to stick around all the way down the coast, even though California. I'd wintered in Oceanside, California, for two years with Beth, and the marine layer was always sitting out there so you could always see it from your condo.

Once we'd arrived at another cozy Airbnb and freshened up at the end of our ride, I enjoyed a wonderful dinner at a delightful restaurant in Tillamook. Donna MacLean and Sandy Brodie shared what looked like a divine shrimp pasta while I indulged in a steak I couldn't even finish. The best part was they picked up the bill as a birthday present! The only downside to the night was that Danielle was tired and Yiota wasn't feeling well so they stayed behind at the hotel, and Wayne just had a sandwich. But I thoroughly enjoyed the delightful company, atmosphere, and food, making me glad I'd passed by a major tourist attraction in the interest of time, time I got to spend enjoying the fantastic company at dinner.

Earlier that day, we'd passed the renowned Tillamook creamery; it was an enormous blue building with a parking lot to match. Oodles of folks streamed in and out, sampling and buying cheese.

Dinner with great friends in Tillamook

Even Donna and Sandy stopped in and bought cheese because everyone says you're missing something if you don't stop there, but as I passed by around 5:15 p.m. after a long ride, the motivation to find a place to lock up my bike and go in just wasn't there so I kept on riding. I might regret it someday, but that day I thought, *C'est la vie. I gotta keep the wagon train moving down the highway.*

There was lots of traffic in Tillamook too given it's apparently one of the most scenic popular tourist destinations in the US, but the road's shoulders were so wide it wasn't a problem.

But after my fabulous dinner that night, we went back to our Airbnb and retired a little early. Not that I got much sleep. Despite the very comfy bed, my prostate had been acting up the last two months and I still hadn't gotten past it, so I must have gotten up a dozen times or more. I just couldn't figure out what was triggering it this time or why it was happening. It had been fine when I'd left Costa Rica to embark on this journey; I was only getting up maybe twice a night. I was still hopeful it would disappear on its own again as it usually did though.

The next day was to be a 129 km ride to get to Newport to meet my family and friends. Despite my lack of sleep, I was driven by my anticipation of the celebration at a brew pub the following night. Then I had another rest day to look forward to where I could enjoy my time with my family and friends, and hopefully get some sleep irritating prostate or no, before riding down through the rest of Oregon and pushing on south toward California and the redwoods and Crescent City. And though I hated to say it, what I was most looking forward to now was not worrying so much about staying on schedule. After the party, I could relax and enjoy the touring experience.

But you know what they say about best laid plans, so I maybe shouldn't have hedged my bets just then.

REUNIONS and REDWOODS

We made it.

It was the most important milestone on this odyssey of mine, and we made it, on time and none the worse for wear.

The ride down from Tillamook had been both eerie and spectacular. The six of us—Wayne, Danielle, Donna, Sandy, Yiota, and I—had journeyed down the coast through the densest fog we'd come across yet. In some places, especially along the edges of forests ravaged by wildfires, it had felt much like we were riding on another planet. Fog had clouded the air from sky to sea and blurred the world around us. The barrenness of the fire-consumed forests had only served to amplify the nearly audible cry for help of the few stubborn green ferns and moss trying to grow back here and there. Each new twist and turn of the road had led us to another inspiring sight. As we'd ridden down gravel roads at times, the fog had hovered over the scenery on each side of us as though it was hiding the foliage from us, as though it was saddened and ashamed of the devastation left by the fires. Other times as we'd ridden on the highway, the fog had sunk down to meet the sea so we could make out only the odd peek of the water and waterfowl wading on it or the occasional bay, beach, or outcropping.

And then there were the times when the sun had cut through the fog, utterly juxtaposing the eerie with the spectacular, the dreary with the delightful. In those moments, we'd been gifted from out of nowhere with the sudden sight of sand dunes or monumental peaks rising out of the ocean and out of the fog, much like the one we had encountered as we'd arrived at Pacific City.

One lone peak rising out of the Pacific near the aptly named Pacific City

At times, the fog had been so thick I'd even had to turn on my bike's headlight for the first time. Imagine the contrariness of being soaked to the bone not from rain but from fog. That marine layer had been so immense as it sat on top of the shore that we may as well have been riding through a shower. Heck, as we'd come across a beachfront hotel near Otter Rocks, heading south toward Newport, we'd discovered we couldn't at all see the beach of the beachfront hotel. I didn't complain though because it had made it a memorable ride I won't soon forget. Besides, much of the way, we enjoyed quiet country roads off Highway 101. Beautiful, beautiful riding. Did you know you can smell the moisture in the air? Not even the seawater, but the actual moisture in the air? I think at times too you can even smell the life in the foliage around you.

Mother Nature had certainly gone a little nut on us that day, even disregarding all the fog. Danielle had said it was a "menopausia" ride. It had started warm, gotten hot, then had turned cold when the marine layer overcame the sun. Then it had gotten warm again, then hot again, and finally the temperature had plummeted once more, making me even have to stop and put my jacket on. The whole day had followed that pattern: jacket on, jacket off, jacket on, jacket off. Nature had quite the battle with itself that day!

When we arrived in Newport, Oregon, I was taken aback by a car full of screaming people passing us when were still about six or seven kilometers away from our hotel. It pulled over at the next viewpoint, and out jumped my daughter and granddaughter, my sister and niece, and my niece's daughter. It was tremendously moving, and it meant so much to me. So, there were hugs all around, and we took a few minutes to take some pictures before heading to the hotel where I was greeted with another surprise.

The carload of family had gone ahead of us of course, and by the time Wayne and I made it there, the group had grown by about another ten people, all waving us in and cheering. Just moments later, a taxi pulled up, and out stepped my beautiful wife, Gloria, and her daughter, Julie. If I was a tears kind of guy, there would have been a bucketful of them then. It turned out our newest team member, Kyle, had been kind enough to meet them at the airport. Anyway, more hugging and kissing ensued. Now I may not always be around as often as people would like and maybe it seems I forget about them, that I put myself and my adventures first, but I hope they know how much I love them. That moment was so much more than special to me. It's times like that when you really feel appreciated and loved. It makes you think that you left your mark on the world, that you'll be remembered when you're gone, and maybe, just maybe, you did a little good.

Later that night, after we'd all gotten settled, the three friends that had been riding with us since Astoria—Danielle, Sandy, and Donna—threw a little party in their room. They'd gone out and gotten a bunch of clam chowder and pizzas, and most importantly, lots of beer and wine. We all had so much fun; the party carried on for hours.

***

In the morning, we all did our own thing before the party and later that evening. I had to go and check out the restaurant where I'd planned to have my party, and it's a good thing I did because I discovered it wasn't the best place to have a party. So, I changed tactics and went to check out all the restaurants on Newport's historic waterfront, but I couldn't find anything better in the end. Doing a one-eighty then, I went back to the first restaurant and told them we would have the party outside—I'd told the manager when I'd left earlier that I was deciding between in or out given the foggy weather—but the manager chose that moment to tell me that they didn't do large groups. After she explained that the kitchen staff couldn't serve that many people, I felt compelled to debate why someone would have taken my earlier reservation *and* confirmed it just two days earlier if that was the case. As a result, the manager called another brewpub, who said the size of my party was no problem. Crisis averted. We ended up holding the party at a wonderful pub house on Nye Creek called The Taphouse, with a couple big tables just for us and lots of drinks flowing.

Well, I must have had more drinks than I'd thought though because when it was time to order, I decided to make a list on my phone of the pizzas we wanted. When the waitress came over, I gave her the phone and showed her the list. I had a list of six pizzas, two of three different kinds, and she wrote that list down. But when the food came, we ended up with twelve pizzas instead. I was flabbergasted, but I took responsibility for it because I'd written the list and showed it to the waitress. Besides, everyone else thought it was funny because the pizzas just kept coming and coming, and we ended up with five extra pizzas. I wasn't exactly sure what to do with them, but we ended up eating much of them the next day before throwing the rest away.

Either way, I had lots of fun at the party, and it seemed everyone else did too. Rachel and Mike, my two friends who'd had to cancel at the last minute, FaceTimed the party, and we had a long chat. I also sent a video to John Burdett, another friend who'd been going to ride with us along with Rachel and Mike, to say how sorry I was that he wasn't able to be there. Later that night, another two friends from Portland, Greg, and Gillian, arrived. It was fantastic to see them after nine long years. I'd last seen them when I'd ridden with them in Croatia on my first international bike trip after Beth's death. We became great friends on that trip, and have stayed Facebook friends since then, but I hadn't seen them in all that time. I was touched that they'd made the trip out to see me. They even said they might try to get to Antigua in Guatemala to celebrate the fiesta when I break the world record there. I thought it would be nice if they showed up. I would keep my fingers crossed!

And of course, as you might expect, I got lots of funny gifts that people would usually give an old man, like a cane, some Viagra, and some hemorrhoid lube. It all made me quite a laugh. The night included a loud, boisterous rendition of *Happy Birthday* that began with our group of sixteen, but then all the other tables around them decided to chime in, so it was like the whole restaurant was singing *Happy Birthday* to me. To top it all off, I received all sorts of birthday wishes on Facebook, and even some videos from my old bike club in Edmonton wishing me a happy birthday. The night was a rousing success, and I had a sensational time. We didn't even leave until about 9:30 p.m.

All in all, it turned out to be a really great day, plus the pressure was off quite a bit because there were no more deadlines to meet; I didn't have to be in any particular town or at any particular event or anything along the way, besides the odd interview I could do on the road if I had to. So now if something happened, mechanical—touch wood—weatherwise, or anything like that, we could pause for a day or something, and it wouldn't affect anything other than making us a day or so late getting to Panama.

You'd think after all that fun and all those drinks, I'd sleep like a rock that night. But again, that was not to be. My prostate was still giving me grief, but it was getting worse by then. I had to get up every hour or more to try and pee, but you know how it goes. Nothing comes out.

Anyway, it was a good thing Gloria was there because she convinced me to go to the pharmacy in the morning to see what they would say. This enlarged prostate was nothing new to me, but it had really been going crazy the last couple months, and if anything, it seemed like it was getting worse. That night was the worst though. Nothing really happened when I had to get up and go, just some pain. Thankfully, as I'd suspected, it was just a urinary tract infection. Though the pharmacist wouldn't accept a prescription from my doctor back in Edmonton, he did give me an over-the -counter medication for it that worked well enough in a few days. I'm not exactly sure what triggered my prostate, or even what triggered the urinary tract infection, but I'd certainly have to drink as much water as I could get down and see if that would help. I admittedly don't get as much fluid as I should when I ride.

Another thing I found I don't do much when I'm on a long-distance cycling trip is walk, as I discovered when I'd walked around the historic waterfront looking for a more suitable place for the party. My muscles just seem to forget how to do that, or more accurately, I don't seem to use certain muscles when I bike that I use to walk. These legs didn't like walking around town, especially not up and down the hills. I suppose I should just be glad that I can walk well still—and ride. Perhaps I'll have to walk more though so my muscle use is better balanced.

Otherwise, I realized I was so glad to be eighty. Really! I see it as another opportunity, another year to see and do more. And I was so glad to be in Newport, to be with family and friends. But most of all, I was looking forward to getting back on my bike the next day, back on the road. Discovering what the rest of the trip had to offer had me itching to move again. And Kyle, our new member that had just joined us, had all this fancy equipment, so he was taking videos and photos and putting mics on people and everything, so maybe now we could get some exciting, high-quality footage of the trip for Instagram and the blog. He really appeared to know what to do with all that equipment, so I had a good feeling about the trip moving forward. It looked like he would be a terrific addition.

***

Though the day after my party was enormously cloudy as I prepared to head out on the highway again after my three-day rest and partying, the clouds seemed to be higher, and the forecast for the following day was all sun, so I was hopeful the marine layer would disappear and maybe we could stay dry for a day.

And luck was on our side. Departure day did indeed dawn sunny and warm, the marine layer seemingly losing the battle for the moment at least. I took that as a positive sign and hopped on my bike, energized, and excited. Southward we headed, aiming eventually for the redwoods and the Mexican border. But first was to be a few massive bridges, one accompanied by wind-warning signs. Again though, Lady Luck was with us because the wind wasn't bad that day and we crossed both bridges problem free.

So, we rode down the coast in the sunshine for a while, taking in the swampy coastal areas, the multimillion dollar homes, the beaches and the sand dunes and the verdant foliage before coming across a whole stretch of wood-carvings shops, where we saw everything from bears to men to dolphins made all of wood. To say they were something else doesn't give them enough credit. The talent those wood carvers possess makes me jealous.

To say the scenery was stunning along the coast just doesn't give it justice. We rode right on the edge of a mountain that dropped into the ocean, and below were beaches and sea-lion caves and a spectacular, gorgeous surf pounding in. Even the greenery was awe-inspiring the way many of the trees were so windblown that their branches grew sideways while the leaves and the needles all grew in the direction of the Pacific Ocean. In my mind, Oregon is one of the best coastal rides in the world.

Windblown trees on the Pacific coast in Oregon

We stopped at a viewpoint to take some photos of the stunning beauty around us, and that too turned out to be fortuitous. Here's the story. As normally happens whenever we stop, people come over and ask questions about the trip. So, I was talking to a guy on a Harley from Indiana, and we were comparing notes about our journeys when another guy and his wife suddenly appeared out of the sand dunes and wandered over to me. He waited till I had finished talking with the guy from Indiana before saying anything. But then we started chatting away, and when I told him about my odyssey and my goal, he said he's a cyclist too, that he'd cycled the coast four times, cycled from Venezuela to Brazil to Argentina, and even all over Europe.

Then this guy says, from out of nowhere, that he hopes I'm writing a book about my adventure. When I replied that I was, he told me he writes books about his travels, and he had another one coming out shortly. But here's the kicker, when he mentioned the title of his book, what it was about, and described a couple others, I suddenly clued into who he was. So, I asked him what his name was—I'm still not sure why I hadn't by that point—and he said his name was Frosty Wooldridge. Imagine my surprise at running into the same guy whose books were on my phone! Once I recovered from my little shock, I said, "Frosty, I'm Robert Fletcher. I talked to you six, nine months ago, and you gave me advice on publishing and writing a book. I even have two of your books here on my iPhone! I use them for researching this route and finding out what's ahead. So glad to meet you."

Frosty said, "Ah, I remember you now, yeah." So, we chatted for a long time, much to everyone else's dismay. But how often do you just run into someone you'd pretty much call a mentor? I mean, his seventeenth book is coming out! And they're not all about cycling; some are just about life. Apparently the next one is about keeping the earth healthy and sustaining life on earth. It was quite a treat to unexpectedly meet somebody I've spoken with before. It's amazing how that happens; you're just riding down the road and you randomly stop somewhere, and bam! there's suddenly somebody you know in front of you. That was the highlight of the day, even with the spectacular scenery.

Finally, our crew moved on and came upon another fellow riding form Oregon to San Diego, bikepacking though—unlike me and my comfy trip camping and staying in hotels and Airbnb's—and two people from Switzerland also bikepacking. We stopped for a break at the famous Sea Lion Caves, touted as America's largest sea cave, and had a bite and some cold ones and took some snapshots of the blue sea-lion statue, stunning beaches, and never-ending sand dunes.

We finally called it a day near Dunes City, Oregon, and spent the night in a beautiful state park with enormous trees and excellent facilities. The next day's goal was Bandon, Oregon, and I was hoping, despite my rapidly emptying wallet, that we'd find an affordable and accessible Airbnb. There just isn't good enough Wi-Fi when camping to research the route ahead at night.

Sand dunes from above along the Pacific coast

***

After a better night's sleep than I had been getting, we began yet another day on the road for what was to be a 122 km ride with a thousand meters of climbing. Of course, it was another interesting day as we hit the Oregon Dunes National Recreation Area. Apparently, the Oregon coast with its sand dunes is the largest coastal sand-dune region in the world. Everywhere you look, companies are offering sand-dune buggy rides or people are sandboarding down the dunes. Some places even look like ski slopes.

From there, we moved inland a bit, following Highway 101 to Gardiner, Oregon, a tiny little community that had once been a bustling trade and logging town known as The White City after rebuilding from a fire that had destroyed most of the town. The weather was beautiful that day, given we had less of the marine layer to deal with while we were inland a bit. We did, however, must contend with more "monster" bridges, as Wayne calls them. Enormous, wide-open bridges where you can see below you are nothing short of nerve-racking. And that's even before you factor in all the vehicles zipping closely by you!

At least we could often pull onto quieter side roads after crossing those bridges; we didn't always need to remain on the crowded, noisy highways. On that trek from Dunes City to Bandon, we traveled down one where we passed not only the usual fascinating Oregon forests and dunes, but also boat basins and huge piles of oyster shells. And when I say huge, I mean huge. One pile I recall was at least the size of two cars.

We met more cyclists on that road and chatted with them for a while. One interesting character was Tyler from Lake Tahoe. I recall him because not only did he have an interesting bike, but it was also his first bikepacking trip. We chatted with him for a while, and they offered me a refreshing drink, which I gladly accepted, as they were on the side of the road in their easy chairs when I came riding up. We later saw him a few times as we leap-frogged back and forth.

Then there were two young ladies who'd pulled off to the side of the road who wanted to take a picture with me. I never mind the attention, so I stopped and after they took the photo, they generously gave me a bunch of energy bars, an apple, and a drink. See what I mean about how friendly people are on the road? We chatted quite a while as they wanted to know about my journey. They were just traveling down the coast enjoying a nice holiday and were quite interested in the sign on the back of my bike.

Well, that night, after passing through Lakeside, North Bend, and Coos Bay and stopping to take some photos with a cyclist structure made of bark, complete with an old bike and basket and helmet, we pulled into the harbor in Bandon, Oregon. It's a fascinating little town renowned for the sand dunes and golf courses. Bandon Dunes Golf Resort in particular has five links plus a par-three course, so it's a mecca for golfers who love to play link-style courses. As much as I love golf, I appreciated the town's charm even more, with its quaint beachfront shops like Bandon Sweets & Treats, Bandon Card & Gift Shoppe, and By the Sea Treasures. The shops are an incongruous combination of old with their weathered-wood structures and new with the brightly painted signs and molding. As we walked the waterfront admiring the incredible art installations, Wayne and I took the opportunity to stop at the pier and grab a snack before heading to our campsite at Bandon By the Sea RV Park, which, oddly, was decorated with colorful, character tea pots all along the fence. Anyway, when in Rome of course, we ordered some crab cakes and oysters, though Wayne doesn't like oysters, so I got all six, dressed with tabasco sauce and horseradish. Yummy! And here too, lots of people came over asking lots of questions about my odyssey. That sign was sure attracting a lot of attention!

***

The next morning, I was the one slow to get started. I was just feeling so sleepy and lazy! Usually, our overnight stops were rather routine: I'd plug in the two batteries and get them charging when we pulled in, have two beers, change, shower if we have access to one, make and eat dinner, do the dishes, then go to bed quite early around 8:30 p.m. Then the next morning, I'd get up around 7:00 a.m. and try to get coffee going and wake everyone else up. As hard as I try though, I can never seem to get a head start on the day, so we usually end up leaving around 9:30 a.m. And there was me that morning, the last one to crawl out of bed. Wayne had to come check on me!

Well as tired as I was, we stopped for coffee at a charming place called Langlois Market not all that long after starting the day's ride. That, and of course riding, finally woke me up enough to enjoy the sights around me again, including my first ever cranberry bog. Then it was on to Myrtlewood, where we stopped for our midday snack, and Port Orford, where a famous battle occurred between the Native peoples and Captain William Tichenor and nine of his men there to establish a white settlement. The men had been stranded and surrounded on an island now called Battle Rock and had only managed to escape under the cover of darkness. Eventually, however, the captain had returned with many more men and claimed the land, establishing the city as it's now known.

After a lovely, warm weather day and fantastic views of the ocean, we arrived in Wedderburn, then crossed another massive, nerve-racking bridge into Gold Beach. As we crossed over the river, I was reminded once again of how all your senses come into play when you're cycling a long distance. Beyond all the sights, sounds, and smells of nature that you get to appreciate as you ride along, there's also the other side of that, where you always have one ear open for vehicle traffic or a strange noise on your bike, and you always have one eye on peripheral guard duty to ensure nothing's coming at you or nothing unexpected is happening. I'd even have to say maybe there's some sort of sixth sense that gets involved too because there's always this sort of invisible radar scanning for anything that feels wrong about your surroundings or your equipment or you. Strangely, this trip was the first time I've really appreciated all of that, all the various sensations and experiences and how incredibly different they are. I mean, we had the hot air whipping through our helmet straps in Alaska, then the cold and the rain permeating us through the semiarid/arid plains of Yukon and northern BC, and then the warm, spruce-filled air in BC's interior round about Whistler. After that came the fog, the wind, the salt air, and the sand in Washington and Oregon. And once I'd discovered how much more aware of it, I was on this journey, I was excited to experience the redwoods, the Sonoran Desert, Central Mexico, and the rest of Central America. I guess I had uncovered a new goal: to experience as much as possible and file it all away to appreciate again later instead of taking it for granted. There's nothing more fascinating than what nature has to offer, except of course what people of different cultures have to offer.

Again, I digress from my story. We stayed in a lovely, modern Airbnb that night, one that had plenty of room for us all. As much as I love the comfort, the cost of those Airbnb's was really hurting the Airbnb budget. The deeper into the US we got and the farther into summer we got, the more expensive they got. The only reason I was still shelling out for Airbnb's was to help Yiota out now that Kim was gone—and for the Wi-Fi. That said, I was really looking forward to potentially camping the next night, if everything went according to plan that was.

***

The sun took prominence in the sky as we packed up to head back out on the road again in the morning. It's amazing to see what that does for people's attitudes. Every time the sun shines, people are happier, they're nicer to each other, they're more helpful and energetic. Maybe that's why we had such tension and drama in Yukon. Who knows? Anyway, we continued journeying south on the Oregon Coast Highway, going through Cape San Sebastian, named after the patron saint of the day it was when Sebastian Vizciano discovered it in 1603, and we got rather doused once more. This time though, it was the fault of sea spray, not fog or rain, which wasn't nearly as miserable, especially with the heat of the sun warming us. So, we took it in stride and enjoyed the view it gave us as we rode around each bend along the coast, listening to the surf pound, watching the waves crash around the rocky peaks piercing the sea near the shore, and wiping the spray off our faces.

Further and further south we pushed, stopping at many of the spectacular viewpoints on the way as we rolled by Pistol River and crossed yet another bridge of the sort that made Wayne apprehensive. Not long after, the Oregon Coast Highway, or the 101, turned into the Persian Gulf, Afghanistan, Iraq Veterans Memorial Highway for a while near Crook Point. By the time we'd crossed Burnt Hill Creek though, it once again became the Oregon Coast Highway. We stopped for coffee that day at the Compass Rose Café in Brookings, Oregon, and the staff in the little grocery store there were quite interested in what we were doing and gave us free coffee to help us a little along the way.

Salty sea spray, not fog!

That day was great for meeting more people as we rode. I know I've said before that Wayne doesn't like it as much as I do so he usually rides on and I catch up, but I can't say it enough: it's one my favorite things about long-distance cycling. Well, that and always finding something new around the next bend. Imagine always getting to go for a different hundred-kilometer ride every day!

First up that day was Dave. He was a bit of a hyper guy on an inexpensive e-bike; he said he'd paid just $900 for a souped-up 48V battery, 350W motor, so he could make it go quite fast. I supposed that would be more expensive in Canadian dollars, and heck, probably cost more in Canada too. Anyway, he was so excited to see us, he took our cards that we'd been handing out along our odyssey, told us where we should stop for beer, and said we should mention his name there. That fascinating character even said we could stay at his place in his shop, but I wasn't exactly sure if "shop" meant a garage or if he had a business or something, so I wasn't sure I'd take him up on his offer. As it turned out, Dave had already spotted us earlier, so he'd gone to a bike shop and told them all about our little crew. So, he told us before we parted that my team should stop in and say hello and they'd give us free maintenance. That sounded great to me, but somehow, the road we took must have bypassed the bike shop, so we never did stop there.

We also met a wonderful young couple, Xavier, and Kristine, who had just recently met, but because they both liked bikes they seemed to have clicked. They were on their first bikepacking trip, going to a wedding in California from Oregon. I found Kristine unique because she was the first lady I'd seen thus far on an e-bike. She said she really liked it though and had bought it used, at first just for commuting but now for touring.

And then we hit another milestone. We crossed the Oregon/California border and of course had a little mini celebration under the Welcome to California sign. I wasn't quite sure why California felt more significant than Oregon, or even Washington, and I still couldn't tell you, but it really did. Maybe it was just the subconscious contrast between Alaska and California or maybe it was that we'd ridden nearly 5,000 km by then.

*Celebrating another milestone! We were
getting places!*

Celebrating another milestone! We were getting places

***

So, after another scenic, enjoyable ride, complete with our celebration, we settled in and made camp for the night, only to wake up to a cool, foggy, damp day. We were, however, about to head into three days of riding through California's giant redwoods, and I was really looking forward to that. We got a good indication of that when we came upon an old redwood stump the size of a camper. Of course, along with riding through the redwoods came the need to climb two mountain ranges. Thank goodness for my e-bike. It would be mighty beneficial over the next two or three days, but I felt for Wayne.

Climbing or no climbing though, suddenly, there we were, seeing our first live redwoods. Even the few we saw as we neared the forests were mind boggling. If I could, I'd fill this whole chapter with nothing but photos because there's nothing, I can say to adequately convey their majesty. Adding to the ambience was the low-lying, persistent fog. It obscured the way ahead enough that with the redwoods on either side, it felt a little, as Wayne said, as if you were going to disappear into another dimension if you kept riding into it.

You must know we stopped on multiple occasions, both to take photos, including the typical tree-hugger photos, and to give our poor bodies a break from climbing. At one tree, even with Wayne's arms spread out as wide as possible to hug the tree, you still would have needed a good four or five more people his size just to cover one side of the tree. Another tree was so big that the gap that time and fire had worn out within it easily housed me, Wayne, and both our bikes with room to fit a few more people still. Even the forest itself looked positively prehistoric between the size and abundance of redwoods, the colossal ferns and various other foliage filling in the gaps, and the immense tree cover way above that kept any-hint of sunlight from getting through. I did, though, find it incredibly odd to discover a tree named, however aptly, Big Tree. All the trees were big trees! Of course, that's what all the directional arrows said too, "This way to the big trees!" and "This way to more big trees!"

Finally, as we left Del Norte Cost Redwoods State Park, we were rewarded with a long, satisfying descent back down to sea level and the ocean. The fog gave us no quarter though, so we gratefully arrived in Klamath, California, where we happened upon what we thought was a replica of a giant log-hauling frame used for transporting those behemoth redwoods and our first sign proclaiming the distance to San Francisco. It looked encouraging at first to read 326, but when Wayne reminded me that was miles, not kilometers, it took a bit of the wind out of my sails.

***

Next up was Prairie Creek Redwoods State Park and another long climb with a matching descent before we rode into Orick, California, and a short break from the redwoods. Waiting at the top of each climb for Wayne gave me an opportunity to do what I'd said a few days earlier I would spend more time doing: reflecting. I got a few quiet moments to reflect on the world around me, behind me, and ahead of me, and I got a few precious minutes to just let the smells and sounds ooze into my memory: the cold, the moisture, the redwood aroma full of life. It was hard not to be grateful to be alive.

Orick was another intriguing town, much like Hyder, Alaska. It seemed each home boasted a carving of one sort or another: an intricate fairy-tale house made of old wooden shakes at one home, a lighthouse, and a windmill at yet a couple more, and everything from fish to whales at still others. After Orick, we scooted through the vacation town of Trinidad, which of course had even more marvelous sculptures, including a magnificent dolphin ... and an alluring mermaid, before pushing on to McKinleyville. Here we took a quieter coastal side road parallel to Highway 101, where the odd palm-like tree and pampas grass were starting to pop up among the redwoods and spruce. It never ceases to amaze me; the wonders nature offers and how it's a perfect example of how things that are so outwardly opposite can live together harmoniously.

After a long, hard, cold, beautiful day, hitting McKinleyville and Arcata meant we were just shy of our Airbnb. That was a day the cost of those expensive Airbnb's just didn't bother me. I was tired, cold, and hungry, as were we all. Once there, Kyle treated us to some wonderful fresh crab a fisherman had given him for free a couple days earlier.

As I tucked in for the night, I was feeling mighty fulfilled and satisfied, despite my fatigue. I mean, it was a good tired I was feeling. Ever since Newport, we'd been blessed with plenty of luck and some really great times. I'd gotten to meet lots of new people, I'd seen some incredible sights, and best of all, there had been no drama among the team. That might all have been countered by all the cold and fog and climbing we'd faced, but there's nothing wrong with a good challenge. It makes you feel alive. My only hope as I fell asleep that night was that things would keep going as smoothly as they had.

EUREKA!

Fog and gloom set the stage for the next day again as we packed up and headed this time for Eureka and another milestone. So of course, when we reached the sign proclaiming the city limits, we had to make a video for posterity, shouting, "Eureka! 5,000 km!" What great timing, reaching that milestone in that place. And it also turned out to be quite the city, with numerous grand old homes and buildings, complete with towers and turrets and arches. In some places, you'd have thought you'd fallen into a fairy tale or Disney movie like Cinderella. But wouldn't you know it, not long after that came another one of those dastardly bridges we hate so much. The fog didn't help the experience either. It was thick enough that it left droplets on our glasses.

Eventually, we made it to Fernbridge, the last community before a civilization void until Fortuna. Once we passed there though, our little party enjoyed riding along the "Avenue of the Giants" on more sideroads parallel to Highway 101. At times, it felt as though there was no end to the redwoods, that we would just ride down some endless road forever and ever into eternity. Suddenly, though, we came upon the Immortal Tree. It's a thousand years old and big enough to build many homes, just that one tree! It's called the Immortal Tree not only because of how old it is, but also because it survived a lightning strike, loggers, a forest fire, and a flood.

Then came Pepperwood—where all about fifty people live—more redwoods, Redcrest, and more redwoods—even one with a small house built beneath and a long since cut-down and preserved one whose rings date back to 912 CE. The sun came out around then, creating some beautiful lighting through the trees that brought out the colors and made everything spectacular. Then came another climb through Humboldt Redwoods State Park and another descent down that I, of course, thoroughly enjoyed, to Miranda and Phillipsville before reaching a redwood with a break in it so large a road runs through it. Of course, they've made a tourist trap out of it and charge you three bucks, but I waited in line, went through it, and got photos anyway!

On and on we rode through all the tiny communities peppering the forests of California, just a little inland: Redway, Garberville, and Benbow, all with showstopper old, maintained homes that remind you of a bygone time. Each time we left a community and were engulfed again by the redwoods, I realized the light coming through the trees was phenomenal; it produced some ethereal yellows and greens you just don't get to see when it's cloudy and gray. Not far outside Benbow, we pulled into Richardson Grove State Park to camp for the night in the redwoods. It was both humbling and eerie looking outside the window of the van and seeing nothing but those enormous trees all around me. They just continue to go up and up and up and you must almost lay down on the ground to see the tops of them.

I spent some time that night taking note of some things I'd noticed over the last few days. Kyle seemed to be doing an incredibly good job with the videos for Instagram and the reels for Facebook and such. I'd come to learn that he was a real adventure type of guy; he'd jumped out of a plane 125 times and still wanted to do BASE jumping and paragliding. He rides a motorbike, does yoga and handstands—he can even walk on his hands—and he's traveled a lot. That Kyle is quite the interesting fellow, not to mention a very fit young man.

Still things were calm in camp, and the traveling was pretty good. Wayne's spirits were up, Yiota seemed to be happy, and Kyle seemed to be doing well; things seemed to be moving along quite well. We were still on schedule even though I'd had to redo the route a bit because I'd made a mistake. Yiota and I had had to sit down and came up with a few different towns to visit rather than original ones, but we planned to be back on my original itinerary in another day or two.

I'd chatted with some more fantastic folks earlier that day, for instance, a young German couple cycling from Vancouver to San Diego on the same route as us. They'd been as interested in my Octogenarian Odyssey as I genuinely was in their trip. Then Wayne and I stopped in a small town for a beer or two as we usually do when they get within maybe ten kilometers of our destination; it's kind of a reward thing, especially if the day's been a good one. We never stop when we're wet and cold of course. Then we just want to get somewhere warm and dry and be done.

Anyway, we stopped at what turned out to be a fabulous restaurant with about ten different beers on tap, so we got a few pints, a different kind for each of us. As we were sitting there, a fellow by the name of George came by. He was one of those guys with a sign saying he needs donations for food etc., that he's a vet. In this case though, he had copies of his ID to prove it. Apparently, he'd been in the navy and served over in Iran during the hostage situation many, many years ago. The poor man said he was sixty-two but looked more like 102. He also said he was going to apply for his veteran benefits but that he lived in a camp right now, meaning he was homeless and camping in the redwoods for maybe the last year, moving his camp every so often. I gave him a couple bucks and he seemed to appreciate that. He went on his way then, so our crew continued to enjoy our beer.

Suddenly, two people I hadn't seen come in the restaurant came over and said, "Well done, Bob. Congratulations, and good luck on your trip!"

I sat there thinking, *Who the hell knows my name here?* Well, they were a young couple, about fortyish, from Sonoma,

California, and they'd passed me earlier in the day on my e-bike. When they'd pulled into the restaurant to get something to eat and I'd been there, they'd gone inside and Googled "Bicycle Alaska to Panama" and read everything about me and my journey that had come up.

They were quite excited, so Kyle got them on video, then they snapped some photos of me with them and we chatted for a while. I thought that really showed our social-media work was effective. I reviewed all our social-media pages while I laid in bed that night thinking about the day and the trip to date, and it was getting lots of likes, followers, and attention. People were sharing my pages and my posts, and we were adding lots of friends, which I guessed was what the algorithms needed to put my adventure at the top on Google. I needed to make that happen both so I could raise as much money as possible to buy the toys for the Panamanian children and so I could reach as many people, old and young, as possible with my message. At the same time, yeah, the idea of being searched for and discovered on Google was exciting.

***

The next morning, we encountered the Grandfather Tree. It's a mind-numbingly 1,800 years old, stands eighty-one meters high, and stretches more than seven meters around. I tell you; the wonders never cease when you undertake one of these cycling journeys. Then we came to a curious place just past Piercy, called Confusion Hill. It's said to be world famous and boasts a traffic sign that says, "Confusion Hill: Is Seeing Believing?" There was no way we couldn't stop and at least check it out.

So, we discovered it was a roadside attraction built in 1949 by George Hudson. Its main feature is what's called a gravity house: a house built and decorated in such a way that it creates tilt-inducing visual distortions and confusing physical sensations such as the need to stand up when you already are. It's grown over the years to include a mountain train ride, a narrow track built in a switchback layout chugging along the side of a steep hill, the Redwood Shoe House—which had originally been a float in a local parade—and the World's Tallest Freestanding Redwood Chainsaw Carving, a forty-foot totem pole carved out of a dead redwood tree. You can even still see the stump used as the base.

And the sights didn't stop there. Next up was the 1,200-year-old Elbow Tree, called such for the odd way its trunk grows, upward initially, then falling at a forty-five-degree angle, then straight back up into the sky again. Eventually, we tore ourselves away from Confusion Hill and ended up at the Peg House in Leggett, California. It's aptly named given it was built by a Danish immigrant, Hans Hauer in 1961 using pegs rather than nails. Its well-known motto, "Never Don't Stop" came to be, so they say, because the carpentry, food, and live entertainment are such a draw that you can "never not stop." So of course, we stopped!

The Chandelier Tree

Leggett had another gem for us: The Chandelier Tree. This tree too you could drive through. The opening in it is six feet wide and nearly seven feet high, while the redwood itself is ninety-six meters tall and over six meters around. But the part I still can't wrap my head around is that it's a good 2,400 years old! How can something that was around in 377 BCC still be alive today?

I stayed busy trying to puzzle that out as we rode westward again, back toward the coast and the fog and the marine layer. We'd follow Highway 1 all the way to San Francisco and the Golden Gate Bridge. The temperature dropped as we went, and the fog once again rolled in as expected. That day too was full of lots of climbing as we rode over a high mountain range from the interior of the redwoods back to the ocean again. I enjoyed riding past the beaches again though, and this time I got the bonus of riding through a natural tree tunnel just outside Inglenook and experiencing the Inglenook Fenlands, where sand dunes suddenly replace the ocean.

Along the way, we met two young fellows, only about twenty-four, riding their bicycles from Seattle to San Francisco after graduating from the University of Boulder. One guy was going to fly home to New York afterward, staying for only five days before jetting off to India for three-and-a-half months. They were friendly young men just out enjoying bike touring, and Ted, the one headed for India, had done a bike tour previously, but the other fellow, Bob—believe it or not—was on his first bike tour.

Then we met a couple from England—interesting characters they were—driving a van to San Francisco as we sailed along beside the coast, again taking in the breathtaking surf before we stopped as usual for beer about two kilometers from our campground in MacKerricher State Park. We sat outside at a local mini mart that sold beer, wine, groceries, snacks, gasoline, and such and got to talk with many locals buying whatever it was they were buying. I chatted with an older guy who'd built his own e-bike and a group of young people who were doing a twenty-mile ride as a group of five; the youngest was about fourteen. He was on a one-speed motocross bike and did some tricks for us, like standing on his handlebars, then the whole group did some wheelies and stuff and entertained us for a while. It was a neat way to relax and enjoy my beer. I also realized that even though I'm still in North America, I find myself always greeting people with *"buenos dias"* instead of hello. Must be the Costa Rica in me.

It turned into a bit of a party after that when a couple people who worked in the park, we were going to camp in that night came over and chatted with us about our whole trip. Then Ted and Bob rode in, and then the couple from England pulled in. To say it was exciting sitting in front of a local mini mart/gas station chatting with people from all around who had seen the sign on my bike is an understatement. It really became a fun part of the day. To top it off, two ladies in a big Mercedes camper van stopped and called us over and wanted to know all about what we were doing.

As people rolled in and out of the parking lot and saw our little gathering, they decided they wanted to follow me and my odyssey on Facebook, as did the folks we were chatting with, so I went to give them the cards my team and I had been handing out along the way to raise awareness. Unfortunately, they were in my jacket pocket that of course was in my pannier, so I ended up just telling them to Google me and "Alaska to Panama." They did, and sure enough, I popped up awfully quickly with lots of links.

After our impromptu party, Wayne and I got back on our bikes to finish the last couple kilometers to our campsite and were greeted when we arrived by the skeleton of gray whale. Later that night it got incredibly cold, so I ended up throwing a sleeping bag around myself like a blanket—on top of my down jacket and jeans—as I sat around eating pizza. I tell you, living in Costa Rica has spoiled me.

But I quickly forgot about the cold when Ted, the young fellow we'd met earlier, came to our camp, and sat around enjoying a beer and chatting about his trips and the people he'd met. He'd also met some weird characters in just his brief time riding from Spokane to San Francisco. Ted regaled us with tales of his encounters, like this one fellow who said he'd been transformed by aliens, that they'd gotten hold of him and transformed him into a person, a person he doesn't like, so he was traveling around trying to avoid the aliens. Ted had also met another guy by the name of Warren, who literally lives on his bike and has his own vegetable farm, right on his bike! He just stays wherever he is for the maximum allowable time before he's told to move on. That guy is just a permanent, homeless type of biker just cycling around the country. We'd been unfortunate enough to not have met the folks Ted told us about, but we would certainly keep an eye out for them. Part of me wanted to come across the homeless biker with the vegetable farm; I would have loved to examine his set up. That's another thing I really love doing on cycling tours: checking out other bikers' rigs. Some of the setups they can come up with are ingenious.

***

Well, after a cold but entertaining night, we started out the next day in the fog and drizzle as usual for this part of the country. The day's highlights would start with Fort Bragg, where we discovered some love-lock craze. I'd had seen these in Europe and here they had taken over a pedestrian bridge. I know now that the history of it dates back a good hundred years to a disconsolate Serbian tale from World War I. I guess the idea is to etch a couple's names or initials onto the lock, and maybe a date, lock it somewhere significant, then throw the key into the river to symbolize unbreakable love. Some places in the world treat these love locks as litter or vandalism, but other places, like Fort Bragg apparently, embrace them. Perhaps it added to the tourist value of the area.

Love locks?

We even happened upon a rather solemn place: a pioneer cemetery with only three remaining gravestones. They belonged to soldiers from the original Fort Bragg army post, but the site may also have likely been the last resting place of sailors and fishermen lost at sea or the victims of sawmill accidents at the sawmill that had once sustained the town.

But then it was on to Mendocino in the fog. Again, the chilly, moist marine layer coated us from head to toe. Fog like that almost feels like it's seeping into your bones, much the way polar-vortex cold kind of settles into them. Though the cold associated with the marine layer isn't nearly so frigid, the moisture of it wrinkles your skin and fills every little part of you from your eyes to your toes in your wet, wet socks. Still, it's all part of the experience, and it's not so terrible when you can smell the sea and the salt and the vegetation, when you can watch the seagulls diving and the waves pounding. In some places, the sand dunes compete with the surf for space, prehistoric peaks jut out of the sea, and the odd mixture of forest and beach flora reach for the low-hanging clouds and the sun somewhere behind them. I think I'll always take the experience at wherever cost it comes with, whether marine-layer fog, desert heat, or Yukon cold.

We stopped that morning for coffee at an old-timey mini market in Little River that not only included a gas station, a post office, and restaurant but also looked exactly as though we'd traveled through time back to the pioneer days. It truly looked like an old saloon or mercantile would have back in the day all built out of aged, faded wood with no ornamentation, the signs all made of the same wood. Inside though, it was a whole different world. Aisles of food and rack after rack of wine filled a building just as modern as any North American grocery store. And the view out the back? Wow. Incredible. A window spanning the length of the building framed the churning gray sea and the rocks farther out. Again, I met some more lovely people, including a an ambitious twenty-three-year-old lady from Montreal. Chatting with new people really energizes me!

When the sun came out later, much, much farther south down the Shoreline Highway in Elk, California, we took the opportunity to stop at a beautiful resort with lush gardens you could walk through. And it was right on the edge of a cliff overlooking the sea. From there, you could stand and absorb the salty, floral aroma while you witnessed the power of nature as it crashed into the cliff and bore holes into the peaks in the water, creating majestic arches. It was simply breathtaking.

When we could tear ourselves away from the sights, we continued along the Shoreline Highway, following its zigzagging twists and turns as it weaved in and out, sometimes perilously close to some treacherous cliffs and over more bridges until we hit a nice straight stretch all the way to Manchester, California. There, we followed the peninsula around and down to Gualala River, California, where we camped for the night among the redwoods one last time at Gualala Redwood Park. We had a lot of fun that night, sitting around the soothing campfire Kyle had made, telling stories and downing drinks. I was so glad it wasn't quite as cold that night.

As I sat beside that fire, I listened to it crackle and let the sounds of my team's voices and laughter wash over me, enjoying every moment. That's such a big part of why I do this. For those nearing retirement, I tell you, take it as soon as you can. I retired early, and I've gotten twenty-five years of great life activities exploring the world. You don't have to have everything the Jones's have; you don't need to live lavishly. Life is about the experiences, not the stuff. So, retire as early as you can. And after you do, you need to be active. You can't just expect to sit at home and do nothing; you need a hobby, a sport, something the motivates you, something that drives you to do different things to keep your mind and body active. For me, it was golf, cycling, traveling, running, going on bike tours, and seeing the world at every chance. And for those already retired, please don't just sit back believing the stereotypes or being afraid. Try and get out of your comfort zone; try something new. It doesn't matter what it is, there's always something that's a challenge and can push you on, and when you achieve it, it'll feel great, and you'll be ready to move on and try something else even farther outside your comfort zone.

***

As the sun began its daily climb, we packed up camp and hit the road. Soon, we rode past a sign boasting our goal for the day and a milestone in general: Bodega Bay 49 miles, San Francisco 114 miles. Bodega Bay was to be our stop for two nights, and San Francisco would be our second last major center before hitting Mexico. I'm still not sure why, but it had always felt as though we'd been pushing to get to San Francisco. Maybe we'd felt like it would be easier after that? Maybe I'd thought it would get warmer and drier after that? Or maybe it was as simple as the rest day it offered. Who knows?

Whatever it was, we pushed on through the fog and the now-desolate environment, with its gray skies and burned-brown wild grasses, positive and energized in spite of our surroundings. The dreariness was punctuated by more powerful surf and jagged rock islands, more intriguing sights. Take the old Russian settlement from the 1800s we chanced upon. With all the tall, forbidding wooden walls surrounding it still standing, not to mention the gate houses, a majestic church, and a few homes, you could just imagine a once-bustling community. And it got eerie if you thought about it too long, especially when we discovered the old cemetery, the Eastern Orthodox crosses dotting the landscape and the barren brush waving its bare branches in the wind like a specter. It almost felt like you could see their ghosts wandering the settlement.

Thankfully, the sun popped out from time to time, dissipating the somberness. It brightened the brown grasses and turned the ocean a beautiful turquoise blue in places. Again, we rode beside more perilous drops to the rocks below as we followed the Coast Highway along the cliffs.

At top left, you can see the edge of the road and the minuscule barrier keeping us from falling to our deaths.

Of course, with all those cliffs as we made our way through Salt Point State Park came a ton of climbing and descending and more twists turns in a dizzying fashion. If it hadn't been for the ocean and my instruments, there were times I wouldn't have known which direction I was headed in. The day continued in that roundabout way as we cycled for Jenner, California, and the Sonoma Coast State Park, more than halfway to Bodega Bay. We stopped to eat and look around in Jenner, where we spotted more quaint, old-fashioned shops, and the sky brightened even further to grace us with a spectacular view of the sea as we ate outside at Café Aquatica.

And then there we were, at Porto Bodega Marina & RV Park, our home for the night and our next rest day. I could surely think of worse places to stay than camping out among a bunch of eye-catching boats of all sorts. You could lose a whole day just watching them come in and out, whether you're walking the pier or stopping for a quick bite.

***

While it had been sunny and warm when we'd arrived, the next morning brought with it yet more fog, so I had to don a jacket yet again as I sat out of the cool breeze watching the water and the boats. It was a wonderful campground with all the facilities, electricity, and water, a firepit, a picnic table, and a great view of the sea, but the price still killed me. I liked camping for its smaller punch in my wallet, but that place cost me $92 a night. So much for thinking accommodations would become more affordable as we went. And worse yet, we were looking at staying in a hotel the next night when we reached San Francisco, and that was going to be $150 a night or more. I was starting to wonder if I'd have any money by the time, we finished the odyssey. Maybe I'd have to end up living like the homeless biker with the vegetable farm on his bike!

Either way, I took the chance to relax on that rest day, sitting and watching the boats and listening to the seagulls. I realized that we hadn't always heard a lot of birds on this journey, more crows and magpies and seagulls than anything else, at least since way up north. And here, mingled with the seagulls' squawking were the foghorns, boat horns, and barking sea lions. It was a far cry from the cycle tour I did in Germany where I listened to songbirds singing in the trees all day long.

It occurred to me then what an important part sound plays in a day when you're cycling long distance. Besides the beauty of nature's music, you really need to rely on that sense to stay safe on the road. For instance, you always hear the traffic because it's always right beside you. You can especially pick out the motorcycles because you can hear them coming before they even get there. Heck, you can even hear them talking to each other when they're in groups and hear their music playing. I hear so many cars and big trucks and motorcycles in a day on my rides that because I don't play music or anything, lots of times I'll play a little game of "I hear something coming. What is it?" You really do need to have your ears always open so you stay safe because there are times your ears will warn you of something you can't see. That said, my favorite sound is when I ride down a hill super-fast and the wind rushes by, creating this turbulent sound as it goes through my helmet straps and blocks out any other noise. I even love it when I ride through little villages in Central America or Europe and music wafts out of the cafés and people are milling around on the sidewalks filling the air with the hum of many conversations.

***

My friend the sun gave us a lovely day the next day, and I knew it would be a wonderful day. We were going to hit San Francisco. On the road again, we passed an interesting seaplane base in San Rafael and then a curious community of houses on the water. And these were big houses! They had multiple floors and oodles of windows and vinyl siding and balconies. It seemed to me these were perhaps becoming more common lately, and I wondered if maybe that wasn't something I should consider since it would be something else to always be on the water. Then I remembered my biking and realized I prefer solid ground.

We'd turned inland and were aiming for Highway 101 again given we'd veered off and followed the coast previously. Going inland now shortened the route and offered us less climbing. So, we rode through a bunch of outlying suburbs— Saint Vincent, Santa Venetia, San Rafael, and Sausalito— and suddenly we rounded a curve and voila! Our first view of San Francisco loomed before us.

The Golden Gate

We were all incredibly excited to get to San Francisco. Not only was it a major milestone, but we would also get two rest days, which meant we'd get the opportunity to look around. And yet I'm still not sure which view excited us the most: our first glimpse of San Francisco or our awe-inspiring first glimpse of the Golden Gate Bridge! Personally, I was grateful for our luck. There was no fog to obscure either view.

Usually, crossing massive bridges isn't our favorite thing to do given how loud and unsafe it is and how it's rather vertiginous to look down while you're on just a little old bike, but the Golden Gate Bridge wasn't terrible. It was incredibly loud, yes, but with the divider between the bike/pedestrian path and the traffic, I felt a lot safer than usual, enough to enjoy the view and appreciate the fact that I was riding across the Golden Gate Bridge. The downside to this bridge was the powerful winds. You know it's really windy when the water below you are filled with kite surfers. It felt like it took forever to cross it!

In the end, we reached the other side and entered San Francisco proper. The serenity of the south end of the bridge with the sun beaming on the sparkling ocean waters compared to the noise, the business, and the vibrations on the bridge were at complete odds with each other. It sure made me appreciate the peace once again.

From there, we continued riding toward the city center and zipped through The Presidio, a beautiful park full of pines and palms and hiking trails that once was a US Army post. Then we moved on past another marina and were greeted with San Francisco's iconic houses and hills while navigating our way through monstrous crowds of kids riding their bikes home from school. The city's architecture is entirely unique to them and combines old-world glamour with modern sleekness and appeal. Those hills though, wow. I was again awfully grateful for a little assist from my EVELO e-bike! Poor Wayne.

Dinner that night was at a cute Italian place with an outdoor patio, even though it was cold enough for me to again put a jacket on. Living in the tropics had certainly made any cold feel even colder because most people around me weren't wearing jackets. Goodness, many were wearing short-sleeved shirts! I mean, it was still the beginning of September. But jacket or no jacket, San Francisco's atmosphere made the evening delightful—that and some red wine that helped warm me up. I was so glad we hadn't had any more team drama like we'd had on our first leg. It sure made for a lot more fun, memorable moments.

The next day we'd back on the road again and headed for Santa Cruz. It suddenly felt like we were racing to the Mexican border. Where does time go? Especially when you're having fun.

BEACHES, BEACHES, BEACHES

And just like that, our smooth, pleasant ride became full of speed bumps. Nothing good ever lasts. But then, I suppose, neither does anything bad.

Though we left San Francisco on a lovely, sunny morning with our sights set on Santa Cruz, it wasn't long before things went downhill. Not literally of course. I would have much preferred that. Those speed bumps started popping up one after the other. First off, I discovered pretty early in the day that I'd made a tactical error and Santa Cruz was 149 kilometers away from San Francisco—in the wrong direction.

So, I did some searching and found a reasonably priced Airbnb in Los Gatos. It had three bedrooms and four beds, so we'd all be comfortable. I booked it. And lo and behold when I did, up came an address that on the map showed our planned ride for the day was going to the opposite of what we'd expected. Instead of a nice ninety-kilometer, flat ride, we were then facing a 110-kilometer ride with about a thousand meters of climbing. All in the last fourteen kilometers. That ascent took a good two hours to accomplish. Talk about a horrible end to what started out as a soothing ride beside the water along Fisherman's Warf.

Next up was having to wind our way all the way around the outskirts of San Francisco's city center and through some suburbs like San Mateo, Redwood City, and Palo Alto. It took so much longer than it should have just because there were so many stoplights. Between the stop-start fashion of our ride that day, the noise of the traffic, the fear that comes from riding so close to so many vehicles, and the fumes of the exhaust, I couldn't wait to be done for the day and just rest in some peace and quiet and solitude. We were all getting a little cranky too.

Then came the third speed bump. A clicking noise started up somewhere at the back of my e-bike, so I stopped and took a quick look. We were still aways out from our Airbnb though, so when I couldn't figure it out right away, I just hopped back on and hoped it was just a fender and not the transmission. A closer inspection would have to wait until we were stopped for the night, provided the bike didn't completely break down before we got there.

Finally, after that two-hour climb, we got up to the gates of the property and through, only to discover a crazy steep descent. Not that I really minded as I raced down the hill, brakes screaming away.

Then we got to the house. The yard was a mess from some construction the owner had going on. The garage door was wide open, and it was just full of junk, so I slammed to a stop so hard my kickstand broke. But I just left it. I walked into the house to inspect it; sure, it was going to be just as bad as the garage. Thankfully, that wasn't the case, though there were dirty dishes in the dishwasher, and Yiota wasn't very happy with that. The house itself though was big, comfy, and clean, and the rooms had nice soft beds. However, the water spewed brown out of the faucet when you turned the taps on. Let's just say that Airbnb didn't get a five-star review.

The next day was going to include a big descent again, so I examined my e-bike more closely after dinner to see if I could find the source of the noise this time. It was then I noticed that not only had my kickstand lost a bolt screw, but the other one had also gotten sheared off from the pressure. While looking at those problems, I realized the brake rotor was really loose. When I investigated further, I found that two screws had fallen out and another was almost ready to fall out. That was what was causing the noise yesterday, so I tightened those up.

***

The next morning as we headed back out, my bike was silent again, which was great, but now I had no rear brake, only the front brake, and we had another long descent ahead of us. I made it to the bottom in one piece though, and when Wayne fortuitously happened upon a friend he'd cycled with in Istanbul, I left them to visit while I went and found a bike shop. Luck was with me finally because they were able to put new brake pads on right then. It seemed the bad luck of the day before had been thankfully nullified.

That night's stop was to be just past Monterey, California, as we followed the highway to Big Sur and what should be some wonderful camping—if we could find anything. There wasn't much out that way, and though the ride there wouldn't be long, we potentially would have to go quite a way to find a place.

Well, I resigned myself to waiting to see what would happen with a little research and set my mind to enjoying the ride again. That seemed to be exactly what I needed because I started feeling my worry and anxiety easing and my irritation lifting. With blessedly no fog, no cold, and no rain, the ride from San Jose to Monterey Bay flew by, and before I knew it, I was smelling the sea air again and hearing the enormous packs of male sea lions barking to each other in the marina. For those who have never heard them in person as opposed to on TV, just know that the sound echoes through the air for miles and echoes in your ears until your head wants to explode. I'd hate to be a fisherman, spending every day at that marina.

But we couldn't ride through Monterey Bay without taking some time to ride around the Wharf. We were treated to an impromptu hand-pan performance by a busker, experienced the noisy marina, and admired the brightly painted shops, cafés, and restaurants. The best part was enjoying the variety of food on offer in Monterey Bay, everything from seafood, steaks, and pasta at the Old Fisherman's Grotto to beer, oysters, and lobster rolls at the Grotto Fish Market. As I absorbed the atmosphere around me, I appreciated how the sea lions, the hundreds of boats, and the vacationers all shared one space. People were tanning on the short stretch of white sand, kayaking in the bay among the sea lions, and sailing out into the bay, and perhaps the ocean past that. It all came together to create an atmosphere of carefree fun.

It was there we discovered a new source of camping. The Moose Lodge, it seemed, charged twenty or thirty bucks to let you camp in the parking lot. They even had a bar, swimming pool, hot tub, showers, and toilets, so that was a great deal. I was told then that the Elk Club does the same sort of thing, so those little nuggets were something I made note of for our short time left in the US and for other tours. And just like that, a problem that had been weighing on me that day was solved. Somehow, I knew it would solve itself in time.

And we did indeed take advantage of a Moose Lodge that night, where once again, the kindness of strangers lifted my spirits. It had been a rough couple day, but all that negativity washed away when some folks brought over a great big pot of homemade clam chowder, garlic bread, paper plates, and plastic spoons that night. And that food was good. I mean, good. Those kind people said they were intrigued by the fact that we were cycling such a long way, and they wanted to know more about it. So of course, I gave them the name of our Instagram page so they could follow our progress. I have to say, that really made my night. I think I'd been missing that the last few days, except for the time a few days earlier when a guy who'd seen the sign on the back of my back bought me a beer as we'd been stopped for our usual late-day beer break.

***

And the generosity continued the next morning when a neighboring camper brought over four homemade blueberry muffins for us to have with our breakfast and coffee. He said he thought we needed the energy more than he did.

But we had places to be, so we packed up and followed the bike path, a seventeen-mile ride, moving on to Lover's Point in Pacific Grove and even to Pebble Beach, which of course as a golfer made my day. As we passed the enormous, expensive, seafront homes, we got a bonus: we watched some deer frolic beside the sea. That was unexpected!

Then we faced a killer uphill to Big Sur after we rolled through Carmel-By-the-Sea and the old Carmel Mission. A climb like that also meant more dizzying bridges to cross so high up it never fails to make you feel that with a strong gust of wind you're going to be tossed down to the bottom of the cliff. In this case, Rocky Creek Bridge and Bixby Bridge, both built in 1932, were hundreds of feet high and built of concrete. However, the low guard rails I could see through and the lack of separation from car traffic had me holding my breath.

Bixby Bridge, Breath-stealing!

After those bridges, it was up and up and up some more until we arrived in Big Sur. And just as I thought, all the cabins, RV hookups, and tent spots were full. And there wasn't much for accommodation in Big Sur. There were maybe just three campgrounds and a couple hotels. We were, however, treated to a reminder of our next milestone: a highway sign proclaiming it was 310 miles to Los Angeles. Getting to Los Angeles meant we were close to San Diego, which would put us within spitting distance of the Mexican border. I was looking forward to that leg of the journey, and I was also looking forward to meeting up with my sister-in-law, Johana, who was going to join us at the border until the end of our odyssey.

Anyway, we did finally find a spot to set up camp for the night, but it came with a price. Wayne thought I was lying at first, but I paid $200 US to camp for one night. Never in my life did I ever think I would pay $200 US to camp for a night, and that was *after* Kyle had talked the proprietor down from $240! And it was just a tiny little spot barely big enough to pull in and set up the tent trailer. Mind you, it was Labor Day weekend, and with the heat wave in the interior of California, everyone was trying to escape to the coast, so we were lucky to get a spot. I didn't come out of the deal too badly though. The guy did give us four coffee mugs, four small flashlights, and free showers, which all amounted to maybe ten bucks in swag they presented me with, all wrapped up nicely in a bag. And hey, I got free wood that night and coffee in the morning! *C'est la vie.* I'd hate to think what we would have paid for a hotel.

***

Back on the road again after another delightful breakfast, with the aromas of coffee and sea mingling with the quickly warming air, it occurred to me that as of the day before, we'd been on the road for two months exactly. Strange how it truly didn't feel like that much time had passed, and at the same time, it was awfully hard to keep track of the days without looking at a calendar. I couldn't wait to see what the day had in store for me.

It didn't fail me. We followed the highway south along the coast again, in the sunshine. That section of highway was even more spectacular than the northern section we'd ridden the previous day, though everything since our Airbnb in Los Gatos had been spectacular. The scenery whipping by was full of rocky islands and larger outcroppings, elephant seals, seals, sea lions, cormorants, and pelicans. You don't always get to see much wildlife on a bike tour, but this odyssey had included more than any other. And there was certainly plenty of it between San Francisco and Big Sur, and farther south to San Simeon and Cayucos.

Sunbathing elephant seals

Good thing there was lots to distract me because that day was chock full of climbing. Fifteen hundred meters to be precise, so that was a significant climb. And you know it was hard because Wayne even rode the other e-bike all day. He's always been reluctant to admit an e-bike is a good way to go, especially when there's a lot of climbing. But he did tremendously well on it!

Better than me, that's for sure. I didn't have a good day on my bike. On a normal day, I wait for Wayne at the top of the hills, but this time, he waited for me. It really proves that the distance you can get on an e-bike battery really depends on the rider. Wayne is much stronger than me, so he can manually power up hills better, and that means he uses less battery power than I do. Case in point, by lunch around 1:30 p.m. or so, I'd used about 15 percent more battery power than Wayne had.

Anyway, we followed the coast down to Morro Bay, edging along the sides of cliffs as we climbed, and we even rode through a smallish seaside tunnel that seemed as though it were built to look like some sort of castle. It was built with perfectly cut and shaped etched stones that truly made it look like a fortress. It even came complete with arches! Then we stopped for a snack at a cute place called Whale Watchers Café, halfway between Lucia and Ragged Point. The name was apt because you could do some whale watching there, situated as it is on the edge of a cliff.

That day was supposed to have been an easy day, a shortie with just eighty-five km to ride and not much climbing. It should have been smooth sailing down through Ragged Point, San Simeon, Harmony, and Cayucos, California, before stopping in Morro Bay or Pismo Beach. But of course, that wasn't how it worked out. We didn't make our destination until 6 p.m., again. This time it was because I got a flat tire. As fate would have it though, as I was standing by the side of the road fuming a little, another bike packer came Rolf, from Switzerland. He had biked from Geneva to Lisbon, then had flown to Seattle to follow our same route pretty much down the coast of Washington, Oregon, and California.

When he heard I was going all the way to Panama, he confessed he was quite reluctant to travel through Mexico, so he was quite interested in what I had to say about it. Rolf's plan was to fly from San Diego to San Jose, Costa Rica, and he was going to ride from there, bypassing all the Central

American countries of Mexico, Guatemala, Honduras, El Salvador, and Nicaragua. And those were all on my itinerary!

What I told him then is what I completely believe, and I think it helped open his eyes a little. I believe, from experience, that the prevailing press is American; they have the loudest voice. So, they put out this story that Mexicans and Central Americans are nothing more than drug dealers and rapists and brigands solely out to breach our borders and disrupt society. That is simply not true. Most of those populations respect their elders, go to church, honor their dead, and care for their family and friends. Many will even give what little they have to a stranger in need. Can we say that about those of us in first-world nations? So, for those of you who have never been to Mexico or a Central American country, you have to go yourself and meet the people yourself. You must see their homes and learn their cultures for yourself. Heck, start by checking out the Mexican Facebook group and the Pan-American travelers' group.

The truth is that it's more dangerous in many parts of the US than it is in Mexico, provided you don't get yourself mixed up in criminal activity. Hell, in the States, you can go to a church and get shot; you can go to a concert and get shot; you can go to a gay bar and get shot; you can come out of a bar at night and get shot. Who knows where it'll happen to you; you could be at an elementary school picking up your kids and get shot. Those things just don't happen in Mexico, yet a couple people die after making bad choices and messing with gangs or drugs and the rest of North America suddenly wants to ban travel there. Well, why don't they ban travel to the US? Like that's ever going to happen.

My conversation with Rolf was even on par with a discussion I'd only recently had on Facebook, where some guy had told me I was insane for riding through Mexico and the other countries. Heck, he'd even said I should buy a gun when I was riding through those crime-filled, left-wing cities like Seattle, Portland, San Francisco, and Los Angeles. Then he'd added that he was going to buy a life-insurance policy on me as that was money in the bank: I would die and he would collect.

I'd asked him then when he'd last been to these US cities or Mexico.

"Never," he'd said. "Who would ever want to go to those shit holes of places?"

I thanked him for his enlightened opinion and ended the conversation then. I have to say, it was uplifting though when a few other people joined the conversation on my side.

And there I go, off on a rant again. But it's something I feel incredibly strongly about. Discover other people and cultures for yourself. Don't just believe what you're told. Anyway, I had a good talk with Rolf and gave him my card. He lightened the mood in the moment, and I really hope to communicate with him in the future. I'm not sure how old he was, but he looked old, like me.

So back to the flat tire story. There I was, stuck on the side of the road with a flat tire thanks to an industrial staple that had gone through the tire and punctured the tube. Because I'd have to wait for Wayne to come back and then for Yiota and Kyle to come back with new tubes to do a real repair, I patched up the leak in the hopes that I could make it a little further.

Then bam! With only another fifteen kilometers to go, I got another flat. Only this time the problem was that the tube was all wet from the previous puncture thanks to it being full of sealant, and the sealant of course had leaked into the tire, thus causing the new flat. That had to have been the problem, I thought anyway, because I'd already put a patch on it and pumped it up again, but then it went flat again in less than a kilometer. So I pulled into a service station and pumped it up again, only to have the same thing happen. I pulled the tube out, and yes, the patch I'd put on was leaking. So, I tried it again, putting another patch on, and sure enough, it leaked again. I couldn't understand what the problem was, and I was getting more and more frustrated by the minute. Was it the sealant causing the patch to not hold? Was the patch not any good? Who knew? Certainly not me.

Finally, the support van arrived, and when they did, I put in another tube, filled it up, and strangely—and thankfully—it worked perfectly. Wayne and I finished the last fifteen kilometers, then savored a delightful dinner at a lovely little restaurant in Pismo Beach, which was entirely typical of SoCal, or Southern California, with its wide beaches, seafront condos, and multitude of restaurants and bars, all with that light, airy SoCal look. You know you've hit Southern California when you can sit outside a little place that offers not beer on tap but Kombucha.

We also hit another first that day, a happy first. As we passed through Cayucos, we saw our first Southern California pier. That told me how much closer we were getting to the border. We'd see quite a few piers thereafter because each town from there on out has a pier. I love walking out on the piers—and I did the same on this one—and looking around, not really seeing much, just watching people fish, watching the pelicans sit on the pier, and watching the families wander about. Some of the piers further on would even have some restaurants where I could get a good milkshake!

***

But then, after a wonderful night in Pismo Beach, we seemed to be out of the coastal mountains finally and were looking forward to what we hoped would be a nice, long stretch of flat road. On the other side of that coin, we'd left the coastal mountains because we'd turned a little inland headed for Solvang—and of course the highlight of the trip for Wayne as we rode through Grover Beach, his namesake. That meant that day was our first sweltering day, at least since Alaska. It was incredible; sometimes the breeze would pick up, but the air was pure heat like a sauna. I might have thought about the cool breeze on our Northern California stretch last week a few times to keep me going that day.

Solvang turned out to be a beautiful Danish town settled over a hundred years ago and surrounded by vineyards. Everything in the town is built as if someone picked up a town in Denmark and dropped it in California. The architecture on main street, the restaurants, the shops, everything was so very Danish: Svendsgaard's Lodge, Valley Hardware, the Solvang Brewing Company, and especially the Wildling Museum.

Solvang Brewing Company

I learned that the area was a popular tourist destination, not only for the archetypal design of the town, but also because just up the road is Los Olivos, which means "the olives." Kyle said there were forty-two wine-tasting establishments in that small town alone, including some in little out-of-the-way restaurants. So together, the two towns make a great tourist package. Again though, I couldn't believe the heat. I thought I'd gotten used to heat living in Costa Rica, but that particular day soared to 35°C. And on the road, it gets a lot hotter because the pavement reflects a lot of heat. However, it made for one of those beautiful nights where you can eat outside and be wonderfully comfortable.

That night, we stayed in The Viking Motel, which was 112 years old and surrounded by palm trees. A wonderful lady named Angie had just bought the place two or three months earlier; she called it a boutique motel, and to be fair, our room was incredibly nice. It turned out her ex-husband was a biker who had biked San Francisco to Los Angeles, so she wanted to take a photo of us to share with him. I'm not shy about how I love doing that, so we had a little photo-taking session in front of her motel. Then she gave us four coupons for a Danish bakery around the corner, so Kyle and Yiota went over and cashed them in so could have some tasty Danish pastries for lunch the next day. Angie also said that if we ever came back around after we finished our journey, then she'd give us a free night in her hotel. She was a marvelously friendly host, and we wished her all the best for her motel business.

***

The next day gifted us with slightly cooler temperatures with a head wind that helped cool things down and created more shade along the road. That didn't mean we still weren't surrounded by drought-ravaged surroundings. The ongoing heatwave was terribly self-evident, so we stopped that day for a beer at the cutest restaurant yet, or perhaps I should say "tavern." It was called Ye Cold Spring Tavern. Doesn't that just scream personality? The whole thing was built of logs and the red-checkered drapes of yore hung in the windows. Inside was an ancient stone fireplace dominating one wall, wooden tables dotting the one large room, and animal heads adorning the walls.

Break over, we pushed on. Apparently, being out of the coastal mountains didn't mean we had as flat a road as I'd hoped, plus we always had those awful bridges to contend with. Finally, we crested the San Marcos Pass, 2,225 feet at its summit, heading for Santa Barbara and got a great downhill for maybe six or seven miles at a 4 percent decline. Before my accident a few years ago, I used to try to go down hills as fast as I could, but here I decided to open it up just a bit and go down fast but not as fast as I could like I once used to. Still, I went pretty fast, and I loved it.

That spectacular downhill led us into Santa Barbara, a beautiful town along the ocean. A large pedestrian mall goes through the center of town, and it's full of restaurants, palm trees, and pedestrians out enjoying the day. As we were riding through Santa Barbara, I passed a cyclist before pulling up to a stoplight. Suddenly I heard from behind me, "Hey! I'm following you on Facebook!"

So, I turned around and said, "Hey!" then, "Do you wanna chat?" She nodded, so we pulled over to the side and chatted for a few minutes. Her name was Jasmine, and at twenty-eight years old, she was on first bikepacking trip, starting up in Seattle and ending in Los Angeles. Her bike wasn't the best one for the job, but it was fitted out with all her gear and camping supplies. She told me she'd been following me and my Octogenarian Odyssey for a while, since before she'd started her own journey and had been researching her route. Apparently, my name had come up as she'd researched, so she'd become my Facebook friend. Ever since she'd started, she'd been hoping we'd cross paths along the way. Turns out the only reason we did run into each other was because she'd spent five days in Big Sur while we had only spent the one. Jasmine was an impressive young lady and a tour guide for a tour company that takes students to different countries around the world, and in between her seasons, she thought she'd try this bikepacking tour. I just thought, Good for her, a young lady doing this all by herself. That's impressive.

As the team and I reached the beach later, it became cloudy and cooler, and we were even lucky enough to get couple rain showers along the way, just sprinkles really, but it was a relief. We enjoyed the cooler weather and the moisture the rest of the way that day and rolled into Ventura,

California, with no incidents to speak of. We were camping that night before heading to Malibu and our next rest day. While we had a place to stay that night, I was concerned about the next few nights because I didn't know if I could find reasonable accommodations that were still on our route. The last thing I wanted to do was deviate and go inland to get to Los Angeles, nor did I want to pay through the nose just for a place to lay my head. Most of the bike paths and such to get through that behemoth of a city were along the beach, but that didn't mean there would be many hotels or campgrounds on that route. I had originally hoped to reach a campground I knew of, but there was some debate as to whether they permitted tent trailers in there. Our initial research had indicated that any other choices were few and far between, so I just didn't know what we'd come up with. As usual, time would tell.

I chose to worry about it later as it was time to stop for beer just then, and we sat relaxing while we watched all the surfers on Ventura Beach. By then, we seemed to have developed a sort of a routine at the end of the day, where we'd pull into any kind of establishment—maybe a service station, maybe a cute little outdoor restaurant off the highway, or maybe even like the previous night, the campground check-in area—and have a couple beers before heading for our nightly stop. It doesn't matter where we stop, just as long as it has beer and it's anywhere just outside our day's destination. There's just something about having a beer in a location that's different from where you spend the night. Maybe it's the adventure of it.

***

My brain was whirling the next morning. It was 6:14 a.m., and there I was, worrying about our accommodations for our two nights in Malibu as I relaxed in the van. Then as I looked around my sleeping space, I realized we were going to have a new set of logistics problems when Johana joined the team in a week. Now the back of the van wasn't exactly the most comfortable place to sleep, but it was what it was. At least it wasn't cold like up north. That reflection led to the question, "Where is everybody going to sleep?"

I wasn't sure what the best solution was. Maybe one person could take the tent, one could take the van, and the others could sleep in the tent trailer, maybe in rotation? I had no idea how that would play out. The silver lining in all that was that we did plan to spend more nights in Airbnb's and cheaper hotels. Once we crossed into Mexico, the prices would become more reasonable.

Then there was another problem. There would then be three people in the van as we traveled. How on earth could we arrange all the stuff inside so we could create another seat for Johana? One solution was for Wayne to go back to riding his road bike because then one person could ride the second e-bike. But in recent days, Wayne had ridden the e-bike four days in a row, which was quite surprising. He must have been enjoying it, but he sure wasn't going to admit he appreciated the ease of the e-bike compared to the grunting and groaning and sweating of riding the road bike, especially on days like yesterday when we had to climb over the San Marcos Pass.

My last problem I had no control over. I was keeping an eye on a hurricane that had touched down in Mexico. I wasn't at all sure how that was going to affect us, if at all. At that moment, the weather forecast was still pretty good, but I had to keep an eye on it to see if it would bring any heavy rains or anything into where we were headed.

Well, I just crossed my fingers on all counts, looked at my watch, and sighed. It was time to get this show on the road again, so I heaved myself out of bed. Somebody had to get everyone moving. We had another long trek ahead of us that would take us to Malibu and on to Santa Monica the next day. It hadn't been in the original plan, but now the general consensus seemed to be that we'd stay in Anaheim for our double rest day coming up soon.

Once I got the troops alive and moving, we rode back out into a dark and cloudy day. I didn't much mind though because it was a break from all the heat we'd been getting. My only hope was that I wouldn't get soaked. Clouds are fine, a few sprinkles in a warm zone like Southern California, those were enjoyable and appreciated. But getting soaked on a long-distance bike ride just is not pleasant. I'm not sure which I dislike more, the wrinkly fingers, the squishy socks, or the shivers that set in when you can't get dry and warm. But we were in luck. The rain stayed away, and we enjoyed a pleasant ride to the Los Angeles county line and Malibu with its twenty-one miles of scenic beauty—according to the sign— that day. We made the forty miles to Malibu unscathed too, despite facing more climbing up, over, and through a small mountain pass. It might have been smaller than some we'd gone through, but it was no less labor intensive. But there were no flat tires, no broken brakes, no downpours, and we camped for the night beside more brown, parched mountains. Only patches of stubborn green dotted the scorched landscape, completely at odds with all the water rushing up to meet the endless stretch of beaches not far away.

After going through our now usual routine of stopping for beer before the campground, going and setting up camp, grabbing some rest, and then taking the camp down, we set off for the next day's destination: Anaheim. Not long after began, we came across a touching site, reminding me of what day it was. As we were taking a little detour up Malibu Canyon Road to head back to the Pacific coast Highway, we rolled past a 9/11 memorial in front of Pepperdine University. Hundreds of flags dotted a grassy knoll for at least a good kilometer. There were mostly American flags of course, but other nations were represented too, including Canada. I was filled with emotion as I rode past. Having remembered the day, I got the call from my friend, Dave, I couldn't help but stop and reflect.

It had been still relatively early morning yet, so I hadn't left for my daily ride. September 11, 2001. I'm sure I'm just one of millions who can remember where they were on that terrible day. After I'd gotten that call, I'd been glued to the TV screen, watching as the towers crumbled one by one, watching as that plane flew into the Pentagon and another into an empty field, watching as the sirens blared and dust and smoke filled the air in New York and coated every face. The haunted look in the eyes of some, coated in that dust, the fear in others, the adrenaline in yet others as they'd tried to rescue people had rooted me to the spot. Every face, regardless of what shone from their eyes, had resembled zombies from some futuristic dystopian movie. All I'd been able to think was, *Is this really happening? Here? These things don't happen in North America.*

So, though it hadn't personally affected my life, other than making travel harder, as it had so many others, it had changed me, and I felt all those emotions again and more as I took in that memorial. There was pride, humility, respect, honor. And there was sadness too because that day changed the world for the worse. I felt sadness for the way that day changed the world, sadness for the change in how Muslims came to be viewed with suspicion, sadness for the loss of innocence. Take the movies for example. When I was younger, the villains in movies were often Russians and communists. After 9/11, it became Muslims. I'm absolutely certain that that day a seed was planted in the hearts of traditionalists, a seed of hatred and a seed of fear driving many in the US and Canada, and even in Europe, to desire a return to the "the way it used to be" at whatever cost. It's a seed that was quietly, slowly nurtured until it was passed on to and shared with successive generations, to blossom into what we see in the world today in world leaders, protesters, and ordinary people.

After a few quiet minutes of reflection and remembrance, we moved on and watched the surfers on the water, admired the memorial stones in the memorial rock garden on the boardwalk, and rode past the pier, restaurants, shops, marina, and waterfront homes of Malibu. The sky had cleared by then, making everything glimmer and shine, especially the hundreds of beautiful white boats in the marina.

***

On yet another overcast day, we reached Santa Monica and the famed Santa Monica Pier, where exactly a year before, our Wayne's TransAmerica ride had started.

Wayne and I recreating TransAmerican tour kickoff

After taking some photos for posterity, we moved on to Venice Beach, riding down the boardwalk and taking in the colorful shops, unique murals, and curious passersby. Before we knew it, we were looking at Muscle Beach. Yes, it's a real place, and it's just as you've seen it on TV. A few of the guys here were really interested in Wayne and I and the sign on my bike, so we stopped to chat for a while. A couple big guys even jumped the barrier to come talk with us.

Then we hopped back on the bikes and crossed Marina Del Rey, rode beside Playa Del Rey Beach, Manhattan Beach, and Hermosa beach before reaching Redondo Beach. Despite the clouds, there were still plenty of people on every beach. If you're a beach person, this is certainly where you want to be. The whole area is beach after beach after beach.

Finally, we reached Anaheim and pulled into a packed RV park. The sheer number of behemoths and expensive RVs and vehicles blew my mind. I supposed I shouldn't have been surprised since we were camped directly outside the Disneyland gates. We were still trying to decide whether we were going to indulge in visiting it the next day, but for tonight, we settled on a nice dinner in a beautifully decorated restaurant. Expensive, yes, but if I'm going to indulge in anything, it's always going to be in a new restaurant with an exciting or pleasant atmosphere, good food, and wonderful staff. It's an experience itself if you ask me.

After dinner, and more than a few drinks we indulged in since we were going to have a rest days here, we sat outside and took in the fireworks from Disneyland. They were simply spectacular. I had to wonder though, if the thrill wouldn't wear off after a while if you were treated to them every night like those who lived in the neighborhood were. Nonetheless, I loved the show anyway.

***

I spent most of our rest days doing laundry, writing postcards I promised everyone, and patching flat tires and tubes. Then I went and got a hair-cutting kit. Boy, I was getting shaggy! And while we had all tossed around the idea of going to Disneyland, in the end it was nature that decided for us. Lightning lit up the sky for hours, making us think it was going to rain. It never did, so though we missed out on Disneyland, we did get two great nights of fireworks around 11:30 p.m.

Then, rest day over and haircut, we set out for Oceanside, battling the crowds of pedestrians heading for Disneyland and following the Los Angeles River and its adaptations for flood control that we've all seen in the movies Grease for example. It's something else to see things from movies and TV in real life. It shouldn't be a big deal, but for some reason it is. It's like you've accomplished something or confirmed something, or maybe done something others haven't. I don't know really, but it's a weird feeling. We ended up following that river for twenty-five kilometers to get from deep inside greater Los Angeles and Anaheim back to the coast.

That day's ride was to be about a hundred kilometers, including that first twenty-five within Los Angeles. Once at the coast, we rode down Highway 1 and a bunch of bike paths that took us through more beaches—Newport, Laguna, and Treasure Island—and then on to Dana Point and San Clemente. Along the way, we saw a highway sign that, as Wayne put it, told us we "were almost running out of USA." We only had seventy miles to go before we hit San Diego, and right after that would come the Mexican border.

After the beaches, we had a nerve-racking, noisy ride on the interstate. I always hate to have to do that, and it's even worse riding through the most populous county in the US, but it was the only way to skirt Camp Pendleton Marine Base and get to Oceanside just south of that. Then finally, we arrived in Oceanside—where Beth and I had spent two winters, the first for three months and the second for six months—none the worse for wear after a 109-kilometer ride.

Me pointing to where Beth and I wintered once

It was nice to be back there and see that the town still looked pretty much the same, at least the beach did anyway. I thought maybe it would be somewhat bittersweet but being there only brought back lots of good memories. After a look around, and a couple beers of course, off we went to yet another expensive campground. It was slightly cheaper than some of the previous ones at $125, but at least it had a nice swimming pool and good showers. It still certainly wasn't worth what they were charging for it, but there weren't a lot of choices. But we were booked for two nights in a San Diego Airbnb the next night to organize ourselves and our stuff, especially our documents, in preparation for crossing the Mexican border.

Speaking of our looming border crossing, I was pretty sure we wouldn't have any real problems, but you just never know with these things. We did, however, have one hiccup that could cause an issue: we'd lost the license plate off the trailer along the way, but we had the registration and California permit. It wasn't like we hadn't tried to get another plate, but to do that, we'd needed a police report stating it had been stolen or lost, and it would take seven days to get one of those things. We certainly hadn't been going to wait around for seven days in the hopes they'd even have it done in that timeframe. On a more positive note, we were getting a drone delivered while were in San Diego, so Kyle was going to be happy to get the drone up in the air.

***

Off we ventured the next morning, aiming for our last American destination: San Diego. It wasn't a long ride that day, only about eighty kilometers of pretty much flat stretches. It was a good thing too because it was to be a busy day. First, we were meeting a drone operator from iFlyCam who would get some drone footage of us riding into San Diego. Then at 4 p.m., I had a live broadcast on Facebook lined up where people could discuss my odyssey and ask questions about the e-bike or the trip or whatever was on their mind. So, we were going to have to rush through the day so I could at least get to a quiet area.

We began our busy day by riding past a six-wheeled, outback sort of vehicle used by Scavengers Beer Adventures—a pub-crawl business I guess? —And a Moose Lodge just like the one we'd enjoyed previously. When we hit Carlsbad, we found the Army & Navy Academy and discovered a bronze statue of a surfer. So, what you say? It's just a surfer. Well, this one was dressed in shorts and a t-shirt. Wayne still can't figure out how they got the shorts on a bronze statue whose feet were connected to a surfboard.

Then we rolled past Legoland—no, we didn't stop—and stopped for lunch in La Jolla at the Promiscuous Fork of all places. Crazy name or no, the food was great, and while we ate, I did a sort of interview with our waitress, a little hurried mind you given my timeline. I guess she did some writing on the side and had seen the sign on the back of my bike, so she wanted to write a piece about it. But tight timeline or not, we sure needed the stop that day because, again, it was hot and sunny as we rode down the coast. At least we got to ride on a shoreside bike path until Mission Bay instead of on interstates.

While in La Jolla, we were treated to so much more wildlife, again in the form of sea lions, harbor seals, and elephant seals on the rocks. We even got some great close-up shots of pelicans. Riding among nature is always so much more peaceful and serene than riding through a city, even small towns. Even if the wildlife, sea lions for example, are incredibly noisy, they're accompanied by the sounds of waves and seagulls and wind rather than cars and horns and music and people. Here, I also got to show Wayne the little horseshoe bay whose beach is closed to the public in the spring because the seals migrate and give birth to the babies here.

Suddenly, we were just north of Mission Bay and dwarfed by the Giant Dipper Rollercoaster, built in 1925, that towered over Belmont Park. It truly was gigantic! And it hadn't felt like it had taken very long to make it that far that day. It's remarkable how you can lose track of time when there's so much to see around you. Driving this whole stretch might have been boring, but cycling down it is like watching a never-ending movie. The reel just keeps going and going until you stop. Reaching that rollercoaster heralded our arrival in Mission Bay and San Diego proper, and our unfortunate departure from the quiet bike paths.

We crossed Mission Bay from there, and admired how the sun made the water almost dance, with all its shimmering and glimmering. Biking among the car traffic over Mission Bay to Interstate 8 and Interstate 5 was just as stressful and heart pounding as I'd thought it would be. But it was just one of the times when you have no choice. As occupied as I was with keeping one eye on the road ahead and one on the road behind, one ear tuned to the highway and the other tuned to my bike, I didn't notice San Diego pop up ahead of me until it filled the landscape. And there we were, in rather anticlimactic fashion. Downtown San Diego loomed before us, all the steel and glass towers sparkling in the sunlight and the naval base imposingly guarding the harbor.

The USS Midway

Always glad for a chance to pull off the highway and onto a side street, we rode a few minutes west of the interstate and checked out the USS Midway Museum. Again, it's so strange to realize that what you see on TV might look one way, but then when you see it up close and personal, it's something else entirely. In all the movies and TV shows I've ever watched, those American aircraft carriers are big enough, but in real life, they're utterly monstrous. When you're standing right before one, you almost break your neck trying to look up at the top of it. Then I tried to wrap my head around the fact that there were planes parked on top. Real, actual, navy planes. I might have been standing in front of one, but I still couldn't believe that humans had not only created something so immense that planes could park on it—and race down the length of it to take off—but had also built something that big that could still float! To cap off the comparison, we discovered the Star of India docked in the San Diego Harbor. As big as that ship was, the USS Midway made it look like a child's toy.

The Star of India

So, on we continued down Harbor Drive and past the San Diego Convention Center, an intriguing piece of architecture, and Naval Base San Diego. I couldn't help but realize that the US had an awful lot of military bases, and large ones. But I digress. We were so close to our Airbnb I could smell it. The noise and fumes and heat were starting to get to me a little bit, and I couldn't wait for some quiet and our rest days. Thank goodness Yiota had done some research and found a nice cozy place not far from the naval base. You know, I can never help but compare what traveling to foreign places was like back before the internet and smartphones to traveling today. Then, you had to rely on paper maps, and if those and the signs weren't in English, you had to ask people for help, usually other travelers you came upon or Peace Corps folks. Now, if I need a place to stay for the night or want to find a coffee shop or a bakery or a grocery store, all I must do is pull out my phone and Google it. And look at what I was riding. Not a bicycle but an e-bike. That's not something I would have imagined existed thirty, forty years ago.

I suppose it's also good that I've never had a tough time adapting to new technology. I know I'm going to date myself here, but in my time, I've had to learn to transition from radio to TV, TV to streaming, not to mention learning to use computers and the internet, and smartphones after that. I was even an early computer user, including their precursor: digital calculators with functions. I used to take computer programs and programming classes too, so technology has always been part of my life. The only reason I say this is because not only do I have to do lots of research on the fly as we journey, but also because I get a lot of people who say, "Wow, you sure know your way around computers for an eighty-year-old," and such. Technology has always fascinated me, so I love learning about the newest thing. If I won a lottery, I'd even build a smart house, complete with voice-activated controls and the newest smart TVs with surround sound.

***

We quite enjoyed our three-day, two-night stay in our San Diego Airbnb. It turned out to be a large, terracotta townhouse in a quiet area surrounded by greenery. There were enough beds for everyone, so we all got some much-needed rest while we got long overdue chores like laundry done and got organized for our Mexican border crossing. We, or Kyle truly, even managed to find a better bike seat in a different shape for Wayne as he'd been having difficulties with a sore rear end in recent days. Time would tell if it helped anything.

Before we knew it, our rest days were over, and it was time to gear up for rough but short ride through San Diego to Tijuana and hopefully Tecate. We would, of course, do all we could to stay off the toll roads, finding smaller, free roads running parallel to them. At least we had a bright, sunny day with which to tackle what could be a tricky border crossing with the tent trailer's missing plate.

I am determined to stay positive though! And I did, all the way through Chula Vista and down to Tijuana, where things did indeed get a little sticky.

HOLA MEXICO!

And just like that, we hit our third milestone and the third leg of our odyssey: the Mexican border near Tijuana. We chose a border crossing just to the east of the main border crossing, hoping it would be easier with the bikes and the traffic, and with luck, the missing license plate. Initially, it turned out to be a smart decision because there was virtually no one there. It was a little eerie though, looking at "The Wall" stretching along the hills into the horizon. So, we got through the visa and FMM process quite quickly, and we even got the temporary import permit for the car with no problems.

But then we ran into trouble with the tent trailer, as I'd expected. The first hiccup came when a border guard pointed out that it was missing the plate so we couldn't bring it into the country. I breathed a sigh of relief when his superior came over and told the guard to just forget it and to use the car plate instead. So, they took some photos of the car, and sent me on my way. I thought maybe that would be it and we could go when they decided they couldn't give us a temporary import permit for it as they had for the car. When I questioned that, I was told I'd have to go to a bank in Tijuana and get it all taken care of there.

Then they said the bank closed at 4 p.m. I was flabbergasted. So, I asked him point blank, "How am I supposed to do that?" When the guy just shrugged, I sighed and decided we'd just have to do it in the morning and stay in Tijuana instead of going on to Tecate that day. That would put us a day behind. Boy was it a good thing I didn't have to stay on schedule anymore.

We left the border crossing then and had to look for a place to stay—and quickly. I had to at least call the bank to see if I could get that done the next day. But then came the second hiccup. It turned out it was Mexico's Independence Day that day, and traffic was horrendous in Tijuana. It took us forever to ride through the city as Yiota and Kyle tried to book us an Airbnb. That was incredibly dangerous riding because we were riding between the curb and the traffic, trying to weave our way through and having to make left turns by cutting across two or three lanes of traffic.

I don't know how, but somehow, we made it to the house our support team had found in one piece. I called the bank immediately and discovered it was open till 6 p.m., not 4 p.m., so Johana and I jumped in the car and went down to the bank. After a long chat with the folks there, I left, unable to do anything that day. The bank had insisted I had to have the tent trailer inspected, and there wasn't time to do that then, so I had to go back the next morning at 8 a.m. Apparently, so they said, they wanted to open it up and see how big it is, see the beds, and things like that. Then I would supposedly get the registration and import permit for the tent-trailer unit. What a pain in the you-know-where.

I was more than a little frustrated by then, but hopefully I would get the permit for the thing the next morning and then we could be back on the road just a few hours later. Now we were going to have to bypass Tecate and ride as far as we could. My hope was that maybe we could make it up somewhere soon.

Yiota also had some trouble in our first day in Mexico, but conversely, her experience had a positive outcome. While she was driving to the Airbnb, she was using her phone and a police officer saw her. He pulled her over and said he was giving her a $140 ticket for distracted driving. Now to be honest, she wasn't talking on the phone but Googling directions. Somehow though, she wasn't intimidated and turned on the charm. She begged and pleaded and ended up talking her way out of that ticket. She hit it off with the police officer so well, she actually ended up taking a selfie of them and getting a warm welcome out of him. I still have no idea how she pulled that off, though I suspect it wasn't the first time she'd faced an instance like that. But, by the time she got to the Airbnb, she was in good spirits and posted the picture of her and the police officer on Instagram, insisting she loved Mexico!

When I had time to relax, I realized what a contrast the two sides of the border were. The US side was full of McDonald's and 7-11s and Amazon pickup lockers, and everything was clean, despite the large population. But the Mexican side was full of noisy, dangerous traffic, and litter was everywhere on the sides of the road. That's not to say many places in Mexico aren't beautiful and tidy and that the people aren't wonderful, it's just the reality of the different systems, infrastructure, and money.

But the Airbnb we'd been lucky enough to find was just beautiful. It too was quite large and had lots of bedrooms, a gym, and a garage to put the tent trailer in. It was even tucked within a nice small community, so we walked down to a local food truck. But in this case, the truck was permanently parked in a small lot with tables and chairs around it. We all enjoyed some authentic tacos and burritos and had a lot of fun with the local owner and his son with a lot of chitchat. Good thing they spoke English. The only sticking point that night was that to get beer, we had to go across the street to the sort of mini-super place, buy six beers, and take them back to the little taco truck. Not that that mattered. We all enjoyed the food, company, and entertainment, especially now that we'd made it to Mexico.

***

At midnight on September 14th, Gloria's sister from Colombia, Johana flew in. Because it was so late, she got a hotel room till morning before heading to our Airbnb. She was going fulfill the role of Spanish-speaking driver, biker, and support-team member. I knew she'd be a tremendous asset. And she proved that within hours of arriving by accompanying me to the bank and explaining everything in Spanish, really speeding up the process. It also helped that we were the only ones there when we showed up. And we'd done all our paperwork correctly, so everything was good, but we still had to wait around for the staff to do whatever they do with inspecting the tent trailer in their own good time. So, we sat there for about an hour, but I got to chat with the lady behind the desk so at least I was occupied. Finally, the inspection was done, and they gave us a ten-year temporary permit. Not that we needed ten years, but what the heck, at least it was done.

We raced back to the house to get changed and load the trailer. I at least was anxious to get started. I was hoping we could not only make up some time, but also start riding as early as possible to avoid some of the heat. We were about to face the northern desert for four or five days, and I was hoping it wouldn't get too hot, especially that day in the Tijuana traffic.

Disappointingly, we started riding at 11 a.m. And we were a day behind thanks to the paperwork for the tent trailer, but I reminded myself that by the end of the day, the stress would be gone, once we were out of Tijuana and off the expressway. Unfortunately, it took a frustratingly long time to ride through the city, and that included some steep climbs. In fact, we ended up climbing most of the day. Besides all that climbing, we had hordes of traffic to wind through yet again, and the riding was even more dangerous than the previous day because at times, there were no shoulders to ride on. There were moments I was pretty sure I might be shoved off the road or sideswiped by impatient, inattentive drivers.

Wayne had an especially rough ride that day because he's even more nervous and cautious with the traffic and potholes and things than I am. The first half of the day was the worst. Then when we reached Tecate, Wayne had to stop and take a break because he was feeling dizzy and faint, so we spent some time sitting in a gorgeous church courtyard in the shade, having a cool drink and relaxing. Thankfully though, I was sure Wayne's problem wasn't his health, rather his concern and cautiousness about always being safe and not putting himself in danger, which was entirely reasonable and expected. Riding through scary traffic and having to watch for obstructions on the road at the same time can be incredibly stressful.

Finally, we made it out of Tecate unscathed. I was mighty surprised no one ended up with a flat tire out of all that. But we were out of town, and it wasn't too hot, only about 27°C. Once outside of town though, we rode through a mountain pass with huge boulders everywhere and barren, brown hillsides. There was honestly not a spot of green to be found. Dreary scenery or not, I was happy just to be out of the traffic and enjoying some less dangerous riding so I could relax. My plan was to use the free roads as often as we could instead of the toll roads because it would mean both less traffic and more opportunity for local flavors and experiences as we passed through the towns instead of skirting around them. The toll roads are in better shape, but the free roads in the end are better for cycling with the lack of traffic.

Or so I thought. Even after we got out of town and onto the highways, riding was iffy with no shoulders to speak of and nothing but boulders right at the edge of the road. Add to those sharp turns, steep cliffs, and crazy drivers, and we had a recipe for potential disaster. We did glimpse the infamous American wall in the distance, snaking through the desert though. It just seemed like such a terrible symbol representing the state of the world today. Anyway, the desert stretched on for miles ahead of us, and the roads got no better. In fact, they got worse.

As the sun sank, we approached the campground we'd found earlier, and I thought for sure it wouldn't be the best one we'd ever stayed in given all the dirt roads Google Maps had had us riding on, but it surprised me. We turned into a little oasis surrounded by trees right there in the middle of the Mexican desert, maybe a mile from the US border. We'd ridden farther than that in reality, but we'd been riding east parallel-ish to the border. It was a lovely campground, with good showers and toilets, laundry facilities, and a swimming pool. The best part was it only cost $50, including power hookup. Thank goodness prices were reasonable again. I didn't want to end up a pauper at the end of this odyssey. I thought we might even have figured out the sleeping problem too now that we had an extra person. That first night, we tried having the two young ladies share the one double bed we had, Wayne sleeping on the bed on the other end of the tent trailer, Kyle on the trailer's lounger, and me in the van. We were going to see how that worked.

So, after setting up and freshening up, Johana treated us to Colombian arepas, which are just flour, butter, and water—kind of a pastry—dropped in hot water to cook. When it's done, you put all your toppings on top, like guacamole, ground beef, cheese, bacon, and whatever else, and then it's like a small pizza. You can eat it with a knife and fork, but I had fun eating it with my hands.

Everyone loved the food, and it seemed Johana was getting along well with Yiota, so that concern faded. And Kyle had the new camera and drones in hand, one of which was a replacement for the original that crashed into the sea! The second is built for flying through spaces like bridges and car windows and things. I hoped that investment would get lots of good shots by being able to fly closer to everything. The new camera was a 360-degree camera that Kyle mounted on the front of my bike that gets fantastic shots of me riding and of the street life around me. I hoped it would help improve our social media following.

Well after the stress of crossing the border and riding through heavy traffic or on roads with no shoulders that day, all I could do was relax and hope the next day wouldn't be as bad, though we would be riding on the same highway again for 124 km before arriving at another Airbnb. My goal was to start early and try and get on the road by 7:30 a.m. just to try and avoid some traffic—and heat—get some more riding time in and knock off some kilometers. We still had six more borders to cross before the journey was over, and they would all be at least a little stressful, though I had to admit all the Mexican authorities and cashiers, the immigration officers and bank folks, had all been really friendly. There'd been no arguing or intimidation or anything like that, so that eased the stress of all the border-crossing hiccups.

***

Our next stop as we continued to ride inland was to be in Mexicali. Afterward, we would be far enough east that we could turn south and go down the east side of the Sea of Cortez. Somehow or other, the weather was even still cooperating with us. The forecast predicted highs around 27°C, 28°C as we were to cross the northern desert, which would make it a much more comfortable ride.

Despite a promising start however, things were about to go downhill fast, and not the kind of downhill I like. The sun shone over the horizon that morning as we got our early start, making the highway ahead shimmer and blurring the air so the world around us looked almost like a smudged painting. Only the center highway line pierced the haze and the shimmer as it went on and on forever in the distance without so much as a slight curve. It was breathtaking. Or maybe that was from the size of the first hill we climbed after leaving the campground.

Anyway, I think we held our breath, though how we did that as we climbed all those steep hills I still don't know, pretty much all the way to Mexicali as we cycled down shoulder less roads that day. It also felt at times rather pointless to be riding inland and parallel to the border rather than heading straight south, but we really had no choice so we could ensure we were far enough east to reach the east coast of the Sea of Cortez and to avoid the massive Laguna Salada blocking our way. This was the only reasonable route to take, so, east we continued to go.

We rode on through the same stable, unchanging weather through El Rancho, Colonia Luis Echeverria, and Manchon Blanco, always up and down, around, and around. At times, I could look out over the desert, and it would look like it undulated in waves like an ocean, complete with rocky outcroppings towering out from within its depths. It was quite the illusion. Then we reached La Rumarosa, the climbing and descending got crazier, and the highway became two highways: eastbound traffic had one highway, and westbound traffic had another. To look at it on a map, the highway after La Rumarosa looks like the engineer who'd plotted the route had enjoyed one too many tequilas.

After all that dizzying riding, we stopped for a snack just outside La Rumarosa before the highways diverged and came across an enormous group of bikers—motorbikes that is—at the Pemex we pulled into. They were all really friendly and curious about what we were doing there, so of course I enjoyed a good conversation with my snack and drink. Then it was back on the road again. Sharing the same lane every time a car came was nerve-racking, but as much as we might have wanted to call it quits early that day, we had to keep pushing to our Airbnb in Mexicali.

But maybe we should have called it a day early. Hindsight is twenty-twenty though. As we were coming into Mexicali, Wayne had a couple close calls with traffic. The first time, a car cut right in front of him to pull off on the side of the road. I was right behind him and saw how close it was. It was rather scary just for me to watch, so I could only imagine how Wayne felt. The second time, a car pulled out to pass a bus, of course passing in our lane, and it was coming at us at full tilt. I was riding right behind Wayne, and that was infinitely scarier than the first incident. Then, when we'd reached Mexicali, we were stopped at a red light. When the light turned green, Wayne started going without looking, and a car illegally sped through a red light. I had to shout and warn Wayne, and he stopped barely in time. The car missed him by just a few feet. I still think that if I hadn't yelled, Wayne would have been roadkill that day.

Well, we finally made it to our Airbnb alive, and Wayne went off for a time by himself, ostensibly to tour the homes bordering the gated community, while I waited for the security guard to get permission from the Airbnb owner to let us in. I thought he needed some time to recover and recuperate, maybe catch his breath and ease his anxiety after his close calls. It turned out to be more than that though. It seemed that last near miss had been the final straw for him. And in all fairness, he had had five close calls in two days. So, he came to me later that night and told me he'd decided it wasn't worth it to continue on, for now, and endanger his life. He said that while I was on this odyssey to break the world record and achieve another long ride, he was in it only for the fun and the exercise. Plus, he was still nursing a sore rear end despite getting that new bike seat in San Diego. In the end, he chose to fly to Puerto Vallarta the next day and relax for two weeks until we got there. Then he would rejoin us.

While I was saddened to lose the company of my longtime riding partner, I could understand where he was coming from. And I did still have company. Besides, there was one upside to his decision: we wouldn't have any problems with sleeping arrangements for two weeks.

***

So, we parted ways the next day, and instead of riding with Wayne, I rode with Johana. It was her first time on an e-bike, yet she rode the whole 145 km that day and only 65 m of climbing, flat, flat, flat. She's like a strong little mighty mouse. She may be all of forty-four kilograms and less than five feet tall, but she's a good strong mountain-bike rider. And she impressed me too because she used far less battery power than I did, even on the steep inclines, which we would encounter later, which indicated her riding strength versus mine and highlighted the difference in the weight the battery must propel down the road.

What a day that was! It started off normally as we rode southeast through Guadalupe, bound for the Sonoran Desert and ultimately El Golfo de Santa Clara. The farther we went, the more desolate our surroundings became. We rode through the brown-beige, rocky landscape in steadily climbing temperatures. There were very few cars and the road was straight, very straight, but then when we were about twenty kilometers from El Golfo de Santa Clara, the police stopped us. They asked a bunch of questions about who we were and what we were doing, then they told us to follow them because it was dangerous. Here I was thinking it was because of the cartels and such, maybe kidnappings, but no. It was dangerous because a hurricane had blown through about a month earlier, flooded the area with water, then pulled it all back to the ocean, carrying all the sand from the desert down with it. The police told us the sand had covered the roads for days, and they were still trying to clean it up. Clean-up was going to take some time until they could get all the graders out to plow the sand off like we do with snow in Canada. To add insult to injury, when the graders come along, they undercut some of the pavement, creating some sharp, dangerous drop offs on the shoulders, and the sand gets pushed into enormous mounds on what shoulders there are. If that weren't enough, the police said, some areas were down to just one lane because the sand hadn't all been cleared off yet, and the little town and all its roads were covered in sand, making them treacherous to ride on. I was grateful for their thoughtfulness, so we followed behind the police car for quite a way before another came in and drove behind us, likely protecting us was my thought.

Once we got to town, I noticed a couple officers, including the first officer to respond, Juan, were outside filming our entry into town. We stopped and chatted and took some selfies and hopped back on our bikes. Before we left, they asked us if we knew our way, warned us to be careful, and took my Octogenarian Odyssey social-media information. Kyle even got to show off his movie camera and got some footage of the police. As we were about to start pedaling again, one officer, Paulo I thought, gave me his phone number, and told me to call him if we ran into any trouble. He'd take care of it, he said. I thanked him and asked his advice about our missing trailer license plate. He just shrugged and said that whatever the border guards had said applied throughout the country, and if anyone disputed that or asked for money, to refuse and call him. I invited them to our camp for beer then, but they politely declined saying they had to work the late shift.

On that note, I must add that Yiota's been stopped twice by the police, and not for a friendly, protective reason. The first time was back in Tijuana for distracted driving, though she talked her way out of the fine, and the second time was for not having a plate on the back of the tent trailer. She talked her way out of that one too, but it still made her nervous.

In any case, we found our campground and gratefully set up camp. It had been a not unpleasant but draining day. We had a nice dinner, delivered from a local restaurant, and then sat around a fire talking to some locals before I crawled into the van to grab some sleep. I couldn't help but think about how wonderful and friendly all the people—and police—had been as I started to fall asleep. No matter where we are, we get lots of waves and honks, and in the last two days, we'd gotten a couple ten-dollar tips to buy some beer. Sometimes people would stop to give us water or Gatorade, and in one instance, a nice fellow reached out of his truck window as it was moving, and I was still riding, and handed me a beer— that of course I stopped to drink just about right away. There we were, already at the northern tip of the Sea of Cortez, and we'd had no safety worries as far as the population and things like that went.

***

The next day, we headed for Puerto Penasco and a rest day. A lot had happened, and the riding had started off pretty scary at the beginning of our Mexico leg, so I knew it wasn't just me who looked forward to the rest day. I still wished Wayne had stayed with us, but it was fun riding with Johana or Yiota too. And that day was one of our longest and flattest rides, 155 km if I remember correctly, as we followed a route down the Sea of Cortez and around the Gulf of California. However, the monotonous, scenery wasn't helping me forget about the heat.

But just as I had that thought, I crested a rise, and the Sea of Cortez came into full view. Before I could fully appreciate it, Yiota flew by with nothing but her shorts and bra on! She was riding with Kyle and I that day while Johana drove, and there Yiota went, completely carefree, arms outstretched, helmetless, and music blaring. Someone was having a good time!

Finally, as we continued south, I went from seeing a whole lot of nothing, just the road running straight in front of me, sand—lots of really fine sand—and a few tiny green bushes to a study in contrasts. I still can't reconcile the juxtaposition between the sweltering, sere desert with the vast body of water at its edge. Dusty air mingled with the smell of seawater. Yet when the wind came up, the sand blew through the air. With almost no clouds on the horizon and the greige of the perfectly flat terrain pockmarked only by the odd miniature scrub brush, if I looked to one side, I could imagine I was on Mars. If I looked to the other side, I was in an ocean paradise. And on that day, it hit 44°Celsius when we still had 107 km to go. We'd hit just about the toughest section for riding a bicycle. Crossing the desert had not been something I'd been looking forward to. There was a bonus to such heat though: there were no irritating bugs to deal with during the heat of the day.

That day became such an uncomfortable ride that when we reached our Airbnb in Puerto Penasco, I discussed changing the route with the team. On our current route, we'd face two long days of riding across the desert, but if we went down the coast instead, I could turn it into three shorter days. I warred with myself, trying to decide how important it was to stay on schedule. So, I brought it up at dinner that night—at a sports bar full of Americans. Funny how neither the food nor the service was very good, and margaritas weren't even good, but still it cost me a hundred bucks.

***

In the end, we stayed on schedule by keeping to the original route once our rest days were over. But first, while in Puerto Penasco, commonly called Rocky Point by Americans, I got my first opportunity to really indulge in my favorite aspect of long-distance cycling: immersing myself in the culture and learning about it. Puerto Penasco is quite unique, a balance of old history and modern North Americanism. The Mexican government has been trying to turn it into another Cancun or something these days, and with its decent Malecon, multitudes of restaurants, and long stretch of beach on the northern edge of the Sea of Cortez, it is worth visiting. Plus, there's an airport only twenty-five kilometers outside town, and when we rode past it, there were a few buses waiting around, likely waiting for a planeload of tourists to land. You could also drive there because it's only about a hundred kilometers from the American border and maybe three hours form Tucson, Arizona. Not to mention you don't need an import permit for your car there.

I even read that in 2022, half a million tourists visited Puerto Penasco. I suppose that would explain the vast array of huge all-inclusive resorts along the beach, just a short ride down a dirt road. Each resort has an immense footprint given they stand about eight kilometers from the highway, and there was probably a good eight kilometers between each resort. Puerto Penasco could be a wonderful place for a vacation for the sort of person who likes that, who just wants to hang out and eat and drink for a week or two. Not a single palm tree to be found though. Me, I wouldn't choose it over Puerto Vallarta or Mazatlán or even Cancun. And I wouldn't choose an all-inclusive for a vacation either simply because I love old areas of town and meeting the people. It's just not my thing, but who am I to say what other folks want to do?

The family that owned the Airbnb we stayed at were super friendly. They brought over their daughter and her children and husband to meet us and take photos, and a newspaper reporter and a fellow from the local radio station!

Puerto Penasco, or Rocky Point, Beach

Though our conversation and my interviews made my crew hit the road much later than usual that day, I—as always—thoroughly enjoyed it, and the reporter wrote a fascinating article about me and my Octogenarian Odyssey. I really hoped word of my journey spreads so people everywhere, especially senior citizens, regardless of where they live or their circumstances, are motivated to live life, do things, get active, and find happiness.

And I can't say this enough: the Mexican people are so gracious and so friendly, it's impossible to believe they have such a bad reputation with so many in the US.

Back to the journey though. After our late start, we skirted around the last curve of the Gulf of California and before long turned inland again, headed for Caborca that night. We finally left the desert that day after spending maybe two-thirds of the day in it. Then we started to emerge and began to see some trees and cacti, then more green, and even some fields where things are actually growing! I discovered as we rode by that one of those crops was grapes, but not the kind used to make wine. Those were the ones used for making raisins, so though they looked like the same rows of grapes, they're not treated the same way. Raisin grapes are left to dry on the vine. And there were sure a lot of them. Interspersed among the grape fields were date palms, of which we bought some of course.

We thankfully rode on a flat road, and a pretty good road too in most cases, with very light traffic. It seemed we couldn't go more than a day or two without an incident though. This time, Johana's bike touched my rear wheel, and she wiped out on the highway. She got a little road rash on her knee and arm out of the deal, but at least that was it. Then when I started riding again, I kept hearing this click click click. So, I stopped to figure out what it was, but I couldn't find anything, so I kept going. Suddenly, the bike stopped. I got off, pushed it to the side of the road, and tried several different tricks to try and get it to work again. In the past, my bike in Costa Rica would overheat and I would just have to let it sit and cool off for five minutes or so before the motor, or the control that protects the motor, would let the bike run again. Nothing I did worked, but then Johana saw that one of the sensors had been knocked out of alignment. I turned that around and bingo! We were off again.

Well, despite our delayed start, we still achieved 115 km that day, though we didn't make Caborca. Instead, with the sun about to go down, we found a lovely place to stay just before that in Plutarco Elias Calles. At least our only issue besides the couple bike incidents had been the heat, which had been at its worst in the middle of the day, around noon.

When it got to around 3 p.m. it got quite a bit cooler. You could even see the angle of the sun change in relation to the flat, flat ground. And, hallelujah, we were even blessed with a tailwind for the last part of the day.

***

The next day was sunny and hot again, so I inevitably switched up the plan. Riding in the heat was becoming harder than I'd originally assumed, so I'd decided to add an extra day so we could have a few shorter rides. The new plan was to stop in Altar, then continue to Santa Ana the following day. I'd thought with the e-bikes, the riding would have been a little easier, and it was to some degree, but it was still a bit much. Plus, I was sure we were going to need a couple shorter riding days because once we left Santa Ana after those short rides, we were looking at a 170 km day. There wasn't much for civilization between Santa Ana and Hermosillo, so we'd have to push through until we reached Hermosillo.

In the end, I was glad I'd cut the days short and we'd stopped in Altar. Making the days short meant I could ride at a slightly slower speed and enjoy myself, especially those times when people would wave and honk. They just seemed to do that no matter where we were. Most vehicles, and even semis, would see my sign and give me a friendly toot toot, so I'd give them a wave. Some folks even stopped because they'd seen our videos on social media, and so many of them offered beer, food, water, money, whatever they had. It touches my heart every time. Many people just don't have much, especially these days, and for them to share the little they have told me more about them than anything else.

On our ride that day, I got a little freaked out when I saw my first snake. I should have been surprised it had taken that long, but it still caught me off guard. It was quite large too, and it slithered across the highway. I swerved so I didn't hit it, which was kind of stupid of me because traffic was coming at me, and although I was riding on the shoulder, I still veered bit into a truck's lane. I'd call that a close call for me between the truck and the snake. Damn, it was a big critter; I'd say it was maybe six feet long and the width of a hammer handle.

Not long after that little heart attack, we reached Altar and ventured downtown for dinner. Using my trusty inner radar, I found a small Mexican restaurant full of people. I've learned over the years that's the best indication of a great place, whether it's the food or the service or both. Of course, we had the molé. How could we not? Besides, I never eat the salad or fresh fruits and vegetables. Getting sick is the last thing I want to do. And the total for that meal, even after adding in some Cokes for everyone? $16 for four people. That was a relief after the US, and even after a couple nights earlier in Puerto Penasco and that $100 tab.

Thank goodness for my pocketbook, we all decided then to try and eat more street food where possible. I mean, even street food in Mexico is delicious. That wasn't to say we wouldn't take a break every now and then and relax in a good establishment with a few drinks. We hadn't even had to camp in a while, which part of me missed but there simply weren't a lot of places to do so in the middle of a desert, because hotels and Airbnb's were generally more affordable than even camping in the US. I'd paid just $25/night for an okay hotel the previous night and anticipated the same that night. Even with booking two rooms each night, it was still a real bargain, especially when compared to the $200 US/night I paid to camp in Big Sur.

After dinner, we spent a little time in the town *zocolo*. That's a church square. All Mexican cities have them. We sat eating ice cream cones while we admired the church, all lit up with the colors of Mexico—red, green, and white—and absorbed the nice warm evening. I realized that while I loved seeing these new places and conquering the desert, I was getting tired of the long, straight roads where I rode a hundred kilometers and never saw a single curve. I always prefer roads that take a little bit of navigation, that twist and turn a little. It breaks up the monotony. Riding past things, anything—a farmhouse, a factory, a town, a sign—helps ease the boredom. At least the landscape had been improving a little. I didn't mind gazing around at the mountains in the far distance or the green grasses now starting to pop up by the roadside.

***

Our ride the next morning was graced with a beautiful blue sky, the sun shining over the mountains surrounding me in the distance. Though we'd just left the desert, the sandy part, we still had lots of heat to conquer during the day. The only wind through the whole desert, and even now, was the wind we made as we propelled ourselves down the road on our bicycles. Everything that day was a lively green, and I finally found myself looking at trees. They were a modest size mind you, certainly not forest-sized, but more like big bushes. Not long into the day, we came across more farmland, and what looked like cattle. Those were punctuated by the seemingly ever-present grape fields. It may be too hot there for wine grapes, but it sure is perfect for raisins!

Though I would have preferred riding longer than just seventy-five kilometers that day, I had no choice but to end the day in Santa Ana, with nowhere to stop between there and Hermosillo. But after that long day, we'd have just one 135 km day before we'd hit our next rest day in Guaymas. That felt sort of bittersweet. Guaymas was one of the first Mexican towns I'd ever heard of. Beth's parents used to go down to Mexico and spend a week or so in Guaymas back in the day. I'd passed through it a few times but had never explored it. I usually always stopped in San Carlos, a kind of suburb just north of it, so I was looking forward to doing so on my rest day.

Santa Ana turned out to be a pretty good place to stop. We got a nice hotel, and people again extended us a warm welcome and asked to take pictures with us. We even met a touring band there that night called La Kinta; we chatted with them a while and learned about their experiences, shared ours, and then we took photos with the whole band in front of their bus. That night, dinner, as promised, was street food. Tacos in Santa Ana were just a buck and a half for two tacos. And those tacos were stuffed! You got a tortilla with a huge spoonful of meat, ground beef for me, and then you could head over to the, for lack of a better phrase, the salad-bar wagon, where you could add onions and jalapeños and veggies and sauces and anything else you wanted. It sure turns into quite a decent meal, with two tacos piled high with all kinds of goodies!

***

And then, after a good night's rest, it was time to tackle the long, 170 km ride from Santa Ana to Hermosillo. I reminded myself that it would be worth it because not only would it get me one day closer to breaking the world record, but I would also get one day closer to Guaymas, a place I'd always meant to get to. Oh, and a rest day.

The stretch of riding over the previous few days had been incredibly boring. Though we'd been riding down a four-lane divided highway with wide shoulders, the road just cut straight across the plains, and there hadn't been much to see. We'd left the sand behind of course, but we still only had shrubs and farms to look at. Lots and lots of farms though: grapes, dates, cattle. But however mind-numbing the landscape, at least we still got stopped all the time on the highway. That always served to lighten my mood. I got at least two or three people a day who stopped and asked about the Octogenarian Odyssey. It was great to take a break from the monotony to take selfies and group photos. Then the team always shared our Instagram account information so folks could follow our progress. We'd even come across a family the day before who'd pulled over and told us they'd seen us on TV, so they wanted to stop and talk to us. I had no idea, and still don't, how we'd ended up on TV in some little Mexican town I never quite got the name of. I certainly hadn't seen cameras or anything anywhere we were. Who knows? Maybe the station just heard about it from someone or saw it in a newspaper or something.

We even ran into three fellows—David, Tony, and Alfredo—who brought out a bunch of beer and offered to share. Well, there wasn't any question about accepting the offer, so we all indulged in one plus some engaging conversation, and then those fellows stuffed some more beer in our paniers for later. We then toasted Mexico with "Viva Mexico, Cabrones." It was the first I had heard the word Cabrones. The term is used in a non-derogatory way to express the grittiness of the people. If you ask Google to translate this, it says: long live Mexico bastards. It was wonderful to see the enthusiasm of the younger people for something this old guy was doing. Of course, they always got excited when they found out I was eighty years old. On the one hand, they couldn't believe it, but on the other, they thought it was awesome. I guessed that meant I was accomplishing one of my goals, which was to both influence younger people to look at senior citizens in a different light and to know that there's a big wide world out there in which to try and experience new things. I hoped too that I would spread the word that there's lots of people doing long-distance cycling. Maybe more young people would be encouraged to start doing something along the same lines.

And you know, it doesn't matter what country you're in, you're always bound to see some strange stuff. We saw one of those that day. It was a souped-up motorcycle flying a big Mexican flag. A woman was driving—and Spiderman was sitting behind her. Of course, we had to stop and talk! I eventually learned he'd had a bad motorcycle accident ten or so years ago and that's why she drove, and he wore the Spiderman mask. It helped him feel better by obscuring the injuries to his neck and face.

Well, as always happens, we finally made it to Hermosilla after a long, mostly dull day of riding through the dreary, hot landscape with barely a tiny town to speak of. The day had been one of the hottest we'd experienced; the car that day registered 42°C. Heck, it was so hot, it was just better to keep riding because stopping meant there was no wind to cool you off, to whisk away your perspiration, and there was no shade anywhere.

Dinner that night was a quick stop at one of those taco-chain restaurants where they charged maybe a dollar more than what the taco stands on the street did. But that night we were beat, so the big chain was the easiest option. Either way, supper cost me only $35. I think we all staggered back to the hotel and just fell into bed.

***

Thankfully, the next day's ride was shorter, and there was a reward dangling in front of us: a lovely rest day in an Airbnb. I was looking forward to wandering around Gauymas and to, if I was lucky, just a bit of air conditioning.

At the risk of sounding incredibly boring, the truth was, our ride to Gauymas was pretty much a carbon copy of the previous day, only without beer and conversation with great people. Again, we followed a four-lane highway, and though I hated all that traffic, at least the roads were in good shape, and we had wide shoulders to ride on. It felt so much safer than back between Tijuana and Mexicali. So, on we rode, past a few little communities, making frequent hydration stops and the odd snack. I'd tell you about the weather or the scenery, but it never really changed. Neither was there any wildlife to experience on this whole last stretch.

Thank goodness that after crossing into Mexico, Airbnb's had become much more reasonably priced since we were going to spend the next two nights in one. When we arrived, I was thrilled to discover it was a nice, clean, three-bedroom condo in a decent development. It even had four beds, so it was quite comfortable.

Well, it was fortuitous that we had two rest days just then because my health luck ran out. I'd done rather well to that point without experiencing any real digestive issues, but our rest day was a different story. I woke up feeling okay and went to the beach in the morning with the others, but as the day wore on, that slowly began to change. So I went back to the condo, took it easy, and didn't do too much. A few hours later, I was getting queasy, and by dinner, diarrhea had set in, so I spent most of the rest of the day in bed and close to the toilet. It might have been the sushi I ate the night before. Kyle gave me some pills he said would help; he's a self-professed, but trained nutritionist, and he seemed to know a lot about that sort of thing, so I trusted him. I guess he used to be a kind of healthcare provider in the sense that he ensured the rap group he used to travel with had good food and a proper diet. Either way, I downed the pills and crossed my fingers that I'd feel better the next day because it was going to be another long hot day.

Yiota made such a great dinner that night that I ate regardless of what little appetite I had. She made some sort of Mediterranean-style dinner, some dish popular in Greece or around that area, of peppers stuffed with ground beef and spices and some other stuff I didn't recognize with potatoes. She even made it so you had a choice of either two stuffed peppers or two stuffed tomatoes; you could have one or the other if you had a preference or have one of each.

After I got some supper down, I went to bed early and as I lay there, I started looking ahead at the weather in Mazatlán. That day, it had been about 32°C there, and Puerto Vallarta had been about 31°C, so that was a little bit cooler than what we'd been riding in before we arrived in Guaymas, so I would certainly welcome the cooler weather. It seemed ironic that it didn't feel like that long ago that we were up in Yukon, and it was rainy and cold, and we couldn't wait to get down to Mexico and even the southern US so we could get some hot weather. I chuckled and thought, *Well, we got what we asked for*. I would have to work harder to consume more liquids more regularly. I'd always been rather bad at remembering to do that, and given the heat I'd been experiencing, I was pretty sure that was one reason I wasn't feeling so great. Some days on my bike, on an average-temperature day, I don't drink much fluid; sometimes I don't drink anything at all. But on those 42-degree days on this trip, I'd been trying to drink electrolytes, water, and Coke—even some beer near the end of the day. It likely just hadn't been sufficient, I reasoned, so I'd work to increase that when we hit the road again the next day.

Our goal for our first day back on the highway was Obregon. Unfortunately, it had a bad reputation for crime. From what I'd heard though, the cause wasn't the cartels but banditos. One concerned guy we'd spoken to in Guaymas had even said, "Please, when you go tomorrow, call 911. Tell them what you're doing and ask for police assistance or at least to keep an eye out for you or something like that." Yet when Johana had gone to the mall and asked some folks about it, they'd said it wasn't really a problem, that they didn't bother tourists. So, then we had this conflict of information and didn't quite know what to do.

In the end, Johana called 911 and talked to the National Guard and the police, both of whom had said that, yes, there had been some robberies and such and that we needed to be careful. They even advised us to check in with them before we left and again when we finished our ride at the end of the day. So, that was the plan we were going with when we took off the next morning. And we'd have to be more cautious than usual. I went so far as to suggest we shouldn't take the cameras and everything on the bikes, to keep them packed away in the van, and Kyle agreed, so there wouldn't be any footage of that day's ride. But I couldn't help but think that that kind of day had the potential for great story material if we did encounter some bandits or something. At the same time, I knew it would be hard for us to be more cautious because we treat everyone like friends. When cars stop and flag us down, we stop and talk with those folks, and—until then—a hundred percent of the time, we'd had great experiences, whether with young people, old people, truck drivers, workers, or travelers. It would be hard, but the next day we'd all have to be just a little more choosy about who we rode up to. But I knew too, that as many stories do, they become exaggerated over time, so while banditos do exist and robberies do happen, I felt the probability of something happening was pretty low.

We'd certainly find out.

BOB and WAYNE, TOGETHER AGAIN

Met you today on the boardwalk heading south through Hermosa beach (Los Angeles) Sept 10. My ride today is a fraction of a fraction of what you are doing. Thanks for the brief chat. You have inspired me to challenge myself. Keep it on two wheels, ride safe, watch out for the bears at night. You are a true champion in my book.

—S. Hicks.

That makes it a perfect stop! I'm loving this trip, Robert. You are an inspiration, man

—R. Futrell.

I have been following your travels with great interest. Thank you for your posts and continued safe travels to all.

—R. Osborn

Posts like these are my motivation

It was posts like these that kept me going through some of the harder days. Whether I read them on Facebook or Instagram or I heard them from people I met en route, it delighted and motivated me to know that I was getting my message out there, that word was spreading. I found too, that I now had two equal messages: to get people, seniors especially, up off the couch and living life and to let the world know that much of the American press has it wrong about Latin Americans and people from other countries. While it's true that there is crime in Latin American countries, African countries, Middle Eastern countries, that's true of all countries. So rather than painting everyone with the same biased brush, go out there and learn about other people and other cultures for yourself. You'll find what I have to date: people are generally good, kind, friendly, and caring.

Anyway, we were headed for Obregon that day, the city of banditos where we called the police when we began our ride and when we got in. It was also the day after my Montezuma's Revenge and another searingly hot day. We had good luck on all counts though. My health was back on track, and I was able to start the ride that day recuperated and refreshed.

We also didn't run into any trouble in Obregon. Not that it was completely smooth sailing, but we did come out of our one and only situation just fine. A group of men dressed all in black, just like I'd heard of on Facebook, stopped our car. On

Facebook, I'd read that they would try and extort money from Americans and Canadians, but Johana was our hero once again. She just showed them her Mexican driver's license, and they just left her alone, waved her on. And she just chatted with them like a local, so it felt more like a friendly encounter than a close call. Otherwise, I think because I was on a bike, they didn't bother me. Whenever they saw me, they just waved, and I waved back, though it did appear they were harassing those in vehicles. Whether we would meet these men in black again, who knew. We were just glad to have scooted through Obregon unscathed.

As we progressed down the highway through all the different cities—Huatabampo, Los Mochis, Guamuchil—over the next couple days, we managed to get off the main highway and enjoy some new scenery. Johana and I rode that stretch together, and we toured through some spectacular farmland with all kinds of things growing, from figs to potatoes to tomatoes, even orange groves and enormous trees bearing nuts of numerous varieties. One day, I forget which because I just lost all track of time out there, we were so curious, we got off our bikes and wandered into a field to talk to the folks harvesting the figs. We took a short video of them, and they showed us how to eat a fig—and gave us a handful!

Later that afternoon, we moved on to lunch at a small restaurant, and would you believe the town was so small, all the locals came out to see what we were all about! One lady even brought some fruit over for us to try. That was a fantastic lunch and so worth the time we lost talking with everyone and taking photos. Then we tried to get back on the road again, but a block or so down the road from the restaurant, we came upon a school surrounded by teenage girls who wanted to take more pictures with us. They were really interested in Johana riding an e-bike as big as it is because she's so small. And she was all geared up in her EVELO riding outfit, so she looked really professional too. The girls really liked that and thought it was awesome to see a woman riding a bike from Alaska to Panama. The rest of us knew she hadn't gone all that way, but that's what the sign on my bike said, so we went with it. It seemed to really be motivating those girls to believe they too could achieve big things. We finally got going again after that, but only until we hit another farmer's field and got stopped to take yet more photos. Though a small part of me was getting irritated that we weren't making any progress that day, I brushed it off quickly by reminding myself that I wanted to get my messages out into the world, and this was how I was going to do it. All those photos would be posted to social media, and hopefully, shared around the world. Besides, I really did love the attention.

Then the next day, we had to get back on the busy, noisy, four-lane highway again before Los Mochis and the border of Sonora and Sinaloa. Though it had great wide, well-maintained shoulders to ride on, the noise of the trucks and everything screaming by was not a very pleasant way to spend a day on a bicycle at all. When we reached the edge of Sonora and stopped by the roadside, maybe a hundred meters off it, a police car came by with three police officers in it. I thought we were in trouble, but they only wanted to know what we were doing, just like everyone else who stops us. They liked my story so much, one wanted to get on the e-bike and take a ride. He was a commander or something, so I gave him Johana's bike and he took a little ride.

When he was done, he invited the team and I back to the police station to have a look around, have a shower, and use the toilet and such. Once we'd taken full advantage of everything they'd offered, the police took out their own mountain bikes and showed them off. They were right to be proud of them because they were fantastic bikes with full suspension, and they let us all ride for a bit. We all had a bit of fun then, taking a video of me getting handcuffed by a lovely looking female officer and snapping some photos. The commander asked that we not publish any of those photos though, for obvious reasons. Then came some lighthearted banter as we swapped stories of our adventures.

Afterward, around about the time I was ready to get back on the road, they asked if we wanted to eat. I looked at the others, and they looked excited—and I was hungry too I guess—so I accepted their offer, and everyone piled into the police truck. There were about fourteen of us all told stuffed in that truck, but it was a memorable experience. We ended up at a wonderful little restaurant we probably wouldn't have found ourselves, and the police treated us to a tasty lunch of seafood soup, or in my case, rice, chicken, and salad with a hibiscus drink.

Finally, much later in the afternoon, we got on their way and thanked them and the people of Sonora for their kindness. In this book, I'm officially thanking all the police we met along the way for all their assistance and generosity, and I'm thanking all the people of Central America for the same. It made the whole experience what it was and strengthened my hope and belief in humanity.

When we finally arrived at our day's destination, we did things a little backward. With our earlier delay, we'd had to stop sooner than we'd meant to, so we stopped and had tacos again for dinner while Yiota and Johana searched for accommodation. They couldn't find a suitable campground or hotel, so we ended up in another Airbnb. It turned out to be a delightfully decorated little place, but it was small. The owner had to come over and let us in, and when she did, she too was interested in hearing our story and taking pictures.

***

The free road was our friend the next day as we were leaving Guamuchil. It's called the free road because it has no tolls, but it's really just the old highway. It too was still fairly busy, but at least it didn't have so many trucks rolling by. Plus, we got to ride through more small towns and see more villages and roadside activity that way. On the toll road, or the freeway, it looks, sounds, and feels just like any freeway in the US or Canada; the vehicles just roar by. I've driven from Edmonton all the way to Acapulco four times and visited

Mexico at least fifteen times—the longest for about five months and the shortest for a day. But every time I've driven down, I took the bypass past all the cities, and even the smaller places, I got to stop in on this journey. I didn't really get to experience them, get a good feel for them. So even though I've been here so many times, touring through on the bikes gave me a much more thorough, true experience. We had a good balance of side roads and major roads too, so I got to soak in both modern, city life and rural, authentic life. And, I have to make a point of this, in all cases, all the cities were nice and modern and clean with plenty of the Starbucks, McDonalds, Burger Kings, movie theaters, shopping malls, and every other amenity we're all used to seeing in Canada and the US. Of course, there are still poor areas around the cities and in many of the small towns and that's where the litter piled up, but that's true of a lot of countries around the world. And the modernization of Mexico's cities sure calls out the supposed story of poverty and crime-ridden streets and rapists and criminals roaming the countryside. I've also learned through all my international tours over the years that as you ride through a country on a bike, you can judge an economy by the number of semis on the road. The more there are, the better that country's economy must be doing. And there were plenty of semis on Mexico's roads.

Of course, wherever we rode—free road, toll road, or side road—we always got lots of honks and waves from everybody, whether the passersby were on bikes or motorcycles or in cars, trucks, or semis. The whole trip through Mexico to that point, I'd felt like a kind of a celebrity or something. It was weird and pleasing at the same time. But I figured maybe we were somewhat of a celebrity because most of the areas we rode through probably didn't see many long-distance bikers.

Well, that free road took us all the way to Culiacan and another Airbnb that also turned out to be modern and clean with two large bedrooms. But what was supposed to have been an overnighter turned into an extended stay.

***

We were supposed to ride 127 km to La Cruz that day, but I awoke to a message on my phone telling me that Hurricane Orlene was headed for Mazatlán, which was just two hundred kilometers or a two-day bike ride from Culiacan. That warranted a discussion among the group to determine our plan of action. We decided rather quickly that we really had no choice but to wait out the storm for at least another night to see what developed. It sounded like it would become a category-three hurricane, so there was no point in chancing it. Besides, the state of Jalisco had closed the schools, and the Coast Guard had closed all the ports and small harbors, so that was pretty telling. The news was talking about the storm at least bringing in huge amounts of rain and high winds when it hit the following day around lunchtime. We could perhaps have made some headway before the storm hit, but I didn't want to chance not being able to find somewhere to take shelter for the night. There weren't a lot of accommodation options between Culiacan and La Cruz, and I was sure what there was would fill up almost immediately and we'd be stuck.

There we were, in a state of limbo in Culiacan, and I was guessing we'd still be sitting there the same time the next day, waiting to see what happened. We were lucky though that the Airbnb had been available for a continued stay and that it was truly a lovely place to be stuck in because it was big and comfortable. Plus, the city was fair sized, and there was lots to do if we chose to go out—as we had the previous evening.

That night, we had all headed out for a celebration. It's always enjoyable to splurge on a restaurant of some quality when you're celebrating, so that night we'd gone to a steakhouse. As you would suspect, three of us had the steak, and someone had camarones shrimp and some type of cheese sauce, but I can't remember who now. Throw in some cocktails, and it made for a fun night at a reasonable price, $100 USD, though I still hadn't been able to help but compare that to a taco stand where we could go and fill ourselves up on tacos for $20.

Anyway, we'd been celebrating what had once been the record-breaking goal. We'd passed the originally existing 8,209.2 km Guinness world record. With that Florida couple setting a new record of 11,003 km six or seven weeks ago though, we had to move the bar. But we could still celebrate our accomplishment! And I couldn't help but think that though Flipper and Skipper had achieved a remarkable goal, what they'd completed was a whole different ball game. They'd just toured around the US, basically in their backyard. But we'd gotten out into the world and encountered different things as we crossed Alaska, Yukon, BC, Washington, Oregon, California, and down into eastern Mexico. Heck, we'd even ridden through the Sonoran Desert! The two situations were entirely different in my mind, and it looked then like we would achieve the new goal somewhere around Antigua in Guatemala, so we still celebrated.

Wayne had been due to join us the day after we reached La Cruz, but Mother Nature forestalled that plan. He was safely in Puerto Vallarta, which wasn't in the path of the storm although it was fairly close, so they would surely get plenty of rain out of it. So, since it would have been incredibly stupid for him to drive up to Mazatlán right into the eye of the hurricane as was the original plan, he waited out the storm in Puerto Vallarta for a couple more days before joining us.

There was also the problem of accommodation again since his return meant we would have five people again, which just made things a little more complicated. With just four people, we'd only had to get two hotel rooms when we couldn't get an Airbnb, and I'd generally been paying $25 US per room or $50 per night. With five people, unless we could find some hotels with family-sized rooms and/or three beds, we'd have to get three rooms, making the cost go up another $25.

On our second unexpected evening in Culiacan—having been stuck there for two days instead of one—we took advantage of the delay and went out to eat again given there was a cool food area nearby close enough to walk to. It had a bunch of different booths set up, and in each, various restaurants and bars were cooking up their specialties. Waiters scurried about taking orders from seated patrons and running the orders to each of the booths. So, we sat in a beautiful, tranquil garden surrounded by trees and soft lighting and had cocktails and dinner. It was a lovely place to spend an evening we hadn't expected to have.

***

Well, after two days of waiting out a hurricane that never really amounted to much, it was time to take up the odyssey again. It had been a good rest that was more necessary than I'd thought. I think my body needed it more than I knew.

So, then we were back on the road, riding for about 130 km in perfect riding conditions. What bliss! It was maybe 30°C with a light breeze mostly at our backs. We were off the toll road, so we didn't have much traffic, and the surfaces were good. The road still stretched out ahead of us in a straight line, though we were now starting to encounter some rolling hills that were probably our first hills in a couple weeks. There was more scenery around us now too as we eased away from the desert. To our left was a bunch of lush greenery, and to our right was a majestic mountain range. Eventually, we came upon an obstacle that we strangely hadn't come across yet in Mexico: construction. It stopped us for a little while, but the delay wasn't long. We caught up with the support van, which wasn't far ahead of us, and Yiota handed me an electrolyte drink.

Once we were moving again, Kyle rode ahead to fly the drone around again. There was finally some interesting landscape to capture, and we also passed through a few interesting towns that each had small food stands lining the road. We stopped in the first town and got some honey and bread from a stall where they were cooking the bread in an enormous wood-fired oven, and in the next, I stopped and grabbed a nice cold coconut. I'd needed to stop and meet the support van anyway because I'd needed a new battery. The hills we were coming across were eating up more power than I'd used in the last couple weeks.

All told, our first day back on the highway after the storm delay turned into a wonderful day, one of those days where you feel the satisfaction of your leg muscles working, you hear the wind whistling through your helmet straps as you fly down the road, and you smell all the nature surrounding you. I even got my quota of new friends stopping us and wanting to chat and take pictures.

The first fellow who stopped us took some videos and photos, and after we'd chatted for quite a while, asked if he could say a prayer for us, which he did after I agreed. Then, where we'd stopped for a couple coconuts, we learned the fellow working there had spent some time in both Chicago and the town where Kyle lives, so they had quite a chat about Chicago and Chicago pizza and such. Later on, we stopped to ask directions from a guy on a bicycle, and we discovered he had spent many years in Oceanside, California, where we had just ridden through not long ago and where I'd spent two winters with Beth. Every meeting that day once proved to me just how small the world is.

Suddenly, it was time to meet Wayne. After a quick stopover in La Cruz, I enjoyed a nice balmy day riding beside the coast headed south to Mazatlán on the free road. I'll apologize now because that day's ride was so pleasant, I completely forgot to take notes. I just soaked it all in and appreciated that we hadn't encountered any of the usual obstacles: no bad weather, no tough climbing, no annoying bugs, no zooming traffic, no flat tires, or dead batteries.

So, I'll jump ahead a little bit, but only a short bit. Nothing to write home about must have occurred between La Cruz and Rosamorada if I hadn't taken notes and don't remember it. All I remember is that I enjoyed my first day's ride with Wayne again and that we veered away from the coast after Mazatlán.

We, of course, took the free road again for the next few days until just before Rincon del Verde so we could stop for the night in an Airbnb in Escuinapa. Then it was the crazy toll road again the next day until just after Tecualilla. We held our breath and kept our eyes and ears open on that bit of road, especially after Wayne's close calls. After gratefully leaving it and taking a few relaxing breaths, we zipped past only a few towns but did experience Roca Cthulhu, or Cthulhu Rock, a rather interesting peak jutting into the sky like a sleeping giant's chin. We rode through a few more scattered little towns and skirted a small desert area, and before we knew it, we were at the Sinaloa/Nayarit border. That was our cue that we were not only getting close to a nice long stretch of rest days, but also Thanksgiving.

We stopped that night in Rosamorada, and both the humidity and the iguana population were increasing. What humidity there was didn't bother me much after living in Costa Rica the previous few years, but it was starting to become apparent that it might be bothering Wayne. It was either that or the heat, maybe both. It still hovered around 30 or 32°C most days, and the last time Wayne had ridden with us it had been a bit cooler since he'd left us before the desert.

More and more hills rose ahead of us, and it was beginning to take a bit more effort, but the climbing wasn't yet comparable to our time in the redwoods. The sky was clear, and the sun beamed down on us every day. What a difference from our Canadian and US legs! Despite the temperatures and the increased climbing, I quite enjoyed riding that day. In my effort to take the shortest route to Puerto Vallarta in a couple days, we had to ride on the toll road until Tuxpan, after which Google Maps directed us down a side road through a few smaller towns. I appreciated the opportunity to see more the authentic Mexico, and it gave me the chance to talk to some more locals when we stopped for a snack or hydration, or of course when we got flagged down.

A so-called road Google told us to use

That was where my appreciation for Google Maps ended. It was somewhere in that area that it started leading me down not side roads, but backroads. At times, I wasn't even sure you could call it a road. Nevertheless, after a brief lunch in Santiago Ixcuintla, we pushed on through more little communities—San Manuel, Sauta, La Guinea, and El Vado before reaching Navarrete. Ahead of us were more than just rolling hills; there were peaks looming, taunting us.

As if to thumb our noses at them though, we turned west toward the coast and San Blas. That way, we could follow the coast on some smaller, less traveled highways all the way to Puerto Vallarta. Yiota lived her best life on that strip, zipping at power level three on the second e-bike around me and Wayne as we puttered along like steady tortoises. She lifted my spirits though, her energy and positivity, especially every time we came across a Google-Maps-directed Road and it was nothing more than dirt and rock, or worse yet, washed out after the hurricane.

Despite taking the scenic route though, we made it to San Blas when the sun was low on the horizon, riding past the gorgeous, wide beaches and among the palm trees. Unfortunately, I was a bit dismayed when we got to the hotel. Talk about a crappy hotel. I mean, it wasn't terrible. It's not as though it were a hovel or anything, but it was small and dirty and rundown. The whole reason we ended up there though was because it was the only hotel in town.

Anyway, we nabbed three rooms at $20 each a night. At least I hadn't had to pay through the nose for something like that. It was a place to lay our heads. I let my disappointment go and we dropped off our stuff, freshened up, and headed off to find some dinner. As I'd expected, and hoped, we ate at another taco stand that night. They never disappoint!

***

The next day, we rode south beside the coast again before dipping inland in a bit of a slingshot maneuver given the lack of roads in the area. After another riding day rather identical to the few before, we had to earn our rest for the night. We'd decided to camp that night, and as we neared the campground, we discovered we had about a kilometer of cobblestones to ride over to get there. Had it not been so late I might have looked elsewhere, but in the end, we decided to tough it out. Let me tell you, it just shook the hell out of the bike. I lost a bolt off my bike rack for my efforts with all the vibration, and Wayne lost the mirror off his glasses and the light off his handlebars. Pieces of my phone even fell loose!

But boy, was that campground a hidden oasis. It sat right beside the ocean and included a hotel and cozy restaurant with a patio overlooking the ocean. As we rode in and off the cobblestones, it was impossible to tear our eyes away from the blazing sunset over the water. All the violets, crimsons, tangerines, and golds of every sunset you've ever thought were incredible were on full display. I've never seen one better. We stood there for a bit, letting the ocean breeze cool us off as we absorbed the beauty of the place. If you've ever pictured a tropical getaway, this was definitely the image in your mind.

That campground made me remember why I love camping. There's just something about being surrounded by nature and away from the sounds and smells and sights of people. We hadn't camped in quite some time; we'd been spending lots of the coupons from Airbnb instead. The immaculate lawns, the well-cared for palms, and the glistening pool only added to the sublime appeal of the place.

And here again, we were shown just how small the world is. Kyle, our content creator, saw some sort of incredible overlander rig from Europe that costs somewhere around $250,000 USD on YouTube last winter. It looks just like a military-type vehicle complete with monster tires and a sunroof, only people use it like we use RVs here. Anyway, we come around a corner as we were walking through the campground, and wouldn't you know? *Bam!* There it was, randomly parked right there in our campground in Mexico. Kyle was dumbfounded. Wayne and I weren't sure why you'd need that luxury though. I mean, we were touring through Mexico and more with only a Dodge Caravan and a tent trailer!

We had a wonderful dinner that night and a good rest and took off the next morning, bound finally for Puerto Vallarta and an Airbnb that night. After stopping at a fruit stand for some bananas, we rode with more energy and optimism than we had in a few days, with more rest days just waiting for us. I even got to feel like a bit of a star again when a reporter for a digital publication stopped me and wanted an interview, on the spot!

It may sound like we enjoyed a pleasant riding day that day, but no. It was a long, tedious day. Traffic was heavy all the way in, but at least the drivers were friendly and somewhat cautious, and people were still honking and shouting, "Congratulations!" out their windows, and waving at us and stuff.

On top of all that noisy, slow riding, Wayne stopped what felt like a hundred times that day to take a break and rehydrate. Granted, we'd done a lot of climbing—about 1,500 meters, which isn't unusual—and the humidity had increased again, but it was starting to drive me a little crazy by the time the sun started sinking. All that stopping had put us quite far behind that day. Riding in the dark is never ideal, so I can get a bit irritated when we must do that.

But what good would getting upset have done? That's my usual motto. And to say we all just wanted to get to Puerto Vallarta—technically Bucerias, just north of Puerto Vallarta—and be done was an understatement. So, we turned on our head and taillights and pulled out everything we had left in us to finish that climb and get to our Airbnb.

It was much later than usual when we arrived at our rental that night, around 7 p.m., and it was dark. We had managed to find it in the dark, but we found ourselves standing at the gate of the condo complex waiting for someone to come let us in. We waited. And we waited some more. No one would help us. We waited some more. Finally, a woman told us to go to another gate we'd had no idea existed. We were all absolutely annoyed by then, but around to the other gate we went.

Boy did that change as soon as we got through that second gate into the complex and saw what awaited us. My entire view was filled with a huge private pool, lush lawns, and tons of patio furniture filling the outdoor living/kitchen underneath a giant palapa. Without hesitation, we ran and jumped into that pool, clothes and all!

After we'd cooled off and eased the pressure, we went to go look inside the condo. It was a mansion. It had five bedrooms, six bathrooms, a cavernous kitchen, an even bigger living area, entertainment nooks with giant TVs, and air conditioning everywhere. We got a taste in that moment of how the other half must live. The best part was the price had been reasonable. I'd had an Airbnb coupon for $400 and spent $300 out of pocket, so really, we got that little piece of paradise for only $700 total for three nights. It even had daily maid service! We were all looking forward to our three-night, two-day stay there. I thought we'd earned it too because when we left, we'd be heading high up into the mountains to reach Guadalajara and Mexico City. It felt much like we'd reached another milestone. We capped off the day with three large pizzas and a bunch of beer! It was incredible, and surprising, to see how just pulling up to a glorious Airbnb could make people so happy so fast.

That weekend was Thanksgiving for us, so I'd arranged for Gloria to fly in on our first day there. She was landing in Puerto Vallarta of course, so I'd also booked her and Johana a room in a nice four-star hotel for the night. Johana hopped on a bus to go meet her sister on the afternoon of our first rest day while I did an interview with a senior-living podcast that Airbnb had previously arranged and had already been canceled two or three times. To me, it was integral to get my message out. That ride had been all about getting seniors active, physically, and mentally. Anyway, I unfortunately hadn't realized the hotel I'd booked for the sisters wasn't quite in Puerto Vallarta, so they were rather upset with me, despite the hotel being four-star. *C'est la vie* huh?

I made up for my error later in the weekend though. Gloria had never been to Puerto Vallarta before, hence the reason she'd been a little upset about not staying in the city. In fact, no one on the team had ever been there before, so I enjoyed showing everyone around Puerto Vallarta during our rest days because I'd spent a couple winters there with Beth.

Our second rest day was Thanksgiving. Gloria and Johana had rolled in late the night before, so they were a little on the sleepy side. The entire team looked to be rather sleepy and lazy that day too. We all slept in and just hung around for a few hours. By the time 4 p.m. rolled around and no one had done anything, mentioned doing anything, or had accomplished anything, I announced I was going to take the car and take Gloria for a nice late lunch in town.

Well ask me how that went over. Of course, the response was, "Well, what about us?"

"Well, what about you?" was my rebuttal.

They chose that moment to mention that they had to go get groceries, and I just shook my head. Someone couldn't have said something earlier that day. So, I said, "You've had all day to that. Why is it that now you decide you need to do that?" When I was met with silence, I relented. "I'll take two of you with us and drop you off at the grocery store. Then you can buy the groceries and take a cab back."

That seemed an acceptable compromise, so we did just that, and then Gloria and I went and found an excellent restaurant. The place was packed full of Canadians and Americans, the Canadians enjoying their Thanksgiving dinners, and the Americans using the Canadian holiday as an excuse to party. It made for a festive atmosphere, so Gloria and I had a delightful time. It was one of those rare times it was nice to dip back into old Canadian traditions. Like most Canadian families, we also had turkey and all the fixings at Thanksgiving, but turkey is hard to come by in Costa Rica, so I hadn't had any in a long time. Turkey and the trimmings and apple pie are probably my favorite nostalgic food, so I eat it any chance I get.

After dinner, we walked off the food as we wandered around town and checked out the main square before heading back to the house for the evening. As we walked, I marveled at how much the town had grown since Beth and I had wintered here. There were many, many more restaurants, towering high-rise condos, and a bunch of fancy stores that just hadn't existed all those years ago. The town still managed to retain its quaint, old-world charm but not the small-town vibe it once had.

The next day, I had to get the van serviced, so I took it into Puerto Vallarta to get the oil changed, filter changed, tires rotated, and all the fluids topped up. While we waited, I took the opportunity to show everyone around. We walked along the Malecon, stopped and ordered a nice lunch beside it, then went back to get the van. That night, we just sat around the condo, relaxing and enjoying the beautiful evening and our surroundings. The beautiful Puerto Vallarta weather didn't disappoint either. Its famed constant sunshine and perfect temperatures didn't falter during our entire stay.

Before I knew it, our mini vacation was over, and it was time to hit the trail again. Unfortunately, the day didn't begin in the best fashion as we forgot we were in a different time zone, and Gloria almost missed her 8 a.m. flight. Then it took far too long to get packed up and get started, but once I'd packed up my gear, bid adieu to my wife, and climbed back on my bike, my mood improved. I love the feeling of getting back on the bike again after a few days off. In a weird sort of way, it's kind of like coming home. It's where I always know I belong, and I always have something new to look forward to and experience.

After that long rest, I was full of energy as I began to pedal and heard the buzz of my motor. Adrenaline and excitement for the next leg of the odyssey pulsed through my veins, and I took a deep breath as we started out for Mascota. I couldn't wait to experience Mascota again. I'd been looking forward to the quaintness of it.

Why does fate or karma or whatever always work the way it does? Just when you think things are going great, they fall apart. In this case, our day really started to go down the tubes early on. When we'd started out on our route that morning, it hadn't seemed as though it would be all that tough, just a 97 km day with a couple thousand meters of climbing. Both Wayne and I were riding the e-bikes, so we weren't too worried about that much climbing. But when we got maybe fourteen, fifteen kilometers into our ride, Google Maps did its thing again. It directed us to a washed-out road. It even looked as though the road we needed to take across the river didn't even exist anymore, leaving us with no way of crossing the river. And it was a fairly large, rapidly flowing river. When a local truck driver came along, we asked him what happened, and he told us that that particular crossing had gotten washed out about two or three months earlier.

Well, that settled that. Frustrated, we had to turn around and head all the way back the way we'd come, back into Puerto Vallarta and all the traffic. To top it off, in Puerto Vallarta, you can't make a left turn from the left lane. You must get in the right lane and turn left to cross the road at a ninety-degree angle, and only in marked areas. And of course, there are very few of those, so it took us a really long time to make the necessary U-turn to get back to our starting point and head out of town on a new road.

Finally, after heavy traffic, car fumes, and cobblestone roads, we started our journey up into the mountains. And for a while, it was a lovely day and a lovely ride, with green-carpeted mountains to ride through, plenty of sunshine, and even a lone mule tied to a tree and watching the world go by. And I can't forget to mention the agave farms we passed as we rode down that pleasant road. Thankfully, we didn't have much traffic anymore, and the road was smooth. We even ended up with lots of shade and cooler temperatures as we started climbing.

Our earlier backtracking had drained our batteries, so as Wayne and I were riding up a mountain, we got stuck halfway up with no power left. The higher up we went, the lower the batteries became. It hadn't helped that the new route we'd had to take had included almost nothing but climbing. And then things went from bad to worse. When our battery power got down to about 20 percent, I went to text the support team, to tell them that we needed new batteries, only to find out we had no cell connection in the mountains, so we couldn't communicate with them, not to give them our location or tell them what we needed. I felt like I was in Yukon again. Wayne and I were stuck waiting on the side of the road hoping the support team would realize before long that they hadn't seen or heard from us in a while. We'd only had fifty kilometers more to ride that day, but twenty-five of that was uphill.

Wayne and I sat there for a good hour without any sign of the team. So, there we were, Wayne and I, sitting on the side of road, Wayne resting on a rock in the shade on one side and me on the other, sitting on the curb. We waited and waited, and I got crankier and crankier. As time ticked on and it became one in the afternoon, we started getting hungry too. Had we been able to take the first, washed-out road, we could simply have crossed a bridge and ridden into a little town just in time to have some lunch—and without as much climbing. But now we were stuck with no supplies.

Finally, almost two hours later, the support van pulled up. It turned out they'd had an issue too, and with no cell service, had been unable to contact us. In their case, it had been a flat tire. I guess it had been unfixable too because they'd had to take it in and get it replaced with a new one.

Well, we switched out the batteries on the bikes and started climbing again. My excitement had fizzled, and my adrenaline was gone. All I had left was the sheer determination to get through the last of the day and all the climbing. I had to run my record-breaking goal around and around in my head to remind myself of why I was doing this. As I did that, I remembered that I wasn't just trying to break a world record, I was trying to motivate seniors, I was trying to inspire people, and I was raising money to buy presents for children in Panama. Let me just tell you how much all that motivated me in the end.

So, after almost three thousand meters of climbing, we finally hit Mascota. It was an absolutely magical town and our first break from the heat in weeks. Old-world architecture lined the cobblestone roads, and a magnificent church towered over the town. I took it all in as we made our way to our cute little hotel with its brick posts and stone stairs. As the sun set red, turning the sky to fire, I decided we'd earned a nice dinner. It had been a long, hard, frustrating day for everyone.

I scouted out a charming restaurant not far from the church with dark, natural-wood beams on the roof, hardwood decor, and those colorful Mexican accents I love so much. Of course, later, I realized I should have chosen a place called Sonia's. It had a bicycle adorning its wall directly above the sign, so hey, maybe I would have gotten a discount if I'd brought in my sign. It could have been worth a shot!

***

The next day the skies were clear once again, and luck was finally with us. By that, I mean we enjoyed a pleasant, uneventful ride all the way to Ameca. We passed through some quaint little towns, a couple rough-looking ones, and stopped for lunch at a lovely restaurant somewhere around Atenguillo built of clay tiles and brick and with an unobstructed view of the verdant mountains. Those mountains might have made for tough riding at times, but they were something else to look at.

*A typical Mexican welcome sign, all far more beautiful
than those in Canada*

The rest of the day was, well, normal. We came across a sign warning us of panthers, though we saw none. However, there were bunnies everywhere. The mountains were pockmarked with tiny farms here and there, and most towns we came across boasted a welcome sign, shaped and decorated with that colorful Mexican flair and flanked by shrines or Catholic images.

Again though, once we got into the city, we had to ride on more cobblestone roads, but we followed them eventually to a decent, typical Spanish-style hotel. After freshening up, we all jumped in the van to head downtown and check out Ameca's church, where we snapped some fantastic photos of the church lit up at night. Then we had a wonderful meal at a place called Iggor. We enjoyed our meal on a balcony overlooking the city's central park before heading back to the hotel to get some sleep.

***

Would you believe it? We got an enjoyable, nothing-bad-happened ride the next day too—except those darn cobblestone roads of course. We stopped in San Martin de Hidalgo for our midmorning break and took a quick tour of another breathtaking church, this one bright white and framed in blue. On the way out of town, we were treated to some creative modern-art structures, from a mural-covered concrete guitar to a colorful iguana on the side of a lighthouse to an industrial-type installation of orange and gray complete with a stack of enormous gears.

As we rode into Ajijic late that afternoon, the view took my breath away. Thousands of Canadians and Americans spend their winters there, and I could see why. Not only is it a beautiful city full of color, but it oozes charm and sits on the shores of Lake Chapala. When we arrived at our Airbnb, I couldn't believe my luck again. That five-star Airbnb was large and bright and had a classic brick-domed roof in the living area. The patio doors and backyard even looked out over the lake. We all had to tear our gazes away from the view to go eat dinner. The house and the view were simply stunning. But we were starving, so we drove into Ajijic and had supper at a little restaurant on the waterfront before taking a short walk down the Malecon at the water's edge as the sun set. Most of the buildings, regardless of the plainness of their structure, were adorned with brightly painted murals of such uniqueness, such creativity, it's rather impossible to describe. Punctuated as all that was with the beautiful sculptures and dozens of little fishing boats bobbing on the water's edge of course, we found ourselves taking far more photos than we'd meant to.

It was a good thing we got some much-needed rest in that idyllic Airbnb because we were headed for some rough times.

BUMPS and BRUISES

The next day started off promising, with Yiota riding with Wayne and I as we headed for La Barca. She wasn't in good spirits after receiving the news that her best friend's husband been killed in a motorcycle accident that had been his fault, so she was crying and incredibly upset. I'd told her how sorry I was for her loss when she'd related the story to me and suggested that riding could help. She had been so upset when she'd come to me that morning before we left that she'd been thinking about flying back to Greece for a week to go to the funeral.

Well, the riding did seem to help her feel a little better as we began the day in perfect weather and toured Ajijic's town center, down the Malecon, then up another road to reach the highway that stretched out along the lake. Then we took a break in the town of Chapala to check out the beautiful sights, the church, and the lakefront and to have our usual snack. That's when everything started going wrong.

I'm still not sure why we hadn't learned yet, but we were still using Google Maps, and it started to lead us astray again, this time causing conflict in the team. While it guided us well in the morning as we followed the directions around the lake, things went to pot once we, as a group, overruled one step. Google told us to ride up a mountain, but the road we were already riding on was quite good, so we didn't want to leave it. We decided to ask a local which was the best way to go, and he said to continue in the direction we were headed because the road up the mountain was too steep.

So, after some discussion, I think it was Wayne that made the call to continue on our current trajectory, everything went smoothly for a while. But then suddenly, the paved road ended. We were facing a single-lane road with two paved tracks for vehicles surrounded by more cobblestone. With no other option available, we had no choice but to continue down that road. It wasn't terrible for Yiota, and I give we had shock absorbers and wide tires, but Wayne had a logically tougher time, as strong a climber as he is. We pressed on down that bumpy road until we reached a little town on the lake called San Nicolas de Ibarra, where we caught the attention of a bunch of local children. Then we came upon a wedding, so we took a much-needed break and watched the wedding and admired all the decorations.

I also stopped into a hardware store because the constant pounding of the potholes, rough roads, and the cobblestone streets had broken my rack in two places, resulting in the need for some new couplers. I ended up getting some hose-connection type couplers used for plumbing because that was the best I could find. Surprisingly, they worked, and they continued to work later.

It was there Wayne correctly decided to put his bicycle in the car and drive up the hill we were about to tackle. Yiota and I continued though. And we had a pretty good ride too on cement pathways meant only for car tires, though they gave way every now and then to cobblestones. It was even rougher in some places, with washed-out potholes or cobblestones, but it didn't last for long stretches. However, we did end up with some serious climbs where I had to use all my body power and battery power to get to the top. Fortunately, they weren't long hills, and despite the required effort, Yiota had a really good time. She loved the scenery as we followed the edge of the lake atop the cliffs, and she loved going through the towns and saying "Hi" to all the kids. I was pretty sure it helped ease her sadness, and she couldn't stew and contemplate the loss of a good friend.

Eventually, we made it to La Barca around 6:30 p.m., which was later than I'd have liked, but it wasn't completely dark yet. I let Kyle and Johana pick the hotel that night, and I had to bite my tongue when I saw the cost. It was $42 for two rooms. At least the rooms were clean, the bed was soft, and there was plenty of hot water. It was actually a funky hotel. To get in, you had to go to the parking garage, then crawl through a tunnel carved into the old building. The tunnel was only about three feet high, so of course I bumped my head. We found out later that during the pandemic, the owner had had a bunch of artists paint murals and such on all the walls. The ended with dinner at a restaurant just a short walk away, where we had not just tacos this time, but also baked potatoes with melted cheese. I hadn't had a potato in a long time, so I really savored it.

***

We got a pretty good start the next morning, around 8:30 or 8:45 a.m. But again, we ran into the same problem as we had the previous few days after just a couple hours of riding. Google Maps directed us onto a gravel road, so then we had to make a decision again, which of course cost us time as we debated the options back and forth, putting us behind schedule yet again. In hindsight, we should just have concluded that we should always take the pavement even if the riding distance was farther because we were always going to waste time and energy riding on a dirt, gravel, or cobblestone road. However, we did not, and the day continued to go on that way. So, a day that was only supposed to have been 120 km of riding turned into about 160 km as we tried to work our way through it with Google Maps. It felt like we spent more time looking at our phones trying to figure out the best route than we did riding. And that made it nigh on impossible to enjoy any of the scenery or culture, but I appreciated what I could when I could.

As Yiota and I rode under partly sunny skies in comfortable temperatures, we passed so many blue agave plants everywhere that it felt as though there were lakes all around us, and in among those agave farms were corn crops and even chicken farms. Only the chickens in Mexico don't have coops and such like they do in Canada. Here, they have two concrete slabs resting against each other in a tent formation, and hundreds of those dotted the landscape.

Once, we went through a beautiful, verdant valley and came upon huge, what I call tequila plantations. Every store we passed in the area, no matter how big or small or what else they sold, advertised, and sold tequila. The day had been so rough from so early on, we took a break in the first small town we encountered that day. We took in the Sunday market with its many colorful stalls set up around the church square and stopped for a cup of coffee, where I spoke to one young girl who spoke English. She'd learned it in school, and I got her to follow our odyssey on Instagram and TikTok. Afterward, three young boys ran up to me and gave me some string necklaces with the Virgin Mary on one end and Jesus on the other. That stop later reminded us that the Day of the Dead was close, so when we took a break after another long climb, Kyle and Johana decorated the tent trailer with flags and banners in all the colors of the rainbow. Thank goodness for moments like those to take some of the stress out of a day.

Strangely, we managed to make it to our tiny Airbnb in San Francisco de Rincon before dark. I'm still not sure how we did it, but we did. But that meant we'd made it to Guanajuato State. The city, we discovered, was rather large, and it had some nice bike paths to ride on. Sadly though, our Airbnb looked like it was located in a bit of a sketchy neighborhood, and there was only one parking spot so we were forced to leave the tent trailer parked on the street. I did not feel good about that. But, once we'd gotten settled, we went off in search of our sustenance for the evening. After taking a little walk around the neighborhood, we discovered that a neighbor was selling tamales, so that was dinner that night. No one had the energy to go to a restaurant, or even to try and find a taco stand.

That turned out to be fortuitous though because those tamales were delicious. So good in fact, that we asked her to make us breakfast too. Both the tamales and breakfast were only $5 a person, so that was fabulous deal. That's another thing I love about Mexico: delicious food without paying through the nose.

We went to bed early that night after everything we'd been through that day. I had an inkling that the coming days might be about the same, so I had to give Wayne's suggestions some thought. One idea was to pick a distance and a road and stay in whatever town we end up in rather than sticking to the schedule. But sticking to the schedule meant I got to see the towns I'd originally plotted, so I didn't much like that idea. It would just turn the ride into a "ride as fast as you can on the best road you can" thing. And though that day had been a disaster, we had discovered some cute towns, experienced some great scenery, and gotten some good climbs in. I did, however, agree that it wasn't fun getting in late at night, being constantly tired, and still being tired when we leave the next morning.

Wayne's other suggestion was that we take an unscheduled rest day the next day, and that was the way I was leaning. I didn't want to create or continue the conflict by being difficult. As much as I loved seeing more new places, I was comfortable giving a few up to keep the distance we rode in a day to a hundred kilometers or less, making the days shorter for Wayne. If it had been just me on my e-bike though, I would just have cranked it up, gotten the distances done in a lot less time, and visited the new towns.

***

In the morning, we woke up to find that the battery on the tent trailer and the propane tank had been stolen. What a pain. But at least that's all that had been taken. We'd only camped four times in Mexico by then simply because Airbnb's and hotels were so cheap. The worst-case scenario in my mind was that we might need to buy a propane tank somewhere along the way if it turned out we had to camp in Central America.

While it had been tempting to take an additional rest day there after our hard day, we decided during the delightful breakfast our neighbor brought us that we would push on for one more day. We were due to hit Guanajuato that day, and that brought with it a couple rest days. So, we hit the road again, and it was a good thing we did because we saw some interesting sights that day—and rode on nice, paved streets and bike paths. After we stopped for coffee at a place very Starbucks-like in decor, we discovered a sort of Mexican Disneyworld. We didn't stop to determine which one it was, but it was something you certainly don't see every day. Again, that's what I love about long-distance touring: there's something new around every bend in the road.

The Mexican amusement park we discovered.

Every town we rode through was decorated with brightly colored flags called *papel picados*, and an anticipatory excitement filled the air. We saw a modern university, stopped to watch some training equestrians, and discovered a giant bronze head on a pedestal atop some circular stairs. It did have a plaque, but I speak no Spanish really, so I couldn't tell you who it was.

Suddenly, we crested another peak, and Guanajuato appeared, a bustling city nestled in a valley at the foot of a craggy mountain range. From our vantage point, one peak looked much like a chimney, but if you turned your head just a little, you could make out a sleeping giant with a bit of a pot belly. Riding down into the city, I was anxious to get to our Airbnb because the noise and the fumes of the heavy traffic on the highway we'd had no choice but to take had given me a headache.

Yet as we rode deeper into the city and I saw the old-world architecture and the houses painted in blues and yellows and pinks, the happier I felt. That was my fourth time in Guanajuato, and I'd always loved its vividness and culture, all surrounded by the natural beauty of the mountains.

Then we arrived at our Airbnb, and I was immediately taken by its charm. I later learned it was about a hundred years old, but it was in good shape. A huge hardwood door surrounded by stone columns greeted us, and a wrought-iron balcony loomed above it. The interior too was enormous, and three types of flooring had it oozing personality. A monstrous, natural-wood dining table with blue wooden chairs filled the center of the space, and more iron balconies and unique doors scattered throughout the place threw me back in time to old Mexican culture. Strangely, a black-and-white photo of Marilyn Monroe on an easel filled one corner of the living room, but I guess it meant something to someone and gave the place yet more uniqueness. Granted, a few places could have used a little tender loving care, but it was still a perfect situation to find ourselves in. And get this: it was right beside an actual castle!

A real-life castle beside our Airbnb.

We sure took advantage of that great big dining table. Yiota made us a fantastic Greek spaghetti-lasagna type of dish, and we had some wine and margaritas and lots of good, much-needed laughs. It hadn't been a long day really, but it hadn't been a good day either. But now we could all rest the next few days, recuperate, and prepare for the next stretch. We'd concluded by then that we would put more time into double-checking the roads Google Maps gave us to ensure they were okay for bikes. So even if that meant riding farther, we'd make sure there were no more cobblestones or tiny dirt trails.

The next morning, Johana and Kyle set off to see some mummies. I heard something about them being naturally mummified during a cholera outbreak. But that didn't pique my interest much. I much preferred walking around the city, taking a vernacular up the mountain, and trying to get some colorful photos. Towns like Guanajuato that exude culture and history almost seem to whisper their stories if you just listen close enough.

Kyle and Johana weren't back by the time I was, so I took the opportunity to do some work on my bike. I got incredibly lucky and found a place that offered good but cheap service, compared to the US and Canada anyway, and they even came to the house to do the work. They changed the brake pads and examined the whole bike for only $25 US. *Excellent*, I thought.

When Kyle and Johana returned from their adventure, we all scouted out another great place for dinner and retired for the night. After a relaxing breakfast, I wandered into town again and happened upon an adrenaline-inducing car race. Then I got a message from a friend that his friend in Australia had seen a small snippet about my Octogenarian Odyssey. I was flabbergasted. How those news agencies were picking my story up, especially in Australia, I did not know. That wasn't even the first time that had happened; people had stopped me periodically throughout our journey to say, "Hey, we saw you on TV last night." But that news report was definitely the farthest away. But hey, not only was it nice to have my fifteen minutes of fame, but it also meant more people might see my message. Maybe I could encourage more than a few people to get active, to try something new, to live life fully. And I sure wouldn't mind if it helped us raise more money for the kids in Panama.

***

I almost turned around and went back to bed the next morning. Part of me really wanted that original second rest day when I saw how foggy and cloudy and windy it was. But, after a hot breakfast and a cup of coffee, I was ready to go. How could I deny the call of adventure just because of a little cold? Besides, there was the world record to think about. So, I packed up and threw on a long-sleeved jersey and a jacket thinking that would be enough.

We set out then on what we knew would be a hefty climb out of Guanajuato given the descent coming in, but I truly hadn't known we were going to have to huff up eleven kilometers, six hundred meters of which turned out to be one continuous climb. You'd think that would keep me warm as the temperatures continued to plummet the higher, we got, but think again. All that effort created an equal amount of perspiration. Combine that with falling temperatures and strengthening winds, and you have a recipe for misery.

Initially, the blood pumping through my body kept me warm, but as the wind started seeping through the seams of my jacket and we neared 300 meters in elevation, the clouds descended, and we were wrapped in a blanket of thick moisture. Eventually, I hit a point where I just couldn't take it anymore. The temperature was still dropping, making me wonder when it was ever going to end. I needed to get out of that cold and wet. To our detriment, there were no towns on that stretch of the route, not a little restaurant or diner, not even a single enclosed building in which to take shelter. I lost track of the number of times I admonished myself for not putting on more than a long-sleeved shirt and jacket.

But the three of us climbed on—Yiota, Wayne, and me—hoping and praying something would appear around the next bend. Finally, we stopped and had a little huddle to try and figure out what we should do. We really couldn't go any farther. Our tanks were empty, and willpower gone. Then I heard a dog barking in the distance. Normally I don't like dogs barking. Often that means the potential for trouble. But in this case, it meant there must be people who owned that dog, and those people must live in a house. And if there was a house, then that must mean there was somewhere, anywhere, that we could seek shelter.

We were right. That barking dog led us right to a town. It was only two kilometers away, and as we rode like the wind to reach it, we discovered a sign proclaiming, "Restaurant." And lo and behold, we found a little restaurant on a bumpy dirty road that turned out to be quite a nice place. We ran inside, and though it was still chilly because the building wasn't heated, it was still a lot warmer than it was out in the wind and the rain. It was only 3°C out there, in Mexico of all places—in the summer! Even in Yukon in the wind and rain, it still never got below six or seven degrees. Who knew we would get our coldest day in what I'd thought would be one of the hottest countries? Anyway, the proprietor brought us all a big bowl of hot, homemade chicken soup and a steaming cup of Mexican coffee with cinnamon. That was exactly what we needed right then.

Anyway, we stayed about an hour hoping our support van would show up so we could get some more clothes to put on because we faced another problem now that we were nearing the summit. We had a huge downhill ahead of us, and of course when you're going downhill quickly, you create a lot of wind just with your speed. That would make it awfully cold. But since the support van hadn't shown up, we sucked it up and decided we better head out. Thankfully, the owner said we only had a little more hills left to climb.

So, we buttoned up and headed out, and sure enough, we reached the summit in just two hundred meters. Then we started downhill, wondering how we were going to keep warm. I had nothing more than my warmer shirt, riding shorts, and sandals on. My bare legs were freezing! My solution was to put the bike in a low gear so I could pedal faster, descent or no descent, to keep my legs warm. Then I alternated putting my hands in my pockets.

Then we discovered the joke was on us. No sooner did we start our descent than restaurant upon restaurant appeared. If we had just gone another two hundred meters to the top, we could have found as many restaurants as we wanted. Ah well, I thought. We'd gotten what we needed when we'd needed it most. So, we tackled our huge descent, flying down the whole distance we'd climbed and more. And what happens when you get to a lower elevation? Of course, the temperature goes up.

Thankfully, we were able to warm themselves up then, and as we did, we found the magical town of Delores-Hidalgo, where they make the pottery that you usually associate with Mexico, like those white and blue dishes and the multicolored mosaic plates and tiles and such. Turns out the town is 312 years old. That's older than most Canadian towns. We took a break, strolling through a park and chatting with some young people who wanted to know what we were doing riding through town. As we wandered, we took some photos of another historic, majestic church and watched a funeral procession, complete with a Mariachi band. We even met a nice couple from Whitehorse, Yukon, who live there now and run an Airbnb. Then I made a quick stop in a hidden little bike shop to get my new brake pads filed down.

Rested, refreshed, and finally warm, we moved on to San Miguel de Allende, a charming and friendly city popular with Canadian and American retirees whose historic district is a UNESCO World Heritage Site. We didn't get in until quite late, mainly due to that stop at the top of the mountain to get warm and visiting Dolores-Hidalgo. But we spent the night in a comfortable, clean condo in a beautiful complex with lots of security. Johana put together her famous chicken and molé recipe, which was fantastic. When you're in Mexico, eating molé is just one of those treats you have to experience. True molé in fact takes days to make. I know I was certainly looking forward to reaching Oaxaca, whose molé I'm sure is world famous.

***

San Miguel de Allende architecture

While we still had to make our stop before the sun went down the next day, I'd planned to take a side trip of about five kilometers into the old San Miguel historic district. I wanted everybody to see the square, the church, the colors along the streets, the intricate detailing of the old-world architecture, the stonework. On a trip like this, we don't usually have a lot of time to spend exploring the towns, but I felt it was important that we took a few minutes to do that there. Otherwise, we were kind of just window shopping through Mexico. We were just riding through the towns and gazing at what was going on around us, not getting much in-depth exploration.

After the tour, everyone said they thought San Miguel was wonderful. Yiota said she wanted to go back, and Kyle said he was going to put it on his list, along with Guanajuato and some other places, of places that he wanted to come back and visit again. The time that short side trip had taken had been worth it. After a quick snack, we set off riding in blue skies and sunshine along a highway with a good shoulder. Suddenly, only thirty kilometers or so out, Wayne said, "Oh look. There's another magical town. Let's go look at it." So, of course into town we went, though I couldn't tell you which town it was. We checked out the church, stopped for a coffee at the local OXXO, which is on almost every corner down here like our 7-11s up north, then moved on.

Then we came to a large city of 300,000 people called Celaya. We were originally just going to ride right through there, especially given our previous two side trips that day. Heck, we weren't even going to stop. But then we found ourselves riding on a beautiful bike path, a bicycle highway really, in the center of town, so I asked Wayne if he wanted to go check out the churches, one of which had a door—and a plaque upon that—commemorating something dating a long way back. Anyway, off we went!

While we only took a few minutes on that pit stop, as we were getting back on track, the—by then—normal thing happened, and somebody honked and stopped in front of us. They wanted to talk, and I always stop and indulge them— okay, I indulge myself. Whenever that happened, Wayne continued on, and I just caught up later. It was easy to do with my trusty e-bike. This time though, this person had an awful lot to say, and because I wasn't quite understanding what he was saying, I wasn't entirely sure how to end the conversation. I was watching the time tick by as he said something about the president and stuff, and wondering how I could politely slide out of the situation.

Eventually, a woman came over, and pretty soon about ten or eleven more people came over, including the assistant mayor and staff from the tourism and media departments. On their heels came another fellow from a cycling club. We took a whole bunch of photos, then they carried my bike into city hall and to the main rotunda where they had a big sign proclaiming, "Celaya." There, while they took yet more photos, I did a couple of short interviews for their tourism department and their local TV channel called Connections Celaya.

Even for me, that took forever to get through. When it was all over and everyone had finally left, I wheeled my bike outside only to find four police motorcycles waiting to escort me out of town and to my support van. Now that was a lot of fun, riding down the highway with two police motorcycles in front of me and two behind, lights on but no sirens. The best part was when we came to lots of traffic like a busy intersection, they would flash their lights, blare their horns, and turn on their sirens. Then we'd just roar through the red lights like I was some kind movie star or Lance Armstrong or the president instead of just a normal person. Kyle was with me too, and he sure looked like he was enjoying the experience. And at the end of that trek, we came to a busy tunnel, and the police stopped all the traffic going in and out of the tunnel, so we had it all to ourselves, Kyle, and me.

Shortly after, we reached the support vehicle, so we said goodbye to the police and thanked them for all their help. By then, it was getting late, and we still had some forty kilometers to go. We needed to get there before dark. So, Kyle and I set off again, and Wayne was still off somewhere on his own. Kyle and I finally made it to Acambaro at 6:30 p.m. It wasn't until we arrived that I realized I'd been so preoccupied with all the fuss that I'd completely overlooked the milestone I'd reached just outside of Celaya. I'd crossed the 10,000 km mark!

Not long after the rest of us got to our hotel, Wayne arrived. He'd taken a different route than we had, plus e-bikes are faster. Once he showed up, we took turns showering and hopped in the car to head to a restaurant to celebrate our 10,000-km milestone. I'd never heard of Acamboro before, but it too turned out to be a charming place, as was our Argentine BBQ restaurant. After we ordered our food—the carnivore plate, beef in a variety of cuts for five people—I discovered Yiota and Johana had phoned ahead and told the restaurant what we were celebrating. So, they gave us a free drink and a little pitcher of sangria to add to the celebration. Then I added a bottle of wine to that, and I always have to have a margarita in Mexico too. And at the end of the meal, the staff brought out a shot glass of their special mezcal that they make in the area for each of us. It had a very different taste I found, a smoky, barnyard type of taste, but it was incredibly good. Oh, and we weren't done yet. Out came dessert for me: a plate of crème brûlée with a towering sparkler candle and "Congratulations on 10,000 km" along the outer edges of the plate—in Spanish. Finally, the night ended with the usual round of photos of the staff and the restaurant. What a night! What a day!

Our spectacular night wasn't even over yet because we'd parked the car near an exquisite church square, where the folks were just winding down for the night. So, we got some photos of the church all lit up and bought some salted pumpkin seeds from the lovely ladies still there. I went back to the hotel with a full belly and a full heart. It had been an excellent day, perhaps the best day.

***

The team celebrated 10,000 km in Acamboro.

From there on, we were looking forward to a fairly quiet country road for a while the next day, which we did indeed get. It was a two-lane highway, but it had little traffic. Besides, it was surrounded by farms nestled at the foot of the mountains, so the scenery made for a relaxing ride despite the rough pavement in one stretch that shook your brain and made your hands numb. Thank goodness for the otherwise pleasant riding conditions because we had 111 km to chew through that day to get to Zitacuaro, and plenty of that was climbing. We did, however, stop for a second breakfast of crepes and coffee at a unique café just off the highway.

The sky was busy and gray again that day, making it a little cooler. Sometimes a little cooler is nice though after you go a few days with the sun beating down on you. A break is nice as long as it doesn't rain. We happened upon a farmer on horseback beside an agave field, a rustic church with a giant monarch butterfly emblazoned on the gates, and an iron monument for the area's laborers.

And then came a moment, a place we still laugh about to this day. Zitacuaro hadn't been on the original itinerary, so we were now finding accommodations on the fly. On this day, we stopped at a hotel. An auto hotel. For those unaware of what these are, they're hotels for people to rent by the hour for sexual encounters, generally illicit, but sometimes people just want a bit of privacy given their families are so large and their homes so small. The hotel is usually hidden behind a wall, and each room often has a place where you can park your car behind a curtain or door so no one driving by will know you're there. They're very common in Mexico and Central America.

On this night, our first time coming across one of these, Yiota felt it wasn't the kind of place we wanted to be, so we decided to push on and see if there was anything else within the next ten kilometers. It was a smart decision in the end because we discovered a gorgeous, old-style hacienda full of antiques we could spend the night at. It was three hundred years old and included 66,800 hectares. It was enormous. The owner told us it wasn't long ago that they used to run five thousand head of cattle and three hundred horses on the property. But then it just got too costly and labor intensive to keep doing so, especially in today's modern super-farm economy, so they'd decided to just turn it into a hotel. He'd only been doing that for six years, so when he said it wasn't long ago the property was full of cattle and horses, he wasn't kidding.

We even enjoyed a delicious chicken dinner with potatoes and rice that night for just $10 a person, plus the owners included a delightful liqueur as we relaxed in their beautiful dining room. It was really quite serendipitous that we'd found this cheap but full-of-character hacienda maybe twenty kilometers outside a town we were supposed to have stayed at. It was just another on a long list of surprises that long-distance cycling can offer. You discover unique sights, meet new people, eat new foods, and learn new things. That's probably one strong reason why I never quit even when I start feeling like I should. I would just miss all that discovery too much.

***

The next day's ride was nothing spectacular, but it wasn't without incident. What should have been 65 km after I rearranged the itinerary to split up another long section of climbing ended up being more like 80 km, again thanks to Google Maps. I'd planned to get into town early, enjoy walking around and exploring, and have a relaxing dinner. But no. Google Maps, Google Bike Maps in particular, had us on a promising road at first until it suddenly turned to dirt. There really wasn't much of a road after that at all, so we had to turn around and backtrack. That road was so full of rocks, there was no way we could just make do. Of course, Google Maps led us astray. It's just not reliable in that part of the world. I might just have to stick to good old paper maps on part two of the odyssey.

Well, after we got back on track, we rode through more quaint towns, one of which had a whole road blocked off for a wedding reception. We rode through avocado groves and prickly pear farms and conquered climbs with grades up to 25 percent. Wayne wisely got off and walked his bike up those. On and on we went in a zig-zag fashion, over the state border into Mexico state, through places like El Aventurero, San Jeronimo Totoltepec, and Donata Guerra without stopping for more than a snack, coffee, or cold one on our mission to get closer to Puebla and our upcoming two rest days. That's not to say we didn't snap the odd photo of more churches or architecture as we passed through a town.

And hey, we got to where we were going with only three flat tires along the way. Can you hear the sarcasm? Two flat tires were on Wayne's bike, caused likely by metal wire or thorns I suspect he encountered on the nasty, un-rideable road Google Maps had taken us to earlier in the day. So, when Wayne got his first flat, we just shrugged and repaired it and got going again. But then a block later, it was flat again, so we stopped, took it apart, and found the second offender. After repairing the hole and putting a new tube in, we carried on.

We continued tackling more crazy steep climbs, and by steep, I mean a cyclist on a normal bike would have to get off and walk—as Wayne did. The electric bikes got us up though. We really had to crank up the assistance level to get to the top of those steep things. Occasionally, we'd stop and rest and appreciate the gorgeous green mountains in the distance, the clouds hovering barely above them, and the itty-bitty towns and farms dotting the landscape below. When we stopped for a quick snack on the side of a road leading us through a forest, I swear it looked like we were in Northern California again, not Southern Mexico. Between the temperature, the elevation, and the enormous pines, I got a little déjà vu. Then Yiota's battery ran out, so we stopped in a tiny town with only one restaurant, but they had some quesadillas and tostadas. Fortuitously, along came our support van and found us even though there was no cell service; they'd found us this time simply by driving the same route.

After lunch, Wayne took off on his road bike, and Yiota and I followed. Not five hundred meters later, I had a sinking feeling I had a flat tire. I pulled over, hopped off the bike, and took a look, hoping I was wrong. Sure, enough though, I had myself a flat tire. Sighing, I got to work pumping up the tire, but I broke the connection. We had to finagle things then to try and get the air in the tire, but we did it. I was anything but confident I'd be able to finish the ride without stopping again because I hadn't found the culprit behind the flat. However, with a slow leak, I could usually keep riding another ten to fifteen kilometers and stop and pump it up again, then repeat that process until I could finally fix it when we got to our accommodations at the end of the day.

But get this. That tire did indeed make it another fifteen kilometers, but when it went flat again, I was right in front of a tire dealership. Does it get any more convenient? So, I pulled in and had them look at it. It took them only a few minutes to find the problem and fix it. Turns out the flat was my fault. I learned that my habit of leaving the top covering of the patch on allows the little particles from the cellophane covering to crystallize over time, and that cuts into the tube causing a leak. Lesson learned. It was a cheap lesson though. They fixed it up for just $2.50 US.

All those climbs logically added up to just one thing in the end: a twenty-kilometer downhill. While it's always nice to get a downhill, on those roads, you had to be observant and use a lot of brake because you didn't want your front wheel to fall in a pothole and send you flying. Still, it was a relief after all that climbing.

Anyway, after six or seven frustrating timewasters that day, on what should have been a short, pleasant ride in fantastic weather, we swooped down and were rewarded with a fantastic view of the lake below us as we arrived in Valle de Bravo. Thankfully, we found our accommodation—another giant Airbnb with five bedrooms, five bathrooms, a huge dining room table and lounge, a swimming pool, and a nice big yard—in short order.

For what had only been eighty kilometers of riding, which was shorter than many days, it had felt like forever before we were done. With the little energy we had left, we stored the bikes, charged the batteries, and looked around the house. It was an intriguing mix of old and new with its natural-wood beams and terracotta tile floor, stone and concrete exterior, and wooden window frames. All the bedrooms even had walk-in closets and showers. Though it was old and not exactly in tip-top shape, it would have been a perfect place for a long stay. A large, covered area beside the pool in the backyard offered respite from the day's stresses, and the dining table was one large slab of wood.

As inviting as that was, we were too tired to cook, so off we went in search of a restaurant. I led us downtown because I'd been there about twenty-five years ago with Beth and really liked the town, so I wanted to be sure I at least saw some of it, no matter how tired I was. My restaurant radar worked again because we found a lovely one off the main road with stairs leading down to a hidden patio around back that sat under the shelter of jungle foliage. We had a delightful dinner that night; Johana, Kyle, and I enjoyed the camarones, while Yiota had steak, and Wayne had pasta.

While were eating, we were told we should go down to the square because it was all lit up for the Day of the Dead, so we wandered down. There was so much activity, with crowds of people out and lots of excitement and life. All around the square were all a multitude of lit-up faces of Katrina, the goddess of death from the Aztec age, and the church was emblazoned in light. The whole scene closely resembled a Canadian Christmas display, only bigger. We took some incredible drone footage, then went back to the big house for some much, much-needed rest.

***

Once again, the next day dawned with a smile, streaming sunshine through the dining room window of our Airbnb. I couldn't help but realize that this cycling tour was far different from most others I'd taken, and vastly different from most tours bike packers experience. This trip had been full of comfortable accommodations, intriguing Airbnb's, luxurious spaces, and tasty food. There was no sleeping on the side of the road or under bridges for us. This trip was an experience like no other, and though it was draining my wallet, I found myself appreciating the difference. I think it allowed me to be even more open to enjoying the experiences and the people.

We were slow getting away that day partly because my knees were sore from the climbing of the day before. But we always knew we were going to face another long climbing day, so we took a little extra time to choose what we thought was the easiest route, hence the other reason we started later than usual. We only had about eighty-five kilometers to achieve that day, but with all the ascents, we decided to stick with the toll roads. Though we preferred the older, free roads for the quieter traffic, ever since entering Mexico, we'd tried to stick to the toll roads because they're better maintained than the secondary highways. And Google Maps can't get those wrong like it does all the other ones, so there was less chance of backtracking.

We hadn't come across any problems accessing the toll roads to that point either. The first time we went on the toll road, the officials even told us to bypass the gate and walk through the ditch to get onto the road, probably so we wouldn't be recorded as a vehicle or something. Since then, we'd just always gone down through the small area beside the toll gates, and nobody had ever said anything or stopped us. Until a few days earlier of course. I don't remember where we were, but we were riding on the toll road as usual, and the official wouldn't let us continue. He did, however, say that if we went back a hundred meters and followed a dirt road, we'd find an opening in the fence, and we could go through there. Well, that what's we did, despite the extra time and effort, and got back on the toll road. I wondered at the time if perhaps he did that because he was being recorded by the powers that be.

On this day as we left Valle de Bravo though, the toll road didn't have any gates to go through, so we just kept riding for maybe twenty kilometers on a beautiful new highway with a big wide shoulder and a gentle grade. It made for wonderful riding. But then along came an official toll-road vehicle, maybe one of those folks that help people with car troubles and such, rolling up beside us. He pulled us over, and over the course of the subsequent discussion, he insisted we couldn't ride on the toll road. I begged and pleaded and pulled out all the tricks I could. I said I was old, that I couldn't do all that extra work, then I told him my e-bike wasn't a bicycle, it was a motor scooter because it had the motor. That one almost worked, but then he finally said, "Nope, I can't let you do that. There are cameras in the van recording this incident." He didn't even give us a different option, so we gave up and turned around. Fortunately, I'd suspected earlier that we might have problems because as we'd ridden up the mountain, we'd seen at least two signs saying, "No Bicycles," so I'd kept track of how we could get off the toll road without going all the way back down. The best option was to go back about fifty meters where the toll road went over a country road and walk down the grassy, bushy embankment to the road below, carrying one bike between two of us and leaving the other bike on the highway before going back for it and carrying it down. Eventually, after exerting tremendous effort, we were on our way again on a country road that no one knew where. Good thing Google Maps decided to be our friend that day. Between it and GPS, we found our way back to the secondary highway.

The embankment we had to climb down carrying a heavy e-bike between two people.

Too bad that was the last time that day Google Maps was any help. It ended up being another long day even after being forced off the toll road because Google Bike Maps told us to, "Turn here." The road looked all right but then we went down a little way, and suddenly the road was gone. There was nothing but a rough dirt track. I thought we'd learned not to follow Google Bike Maps, but apparently, we forgot that day.

So, after a long debate, we turned around and followed Google Car Maps instead. We did, however, come across a turkey farm and corn crop on our little adventure. At the same time, I found it rather fascinating how the landscape looked more like Canada than what I knew of Mexico, with the mountains and pines, the grasses and brush, even the cattle lazing in the fields.

Oh, but we weren't done with that day's work yet. We climbed and climbed and climbed some more before finally reaching an elevation of 9,300 feet. At the summit, I pulled over for a minute because I could see the road disappear in the distance. It was reminiscent of riding a rollercoaster and watching as the drop-off edges ever closer while you hold your breath and hang on tight, anticipating the thrill the entire time.

After a hairy descent, we finally spied Toluca, the highest city in North America at 8,730 feet. Finally getting a stroke of good luck, we discovered a road that went straight across to the suburb we were headed for. It was a bus lane, but we used it anyway! We followed that bus lane the whole way to our Airbnb. Our only issue after that was the numerous stop lights and the boisterous Sunday church procession we had to stop for. So, after a rough day of confusion, climbing, and riding ninety-seven kilometers, we ended the day at 6 p.m., which had become our normal completion time.

What a relief it was to arrive at our Airbnb and the gorgeous little pool and stone patio it offered. This house too was spacious and bright, with bedrooms that opened right out onto the pool area. It was clean and new with tile floors and stucco walls and had plenty of space for us to put our stuff. Yiota treated us to a homemade Greek soup that hit the spot that night.

Sadly, we realized once we arrived that Johana had left her passport in our hotel a few nights back, so she and Kyle had to skip Yiota's lovely dinner and take the car back there and spend the night. They wouldn't make it back until sometime midmorning the next day. While it was a pain for everyone, that's something that's always a worry on a long-distance tour. I really don't know why they don't just put a chip in your lip or ear or something with all the passport and document requirements in every country. That way, no one would have to worry about it all, and border officials would have far less work to do. Imagine, lines at borders would flow smoothly and work would get done efficiently. But while I was a little irritated at the hold up, I understood. I too had lost a credit card, my birth certificate, my Alberta healthcare card, and an insurance card somewhere. They had just all fallen out of my pocket somewhere without my noticing and I'd had no idea were. I'd thought I'd maybe lost them at one of the restaurants, but we'd gone back the next day but found nothing. But a passport is different, so I was hopeful Johana would be successful where I hadn't been.

***

And my hopes panned out. Johana and Kyle made it back the next morning, passport in hand, and set off for what would turn out to be, by comparison, a pleasant ride. We rode down paved roads with good shoulders and came across unique sights on our little eighty-kilometer trek from Toluca to Cuernavaca. The sky was a bit threatening, but it wasn't windy, nor did it rain; I was happy with just a jacket. Our day that day was filled with another castle, fresh watermelon straight from the truck, a lengthy bamboo fence, a field overflowing with orange and purple flowers, a roadside display of bonsai trees, and a three-peaked mini mountain range. On the way into town though, we had to contend with riding through tight streets packed with traffic, though they were festively decorated with thousands of colorful *papel picados*.

We enjoyed a memorable evening at that Airbnb, relaxing in the pool and chatting out in the back field by the pool before enjoying an elegant traditional Mexican dinner around an equally elegant dining table of hardwood. By then I was again rearranging the itinerary, and I was feeling a little behind, so we set off for Jonacatepec as soon as we could the next morning. That day included a short eighty-kilometer ride, but a good 1,300 meters of that was climbing so we had certainly had to cut it short. We would rest that night again in another large Airbnb house with five bedrooms and an enormous yard, safely housed in a gated community.

The stretch eastward across Mexico had a been a long haul full of bumps and bruises and mishaps and frustrations. While those had been countered by the incredible scenery, charming towns, and thankfully, luxurious Airbnb's to recuperate in, I was anticipating reaching Oaxaca. After falling into bed exhausted every night, I needed a change of pace, and I was sure everyone else was too.

A CHANGE OF PACE

Finally, after weeks of pushing ourselves over rough roads and through tough climbs, swearing at Google Bike Maps, and finding accommodations on the fly, we made it to the state of Puebla, oddly, just a few days' ride from Veracruz on the Caribbean side of Mexico. It may seem like we'd been riding through Mexico for far too long, but so many people in Canada and the US don't really know just how big Mexico is. We had no choice but to take quite a bit longer to get through it compared to Canada or the US simply because of both Mexico's size and topography. To get down to Central America under human power, we had to travel in a zig-zag manner at times and due east at other times when you'd think we should just be heading straight south. There were mountains or desert or vast lakes to go around, and other times there were just no roads. So, to get to Guatemala, we had to cross almost all of Mexico laterally with a few southerly dips. From Puebla, however, we were finally set up to head southeast down to Oaxaca, then straight down to the border of Guatemala and Mexico.

As we sat that night in our Airbnb in Cholula, part of greater Puebla, feeling hopeful for what was still to come and enjoying a wonderful meal Johana and Kyle had made, we were startled by fireworks nearby. Then we heard music and the sounds of a crowd from outside, so we went outside and discovered a free concert just a block away. One stage was huge, just as you'd expect at a Canadian or American outdoor music festival, with lighting and speakers and everything. The band, Askis International, was really good too, so Yiota and I stayed to watch. Wayne stayed for a few minutes, but it was really loud, so he went back to the house. Yiota put the performance on Instagram Live so others could see it too, and before we knew it, Kyle and Johana showed up.

A second group, a more traditional band of eleven people playing concert-jazz type music, took the stage then. They were a different kind of entertainment, but I still enjoyed it. When the band had finished, we went up on stage and took some photos with everybody in the Askis International. Then Kyle and Johana spoke with the band manager for a bit, and strangely, just a few minutes before the band was due to start their second set, those two went up and talked to him again. Kyle's movie camera, 360° camera, and drone seemed to open doors everywhere we went. This time, it turned out that Kyle had told the manager he'd capture some footage of their next set. Then of course he mentioned that I was eighty years old and cycling for the Guinness Book of World Records, so you can imagine what was about to happen.

Just before the set started, the band let us go up on stage, so I sat on the front corner of the stage while Johana, Yiota, and Kyle worked the drones, cameras, and Kyle's iPhone, wandering all over the stage and putting cameras in people's faces as they were singing. I don't know that I would have appreciated it, but the band seemed to like it.

Then one band member got Yiota up dancing. She did a great job, and we got it all on camera. Not long after, somebody handed the band leader a message that said, "That guy on stage is Canadian, and he's come all the way from Alaska to Panama to break the world record for riding an e-bike," or something like that anyway. So, they pulled me up out of the corner of the stage and told me to say a few words. I indicated I didn't speak any Spanish, but the band leader told me to speak in English. I thought, *What could it hurt?* and said a few simple things: "I'm just so happy to be here in Mexico, and *Viva Mexico cabarones.*" The crowd cheered, seemingly loving the saying I'd been taught by three young fellows' way back in Sonora, and I walked offstage and took up my previous position. I was hoping I was done in the limelight because even I'd had quite enough by then, but no. They called Johana over to dance, and then they called me up. I knew I couldn't say no, but I felt quite foolish up there wiggling around.

But it certainly turned out to be quite a night I won't forget for a long, long time. The band leader even came over afterward and wished me the best of luck on my adventure and gave me a bracelet with a large piece of jade on it. He said what I was doing fit with their philosophy of life and music, which was live your life to the fullest, whatever that means to you: play sports to the fullest, enjoy everything to the fullest, or seek out and experience adventure to the fullest. That was why I'd been so welcome on the stage. It was fulfilling to come across more folks trying to send the same message to the world that I was. We *could* make a difference. And I've worn that bracelet ever since.

Kyle, Johana, Yiota, and me with the band

At the end of the night, we hung out for a while where food tents had been set up while people came by and said goodnight and wished us luck. It was like being famous standing there receiving all those good wishes. We didn't get back until almost midnight and then we stayed up until about 1:30 a.m. to watch some of the drone footage. Thank goodness we'd finally hit a rest day.

Now it was rather serendipitous that that experience even happened because when Yiota had found that Airbnb, I'd said I hadn't wanted to stay there because it was twelve kilometers from where I'd really wanted to be in the old city of Puebla. But I'd ended up giving in because I could always take the van and go check out the old city the next day on my own. And look what happened. I ended up having one of the most spectacular nights I'd ever experienced. None of that would have happened if we had stayed in the part of town, I'd wanted to stay in. What a lovely surprise!

Late in the afternoon the following day, we finally toured around the old city and admired all the old churches. And while Puebla has many historic churches, all designed with incredible detail and intricacy, one always stands out for many reasons: the Santuario de la Virgen de los Remedios. The architecture and the engineering of it are spectacular, and the details are awe-inspiring. But the history is a little darker. It's said the Spanish built it after the conquest, and they purposely built it immediately atop the biggest Aztec pyramid in all of Mexico, likely to send a message of superiority. And perhaps fittingly, that particular pyramid is the largest pyramid in the world, despite being hidden still beneath the earth. Its base is four times bigger than Giza's, and it has nearly twice the volume.

Santuario de la Virgen de los Remedios

Wayne had wanted to go to the bike store and get his bike fixed up, so we dropped it off before we strolled through the old town and picked it up around 3:00 p.m. to make it back to the house around 4 p.m. I wasn't in a hurry, but I did want to head out for something to eat and still get back around 9 p.m. so we could get started at a decent time the next morning.

We found an elegant restaurant with a museum of ancient culture upstairs that we could tour for free and a jazz band that played during dinner. The museum and the atmosphere were wonderful, but the molé we all tried wasn't true molé; it was more like soup made with the bones of the of a goat.

No matter though, we ate well anyway, and when we left the restaurant, we heard some music. A parade was forming nearby, a parade for the Day of the Dead. It included a couple marching bands, one in the front one and one in the rear plus a whole bunch of people dressed in wonderful costumes representing the Day of the Dead and the goddess Katarina. Kyle took the opportunity to launch his drone and get a bunch of footage for our Octogenarian Odyssey social media. We enjoyed the spectacle for a while, but then we headed back to the house. The next day was to be another long day.

***

Boy was I right. After dodging traffic while trying to exit Puebla, the ride ended up being another example of the same old story as when we were riding east. We'd have a long climb, then a scary descent, and Google Maps would send us down some sketchy roads that in some places you couldn't even call a road before we either toughed it out or reevaluated and backtracked. One of those roads was a twenty-kilometer stretch of rough, rocky dirt that shook a bolt loose on Wayne's carrier. Not long after, we went over some rough pavement, and the carrier broke. The power cord had been pulled out, so we used a bungee cord to keep the rack in place.

Despite the difficulties, I enjoyed watching the mountains in the distance and the changing vegetation and zipping down into the valleys. In one instance, I was coasting down a hill toward a creek and about to make a turn, when suddenly there was cow just standing there. Thankfully it wasn't on the road, so it didn't become another near-death moment. Then I was climbing a hill and I thought I saw some vultures up ahead. As I got closer though, I discovered they were turkeys. There were about twenty turkeys crossing the road from one set of bushes to another! Good thing the roads were in good shape, and I could stop quickly.

Just as I recovered from that and was reveling in my peaceful ride under a cloudless sky with no wind to make me too cold, two high-powered motorcycles, racing bikes, roared past us. I'd been about to give them the finger because of the noise they were making when suddenly they dipped into this hairpin turn, leaning way over, their knees almost touching the pavement as they took the corner at high speed. That made me change my mind. Instead of giving them the finger, I gave them a cheer for that impressive maneuver. Then maybe ten more whizzed by. They weren't quite as daredevilish as the first ones though. I didn't know if it was a club ride or motorcycle rally or something, but it was fun to watch them.

We rested our heads in a minute little town called Tepexi de Rodriguez that night in another a charming hotel, for only $35 US a night per room, just off the highway as the sun was setting after a day spent riding up, over, and around in a rather dizzying and challenging fashion. It was just a few minutes out of town and had a lovely view of the hills. After speeding through our nightly charging battery/freshening up routine, we popped into the cute restaurant the hotel offered, that was also decorated for the upcoming holiday, before sliding into bed. There was just no time or energy for sightseeing that night. We still had two more hard rides ahead of us before we reached Oaxaca, and we needed to get there sooner rather than later because I was positive it was going to be difficult to find accommodation during the holiday. Oaxaca has some of the most well-known Day of the Dead celebrations in the country, so thousands of tourists' flock there every year.

***

We pushed on the next day toward a town in the middle of nowhere I'm sure no one has ever heard of called Heroica Ciudad de Huajuapan de León. I'm willing to bet no native English speaker can say it either. But for us, it represented another milestone: we were now in Oaxaca state. We did, however, appreciate more artfully detailed welcome signs with every small town—like San Vicente Coyotepec and Petlalcingo—we rode through, more unique churches, and more cacti while we climbed up what felt like a million miles and whizzed down the resulting descents. The Day of the Dead decorations and displays multiplied as we went, making me almost feel as though they were celebrating our arrival. Once, after Petlalcingo, we even forded a stream from mud bank to mud bank thanks to Google. We found some steppingstones we could use to cross it, so Wayne walked across them, but I just put the e-bike in high power and zoomed across, hoping I wouldn't fall. The stream wasn't very deep, but it was mucky.

Not long after that, we got a message from Kyle. They'd hit a big bump just as Yiota had unfastened her seatbelt and was passing something forward. Kyle called the bump an inverted speed bump, so I assumed that meant it was a big ditch across the road. Anyway, they'd hit it at a good speed, and Yiota had gone flying. She'd hit her head on the roof and then on the side wall and screamed.

Kyle had stopped the car to see if she was all right, and they'd gotten lucky. A police officer close by had seen what happened, and there just happened to have been a paramedic in the car who'd immediately helped stabilize Yiota. From what Kyle told me, she'd gone into shock and started crying then. The police officer had called an ambulance to take her to a woman's hospital in Heroica Ciudad de Huajuapan de León. They'd strapped her in on her back and braced her neck and off she went.

When Wayne and I got to town, I stopped in the hospital to see how she was. She was really scared and worried, thinking maybe she couldn't walk anymore. She was crying and a bit hysterical. I think she was just in panic mode. When we spoke to the doctor, he said it was his belief that it was just muscles creating the pain. So, after I left, he gave her some medication and a neck brace and told her to rest for five days. Johana went to stay with her while the rest of us stayed behind because with all the stuff in the van, there just wasn't enough room for us all to go. She brought Yiota home after I fell asleep that night but took her back to the hospital the next morning to get another injection and get more advice from the doctor. That advice turned out to be to just rest for another four days, maybe try some light massage, and continue with the drugs. Yiota was also to stay on her back as much as possible and use some warm compresses to help with the pain. I thought the doctor seemed to know quite a bit and had every confidence in him once I read the translation of the conversation he had with Johana. Certainly, having Johana with us as a Spanish speaker and a second woman was a lifesaver. She could get so much more done so much easier than us, and she was able to comfort and be with Yiota.

***

So, we spent a little time once Yiota and Johana got back from the hospital the next morning deciding on a plan for the day. The final decision was that Johana, Kyle, and Yiota would drive on to Oaxaca and Johana and Yiota would stay in a hotel there. That would give them four nights in the same place so Yiota could rest. Besides, it would hopefully give us a better shot at finding accommodations since we were a couple days behind the original schedule, and we were due to ride into Oaxaca near the Day of the Dead. Kyle would drive back once the girls were settled and bring Wayne and I some batteries and such and stay with us for the night wherever we stopped. Then the following day, Wayne and I would ride into Oaxaca and hopefully Yiota would be better. She was still worried and thinking about having to go home. I hoped she wouldn't do that and that she recovered because she'd become such a valuable member of the team with the amount of work she did—driving, getting groceries, booking hotels and Airbnb's, scheduling interviews, and keeping the books—that it would be impossible to replace her.

Anyway, each day of our journey to that point had generally been quite different, if not surprising sometimes, although this last surprise had not been a good one. But we had to continue, so as Johana, Yiota, and Kyle headed for Oaxaca, Wayne and I headed back onto the highway under a perfectly cloudless sky for hopefully a more pleasant ride that day. The landscape had started to become more desert-like the closer we got to Oaxaca, and we continued to discover fascinating churches on that day's ride, some smaller but detailed, some still in all their shining glory, and some enormous but time-weathered. Partway through the day, we encountered a friendly group of motorcyclists who stopped and wanted to chat and take some photos. So, Wayne and I enjoyed a nice break while we talked before, we had to ride off to our hotel for the night.

Of course, when we got to Asuncion Nochixtlan, our rest stop, all the streets leading to our hotel were blocked off for Market Sunday. That was a different obstacle but not one that posed a problem. We just walked our bikes through and ended up in a rather modern hotel before heading back out into the streets and the still ongoing market to scout out a place to eat. It was different with it being just the two of us, but we enjoyed the colors and sounds and smells of the market. Eventually, Kyle joined us, and when I mentioned I was craving burgers, he Googled it and found a delightful outdoor restaurant with nothing more than two walls and big shed roof. There were lovely palapas outside to sit at though, plus the tables under the roof, and it too was adorned with colorful papel picados and a Day of the Dead shrine. It was one of those places most tourists would never find, so we were the only three patrons.

Surprisingly, they made us some fantastic burgers. Kyle had a Hawaiian burger, Wayne had something called a black mala—which had a red bun—and I had the standard double burger with bacon, French fries, and beer. Boy it was good! The best part was the whole bill for all three of us only came to $25.

As we rode down a secondary highway the next day, I was gifted with another example of the kindness and interest of the Mexican people. A truck pulled up beside us and a young person handed us some water bottles. We took the water as we rode, but then they stopped so we did too. They asked about my odyssey, so we chatted, and they gave us a big bag of food. Suddenly, as I was thanking the kind folks in the truck, a little girl came running over from one of the houses nearby to give us three bananas. We were drawing a crowd by then, so another car full of three little girls and their two moms pulled over and asked if they could take some photos with us. I had great fun obliging them, then I asked them to follow the Octogenarian Odyssey on Instagram. Before we could get back on the road again, the banana-girl's big sister came over with a bag she said was from their father. It was filled with fresh honey and the comb for us. The crazy thing is, even though Johana and I had made a morning habit of wandering about to find a bakery wherever we were so we could buy some fresh bread or cinnamon rolls or coffee, I forgot about the honey for days after that. That honey would have been wonderful on fresh bread. Ah well, Yiota eventually found it and we used it then.

I just couldn't, and still can't, get over the outstanding kindness and generosity of the Mexican people. They had treated us, complete strangers, like family everywhere we went. For so many people who, for the most part, have so little to give so much so regularly, humbles me. If we had more of that mentality, more of that desire to care for others in Canada and the US, the world would be much happier, successful place. I never could figure out why those in power think the only definition of success is financial wealth, to have all the money and resources and all the power over the people. I would argue that those folks in Mexico are more successful in life than any politician or Jeff Bezos.

Anyway, I'll quit my rambling and get back to the story. Later the same day, we met yet another pleasant, helpful police officer. He let us use the facilities in the police station and talked to us for a while about our journey before we continued riding toward Oaxaca. We arrived a little earlier than usual after a fast eighty-kilometer ride, staying on the freeway the whole way. Thankfully, Kyle and Johana had already gotten a hotel for us when they'd brought Yiota to town to recuperate, but they'd only paid for the one night. It was expensive though because it was just about the only accommodation left. At least it was in the heart of the city, though we'd had to park the van and the tent trailer in the street and hope we wouldn't get robbed like we had a few weeks back when we'd lost the battery and the propane tank.

But if it weren't for the kindness of the hotel owner, we wouldn't even have had those rooms for the rest of the time we were due to stay in Oaxaca. By the time Wayne and I got to Oaxaca, the owner wanted cash for half the amount due for the three nights we would be there. That usually wouldn't have been a problem, but the bank was closed. Yet when I said I likely wouldn't be able to pay the deposit for that reason, that generous man let us stay on nothing more than the promise I would go to the bank the next day and get the money for him. He would transfer our amount due from his personal bank account to the hotel's bank account until then.

Again, I ask, why do Americans paint all Mexicans with the same brush? One new thing I came to love during this journey was going on Facebook or Instagram and finding comments from Americans saying I was portraying Mexico as a fun place to visit or that they were going to put, for example, Guanajuato on their bucket list of places to visit. My favorite comments were the very perceptive ones saying I was portraying Mexico far differently than the American media did. So, I felt like if I could influence just a few people to open their minds and hearts and appreciate their southern neighbors, then my journey would be worth more even than I had intended when I began. I've always thought we should all do what we can to leave the world a better place than when we found it.

***

When Johana, Wayne, and I left the hotel in search of some breakfast and coffee in the morning as had become routine, we came across a pack of no less than twelve dogs roaming the main street, likely feral. That was a little disconcerting given that's something we don't encounter in Canada, but they caused us no problems. Johana asked a passerby if they knew where we could get some coffee, and they told us to go to a market down the street and on the second floor. Well, that turned into an adventure!

We found the place, popped in, and asked if they had coffee. They only had instant coffee, but that was okay with us. At that point, it was coffee. So, we ordered three and saw that they had freshly squeezed orange juice. That sounded good, so we ended up with three enormous glasses. And I do mean enormous. You could probably have fit five or six oranges in that glass!

While we were relaxing with our coffees, Johana decided she was hungry, so she ordered some spiced quail eggs. Before the waitress walked away with the order, we asked her if they had any bread. She didn't have any, but she pointed us in the direction of a bakery that cooked their bread in an old, wood-fired oven. That kind lady even offered to go get us something, but I politely declined. I wanted to wander over there and experience it for myself.

When Johana had finished her eggs, we walked over to the bakery, which wasn't far, where I picked up $5 worth of little pastries and a special bread that they apparently made only once a year for the Day of the Dead. As we were about to leave, the baker asked if we'd like to see their special oven. Of course, I said yes! So, she led us to the back of the shop down a skinny corridor to where four or five people were sweating around a monstrous adobe oven. They did, however, also have a modern oven nearby. Fascinated with the process, we watched them make bread and buns and pastry for a while, then one of the bakers insisted we try a fresh piece straight from the oven.

Oh, my goodness. It was excellent. And that doesn't give it enough credit. Mouth-watering, delicious, there just aren't enough words to describe it aptly. Combined with the heady, comforting smell of freshly baked bread that filled the room, I almost just wanted to curl up and stay there forever. But before we left, I got to take the giant paddle and slide the bread into the oven. That was a fun moment, one of those unexpected moments that make your whole day. One minute you just want a coffee, the next minute you're sliding bread into a traditional adobe oven like a local. Wow.

Later that day, I got my laundry done, got to the bank and gave the payment to the hotel owner, and then wandered around and bought some tourist stuff, just a replacement hat for the one I couldn't seem to find and a cool t-shirt with a traditional Day of the Dead skull shielded by a bike helmet on it. It felt appropriate to me.

But after a relaxing, peaceful day, the night was exactly the opposite and an experience I won't soon forget. It started with dinner at an Italian restaurant where we celebrated four months on road, then we drove to a graveyard for the Day of the Dead and Halloween celebrations. The first graveyard we went to was closed, so we couldn't get in, but all the streets around it looked like a small carnival was in town. It had all kinds of games, food, and drink and even a small Ferris wheel and such. The street was filled with the sound of lots of people having fun. Johana had even painted our faces in the traditional white-and-black skull design before dinner, so we were in the spirit of the evening and fit right in as we watched the bands play and the people dance in the street. Even the smallest children got in on the action with their smooth dance moves. At one point, a parade of honking, beeping motorbikes paraded down the street in celebration. There were so many, it took a good five minutes for them to disappear.

The Day of the Dead displays in the graveyard

We moved on to a second graveyard after that, and it was completely different. There was still a carnival atmosphere with food and drinks and music, but the graveyard was open—and the main attraction. There were probably thousands of people in the street, walking shoulder to shoulder to the graveyard. It was a larger graveyard, and the crowd meandered through the whole thing, admiring all the displays at each grave. Some families must have planned those displays all year because many were intricately decorated with flowers of all sorts but especially marigolds and candles, food, and shrines. In many cases, family members of the deceased were there and would answer questions about the lives of their deceased relatives. The whole atmosphere of color, lights, and music was remarkable. Many different bands even wandered around and would play a song for the deceased if the family paid them.

A long, long time ago, and I do mean a long time ago, Beth and I were in Guadalajara for the Day of the Dead, and when we visited a graveyard in the afternoon, people were just quietly eating their picnics. That was the opposite of what the crew and I experienced that night. I'd heard about Oaxaca, but I hadn't expected it to be so grand. While we didn't get back to the rooms until well after midnight with all there was to see and do, it was a special night.

Oaxaca is certainly famous for many things: their Day of the Dead celebrations, the molé—the sauce with all the different spices and other ingredients they use—and the mezcal. One night before reaching Oaxaca, I had three mezcals. One was so strong it stung my lips that were cracked from the sun and wind, the second was soft and smooth and easy to sip, and the third was a mezcal coffee liqueur I had in my après-meal coffee. How could I not try as many as I could when I was right in the heart of mezcal country?

***

I sat in the sun the next day in a sidewalk café in the main square, drinking a glass of cold white Mexican wine and watching the people go by, some with painted faces still and some wearing costumes. Most were tourists of course, likely all from Europe, Canada, and the US. I'd only seen more in Puerto Vallarta and Mazatlán on this journey. It was easy to see why too. Even during the day, there was something special about Oaxaca, a feeling in the air that I never did manage to pinpoint. Nothing I'd seen beyond the celebrations compared to my other favorites,

Guanajuato, Puebla, and San Miguel de Allende, so perhaps it just had its own unique charm. I would have to visit again.

***

Day of the Dead in Oaxana, Mexico

My last rest day in Oaxaca the next day was reserved for preparing and resting up for the final push because with just another three days of riding, I would break the world record for the longest e-bike ride—provided no one else broke it before I got there. Then I'd have another five days of riding before we entered Central America.

Until then though, and after packing up my stuff, I just lazed in that town square, enjoying my wine and the sunshine and the atmosphere under the shade of the palm trees. There was so much life in that square that day. There were vendors with handfuls of probably fifty balloons each, folks selling cotton candy, and merchants offering trinkets or t-shirts or hats. Stalls lined the streets boasting goods of all kinds and colors, and the aroma of street food wafted in the air, filling the square.

While I was hanging out in central Oaxaca, Kyle, Johana, and Yiota were off at some ancient pyramid about forty kilometers away. I was thrilled Yiota was up and about and well enough to think about getting in a car or a bus and doing that. It also made me happy that Kyle and Johana like to get out and see the towns and the sights. Wayne was just happy to be getting his road bike in for repairs so he could continue riding it rather than the e-bike. That bike had traveled so many kilometers that the front chain rings were worn, and the teeth would not hold the chain properly.

Eventually, my wine glass emptied. I got up, paid, and headed to the hotel for a nap. Then after my little snooze, we all went out to taste seven different types of molé and a variety of mezcal one last time. Part of me dreaded getting the bill again though. I mean, it's not that I minded paying for everybody's dinner, but by then we seemed to somehow have gotten into a routine where I paid for everything. Maybe it was just because I didn't say anything or because it was something we'd gotten used to. Ah well, it was just things like that I would need to remember for part two of my Octogenarian Odyssey.

And suddenly, our restful downtime was at an end. I was grateful I'd gotten to partake in the Day of the Dead celebrations and wander through Oaxaca's old town. It seemed to me we were all rested and refreshed, and the excitement was building in me once again to follow the road wherever it led me. Only time would tell what the next bend in the road would bring.

SMASHING THE WORLD RECORD!

Then came the day it was time to leave the relaxing and sightseeing behind and move on. We started the day with only a slight headwind as we headed for mezcal-production territory on a quiet country road called Camino del Mezcal, or the road of mezcal. We were set for a long day of riding y and a tremendous amount of climbing, as usual it seemed, as we aimed for the Pacific Ocean again and the Guatemala border. The ride was initially one of the better ones; the first half was relatively flat, we had little wind, and the sun kept the clouds away, but then came all that climbing. As we rode, we read one sign that said, "World Capital of Mezcal" and another said mezcal was the gold of Oaxaca. There were dozens of mezcal plantations, kind of like vineyards, along that road, but unlike most vineyards, these were mostly mom-and-pop organizations. We stopped in at a couple of them and tried a few kinds of mezcal while learning about how it's made, though we stayed far away from the ones containing worms or snakes and watched as a truck loaded with harvested agave plants rolled by. I certainly learned a lot—and tasted a lot—at those places.

Johana, me, and Kyle taste testing mezcal

Only about fifty kilometers into the ride, Wayne had problems with his shoe cleat. One of the screws that held the cleat on the shoe came out, making the shoe useless. That meant he couldn't ride the rest of the day and ended up in the van. But I kept riding into the spectacular mountains all covered in green shrubs and cacti. Range after range and beautiful vistas came and went. Agave plants grew high up on steep slopes and all the way down to the river below. So, even though it was a long, tiring climbing day, it was a good day for me. I had so much to see—and mezcal to taste.

That day, I think we ended up buying three bottles of mezcal in two separate locations. At first, I wasn't exactly sure when we were going to drink it, but then I ended up having a couple shots when we got to our hotel. The place was miserable, but it was one of only two in the tiny town we stopped in halfway between Oaxaca and Tehuantepec. There was no hot water, no Wi-Fi, the beds were hard as rocks, and the pillows were lumpy. No one got any sleep that night, but for $25 per room, what can you expect? It did have a swimming pool, but there was no water in it.

At least dinner was better than the hotel. Wayne and Yiota thought at first, we should maybe look for another place because they didn't like the looks of the one, I'd chosen, but we decided to stay after I said we couldn't judge a book by its cover. Besides, there were few options in town, and everywhere was likely to fill up fast. We were glad we did too because we got good service and good food at a great price. In that little family-run restaurant, we each got three empanadas—beef, pork, and cheese—a few beers and juice, and dessert for $25. I couldn't complain, and no one else did either, so things turned out well that night. Even if we didn't sleep, at least we were well fed.

***

By the time morning rolled around, we were all just glad to get out of that hotel and on the road. The goal that day had originally been Tehuantepec but was now Juchitan de Zaragoza and the Pacific Ocean once again. We were facing a long ride that day of 145 km and 2320 m of climbing, and Wayne decided early on that he would ride the e-bike and wear different shoes since he'd broken the cleat on the other pair. But long day or no, I was excited. One more day of riding and we'd have something to celebrate. I was due to break the world record for the longest distance ridden on an e-bike. With the original route I'd planned out, I'd thought I wouldn't break it until we reached Guatemala; instead, we would still be five days out when I broke it.

The ride that day turned out to be not all that bad. It was long, but there wasn't much for traffic, and once we finished a few hard climbs again, we came down out of the mountains. After a refreshing midmorning cold coconut stop, we rode parallel to the coast in generally sunny conditions, passing beneath a graceful tree tunnel, through Tehuantepec—where a giant metal statue of a woman in traditional garb greeted us—and by a good old-fashioned oxen-drawn cart plodding down the road.

At the end of the day, we were all relieved to pull into a fantastic hotel. The u-shaped building wrapped around a tropical garden that surrounded a lovely pool—filled with water this time! It had a relaxing stone patio and a palapa to find some shade under, and twisting brick columns supported the clay roof of another patio. We checked in and went in search of some supper. Strangely, we had a hard time finding anywhere, so when our stomachs started audibly rumbling, we opted to hire a Tuk-Tuk. That was an adventure itself as they're really nothing more than a tiny, beat-up couch and a roof welded to a trike. It was both fun and a little, well, exciting with the close calls the drivers create with some of their daring driving in and out of traffic. But we lived and finally got some enormous tacos from a roadside stand before turning in for the night.

***

My body was humming with excitement as soon as I opened my eyes the next day. I thought that would maybe get us on the road faster than usual, but we didn't end up leaving until almost 9:30 a.m. But no matter, the smell of rain in the air and refreshed foliage filled the air, only increasing my adrenaline. It had rained last night, so it was cloudy and puddles as big as lakes lined the side of the road, but the lingering wind from the storm gave us a nice tailwind. The highway was pleasantly flat, making for a relaxing ride where I could appreciate the sights instead of working so hard. Not long into the day, we rode by a huge wind farm, the biggest one I'd ever seen. There were so many windmills, I couldn't count them all. When you rode close to some of them, you could almost feel the hum.

Suddenly, we came upon two dogs just lazing in the middle of the road. They didn't appear to be excitable, and there was room between them, so I decided to ride on through between them. I slipped by without incident, but just as Wayne was about to do the same, one dog chose that moment to get up. As he did, he hit Wayne's front tire, and Wayne went flying.

Kyle was riding behind us with the cameras, so he stopped to help Wayne, who fortunately came out of the ordeal with just some road rash, some scrapes and bruises. Experienced rider that he is, he just got up, brushed himself off, pushed his twisted shift lever back into place, and carried on. What a pro!

From there, we only had eighteen kilometers to go before I broke the newest world record for riding an e-bike long distance. Just as I was thinking I should take a picture of the computer display at the end of each day for the rest of the trip in case something happened to the odometer, we reached the very kilometer that equaled the current record.

The moment I broke the world record.

A kilometer later, we stopped on the side of the road and threw a mini celebration. We lit candles and set off fireworks and tossed crazy confetti all over. There might have been some hooting and hollering and some funky dance moves, but I'll never tell. Then we did a couple quick Facebook Live and Instagram Live sessions to thank everyone that had supported me on my odyssey and everyone who had donated to the fund for Panamanian children.

After the mini party and a round of celebratory mezcal, it was back to riding. We still had most of the day left to go and were aiming for San Pedro Tapanatepec, which was just before the last state border before we reached the Mexican/Guatemalan border. I was itching to complete the Mexican leg and begin the last leg, the Central American leg, by then. Hopefully things would go smoothly for the next few days until we got there.

Of course, I was wrong. Every time I had that thought, something happened.

You'd think that a bike crash and breaking a world record would be enough excitement for one day, but that day just wasn't done with us yet. Not long after we packed up our celebration and moved on, we came across a supposed migration checkpoint. The police stopped everyone, in a vehicle, on a bike, and on foot. No exceptions. By the time we got there, they'd already pulled over Yiota and Johana in the van and were checking their passports. Turns out, the men had already searched the van and sent a drug dog to sniff around in it. And you guessed it, that dog had found something. Kyle had some marijuana in his bag for some reason, so they'd been stuck waiting around as the van and tent trailer were opened and searched. They even had us crank up the tent trailer's roof and looked under the vehicles.

Wayne was certain these particular officials were really just after bribes though, so Johana approached the official in charge and tried negotiating our way out of our sticky situation. And Wayne was right. The guy wanted six thousand pesos at first, but Johana bravely countered with one thousand. His answer to that was to start walking away, and when another official began to walk away too, Johana offered fifteen hundred and said, "That's all we've got."

He walked away again. We honestly didn't have more pesos than that on us, so Johana was powerless to say anything more. Luckily, the chief turned back a few steps later and eventually took the bribe. Once we handed over the money, he told his minions to shut it down and let us go. We repacked everything as fast as we could and got out of there but the police kept the marijuana.

Well, after my first bribery experience, I was really looking forward to relaxing in a nice quiet hotel room. But that was not to be. The day was turning out to be one of those unbelievable type of days where you just never know what's going to happen, nor can you even predict it. Anyway, Johana and Yiota later drove ahead to San Pedro Tapanatepec only to find there was no available accommodation. When I got the text, I remembered that the crooked official had said that town was a bad town to go to as it was full of migrants, and we'd be wise to stop in a little town about twenty kilometers before that.

I was left with a decision: stop where I was or go an extra twenty kilometers to the town full of migrants and set up camp in the police yard that Johana had discovered was an option. In the end, we chose to go on the twenty kilometers and set up in the police yard. Given the choice between a so-called "safe town" the scruffy-looking migration police had recommended or the police yard the professional, well-dressed National Guardsmen had offered, it was an easy decision.

As we raced to beat the sunset, we rode past group after group of people walking up the highway, and it occurred to me that these poor folks were not the farm workers I'd thought they were but people heading to the US to try their luck. *How desperate was their situation*, I wondered, *that they'd been forced into that situation, to take their chances and go through anything they had to, to build a better life?* That was the first time we'd encountered migrants, and I can tell you there were only families and young people among them.

Anyway, my thoughts evaporated for the time being when Kyle screamed. I was just about to pull into the police yard, but I turned around and went back. Kyle was yelling, "Bob! Bob! Get back here! There's huge tarantulas on the highway!"

I discovered there was only one, so I talked him through it. Then even though he was afraid of spiders, he stopped and grabbed my phone to get a picture of the giant tarantula walking across the road. Suddenly, a couple cars came whipping by and scared it. It must have assumed we were the threat because he ran right at us. We had to drop the phone and fend the tarantula off with the bike tries to keep it from biting or stinging or whatever they do. Oh, I was done with excitement for that day!

Finally, we pulled unscathed into the police yard and met up with Johana and Yiota. We set up the tent trailer and discovered there was Wi-Fi and electricity and even access to a shower and toilet. Then of course the police discovered I was eighty years old and had just broken the world record, so they offered up one of their own beds in the office.

Well, that group of police officers couldn't be any more different from the ones who we paid a bribe to, earlier in the day. Just like all the other officers we'd encountered on our trek through Mexico, they took good care of us and treated us like we were something special. After a good chat, the group decided it was past time to go eat and relax. We walked a little way down the road and came upon a few small outdoor restaurants. In a twist I didn't expect, we discovered most of the restaurants in town didn't permit alcohol on the premises, though a few would allow it but not serve it. So, we found a place where we could drink our own alcohol. We simply crossed the street, bought some cocktails at the corner store, and brought them back to the restaurant to enjoy with our dinner.

As I sat back and savored my cocktail, I looked around and realized the place was full of Black folks. They were incredibly friendly, so we struck up a conversation with one group and discovered they had walked all the way there from Brazil after flying over from Somalia. They could have chosen to go to South Africa, but there were no jobs there, and they hadn't wanted to live in Europe, so they'd chosen to head to Brazil and try their luck there. They'd walked across Brazil and through Peru, Ecuador, and Colombia. Along the way, they'd had to tackle the Darién Gap in Panama, a treacherous 106-km gap in the Pan-American Highway that's all mountain, forest, and watershed. The road had never been built through that span because it was too expensive and harmful to the environment, hence the reason it was called the Darién *Gap*. No plans to continue the highway exist to this day. On the Colombian side is an 80-km wide marshland, and on the Panamanian side is a mountainous rainforest. The highest peak reaches 1,845 meters, creating dangerous terrain, yet these folks are so desperate and determined, they face the challenge anyway. And many, many people die trying. Of this particular group we chatted with, five had died trying.

We learned that after they'd endured all that, they spent hours and hours in lineups at the Panamanian border. One fellow we spoke to had been waiting there for twenty-one days for permission to move on. They hadn't appreciated anything about Panama, they said, but Costa Rica was excellent, and they'd been treated well. We spoke with them for a long time that night, and the hardship they'd gone through just to give their families a better life brought tears to our eyes at times. There were some good laughs though too. But the contrast between me sitting there, white and privileged and on a journey of happiness and exercise, while those folks were undergoing the exact opposite, traversing all those dangerous areas and not knowing where or when tragedy would strike or what they'd face given they had no papers or passports, wasn't lost on me. They had nothing but hope and determination that they could make it to the US and start making money to send to their families back in Somalia, and there I was with everything and just enjoying my journey because I could.

Eventually, that group left, and we talked with another small group form Somalia before heading back to the police station, where we chatted with a couple migrants from China trying to do the same thing as the Somalians. We learned that night that there were people from all over the world undertaking the journey: from Venezuela, Africa, El Salvador, Honduras, China. Though they didn't have much of anything, they persevered, and every time after that when we passed a group of them, I would give them a peace sign or thumbs up.

I lay in my bed in the police station that night, listening to the printer make a bunch of weird noises as I tried to sleep. The day had been too full of unexpected, unbelievable occurrences, and my brain was too busy processing to sleep. What took precedent in my mind was the stories I'd heard that night. The more I thought about it, the more I knew that if I was in charge of Canada's border, I'd ask each immigrant what they'd endured, what they'd been through to get here, and whoever had experienced what these immigrants had experienced, I'd say, "Sure, come on in. We need determined, hard-working people like you here."

I finally nodded off with those thoughts but woke the next day with all sorts of worries. We needed money after the previous day's extortion, we had to find some breakfast, and we had to get on the road as soon as we could because we had yet another long day ahead of us, 133 km and 2530 m up. I was wishing I could find a way to break these long days up, but not only did there just not seem to be any way around it, we'd had long, hard days before and lived through it, so it was what it was.

***

So, we started that day trying to find the bank. It became an interesting hunt though, riding around town watching all the migrants who were up and about early, filling the streets and the restaurants and the stores. They rise early and get back in line. Then they go eat and get back in line and repeat. I did learn that it seems the government eventually gives them some documents and put them on a bus to Mexico City for additional processing. That was why we hadn't passed more migrants on the road than we had.

After we found the bank, we tried to grab some breakfast at the OXXO, but there were at least a hundred migrants lined up there with the same idea. So, we didn't stop but continued to the grocery store. We came across the same situation there. I was overwhelmingly hungry by the time we eventually came upon a coffee shop with doughnuts and pie. Something more substantial would have been preferable though given the long 133, -km trek we were about to tackle, with a good two thousand meters of that climbing. The reward at the end of that hard day and another tough one after that though would be a rest day in a lovely colonial city, San

Christobal de las Casas, and then two easy days as we neared the Guatemala border.

*Migrants at the OXXO while waiting to be given
permission to continue their journey*

That day, we crossed the border into the last Mexican state we'd ride through: Chiapas. We had beautiful, sunny weather to help us push through our long day too. As much as I love scenery, especially mountain views, scenery like that meant nothing but climbing. Everyone had to take turns on the second e-bike over that day and the next. However, here, as opposed to all the other mountains we'd battled, they looked hairy, like they wore a shaggy coat given all the head-high grass that covered them. As the wind blew through the grass, it was as if the hills were alive and breathing, quivering even. And now that we were in Southern Mexico in the tropical zone, we were quickly introduced to an invisible pest the equivalent of mosquitos or horse flies in Northern Canada: no-see-ums. Those teeny creatures pack a big punch that feels somewhere between a pinprick and an electric shock and would make you itch for hours afterward. We learned quickly not to stop and eat our lunch in the grass or sand because that's were they flourish, especially me because I wore sandals the entire trip, and that gave those monsters a complete buffet.

The rest of that day's ride was full of more unique scenery—mango trees and mysterious conical buildings—a quick lunch at an outdoor roadside restaurant with plastic lawn furniture—rather typical in Mexico—and more old churches. Then we rode through Cintalapa and Jiquipilas before retiring for the night at another small hotel in a town not far outside Tuxtla Gutierrez. Another tasty dinner in a modern restaurant with one wall fully open to the outdoors followed before we pressed on the next day for our last long day with a good three thousand meters of climbing to San Cristobal de las Casas. We were gifted on that ride with colorful murals and fascinating architecture again, and on our way through Tuxtla Gutierrez, a local reporter hunted me down. I sure felt like a celebrity then, being chased by paparazzi!

It was a good thing we had so much to distract us because we climbed so high for so long that day, it felt like we were climbing into the clouds—and beyond. As we climbed up what felt like Mount Olympus, we were at least protected by bright plastic barriers separating us from the traffic, sort of. It was a rather calming thought until Wayne pointed out that not one of the barriers had escaped being hit by a vehicle. Later, we stopped at a chicken farm where Johana decided to sit down among the chickens and feed them an entire cake. Really! Much of the farming there we discovered is actually done right on the side of the steep slopes, requiring all the labor be done by hand. You can't use machines or animal-drawn tools there because it's far too steep and rocky. I couldn't imagine the effort that took.

Finally, and I say finally with meaning this time, we arrived in San Cristobal de las Casas. We'd triumphed over forty-two continuous kilometers of climbing into the heavens. Needless to say, the clouds obscured the view in places, with even homes being barely visible, and it was much, much cooler. Because San Cristobal sits at an elevation of over eighteen hundred meters, people certainly work a little harder to breathe there.

We rode through the city to the historic old center where our Airbnb awaited us. That night, we stumbled into the house, charged the batteries, and fell onto the first seat we could find. After an easy dinner and much-needed night's sleep, we spent the next day touring old San Cristobal. I can't say it often enough: the architecture in Mexico is awe-inspiring, fascinating, and unique. With all the arches, peaks, and beams, brightly colored paint, and intricate details, it doesn't matter if the building is an ancient church that took decades to build, a hotel, a restaurant, or a home, they're all equal in their charm and allure. You could look at them for hours and still find little details you hadn't noticed a moment before. We spent hours the next day strolling down San Cristobal's pedestrian-friendly avenues, taking photos, and trying to commit the sights to memory.

From there, it was on to Guatemala after an easier two-day ride through the stunning countryside. It gave me time to reflect on how it's all the little, quirky things you see on a long-distance bike tour that make the whole trip. Every city, town, and view are unique. On this stretch, we had poinsettia stands, cap-hat trees, and enormous handmade signs expressing the area's support of the people of Ukraine. As we neared Comitan, we saw our first sign indicating the way to the border. We were getting close.

Comitan was to be our second last night in Mexico. We would ride the next day until we reached the border, and I could only hope we wouldn't have any hiccups. It was a small border crossing, so it was only open half the day most days and was closed on Sundays. Our timing would have to accommodate any issues we might have to deal with before they closed.

***

As we set off from Comitan, the owner of our fantastic, well-maintained Airbnb rode with us the first few kilometers out of town. It's experiences like that that really motivate me. I love meeting new people and sharing my love of biking with them. And when they ride with us, it not only switches up the routine and creates additional interest, but it also offers an opportunity to get to know each other better, a chance to understand each other better and learn a little more about another way of life. It's incredibly interesting, I think, to discover that no matter where we live, we all have more commonalities than differences.

Riding with our Airbnb owner in Comitan, Mexico

But back to the journey. We were blessed with gorgeous sunny skies on our last full day in Mexico as we rode toward the Guatemalan border. As for my hope of no hurdles? Well, you know how that turned out. First came the 3.5 km climb to get there, then came a flat tire. I temporarily patched the tire enough to finish the ride again, but later that night I would have to put a new tube in again.

When we got to the border town, the day was nearly expired and the border crossing would close soon, so we spent the night there. It was a real frontier town that reminded me of Vietnam or Thailand and other various border towns around the world where you come into this sort of Wild West where everybody's selling stuff, exchanging currency, and just doing whatever they can to make a living around the unique needs of travelers.

I was concerned we wouldn't find anywhere to stay, but a quick search took us to what looked like a charming hotel with an open courtyard boasting tropical foliage and a fountain, walls painted in yellow terracotta, ironwork terraces, and columns of green. Boy, was I mistaken.

It was actually the world's worst hotel room. And given all the places I've traveled to, that's saying something. The bathroom door was broken; it swung on one hinge and there was a giant hole in the middle of it where someone must have put their fist through it. The bathroom tiles had been pulled off, I guessed to fix some plumbing given the constant leak that kept me awake all night as it dripped into a bucket. There was no hot water, the paint was peeling off the walls, and by 3 a.m., the air conditioning started banging so hard we had to turn it off. To top it all off, nothing worked, not the showers, toilets, or lights. After traveling through three countries, this hotel got the prize for worst hotel. The $30 I paid for that one room was far too much. But hey, the Wi-Fi worked in the lounge!

Before heading out for dinner, I dealt with my flat tire and switched out the tube. I thought that would be it, but by the time I got back from dinner and went to bed, it was flat again. Shaking my head and sighing, I decided I'd deal with it in the morning.

The only upside to that night was the food. The hotel proprietors hadn't been able to recommend anywhere good to eat in town but did tell us about a stand that made great burgers, so that's where we went. A hot, juicy burger and fries was just what I needed after that day. The rest of the team felt the same way given the shared enjoyment on their faces.

By the time I saw my again-flat tire and rolled into that nightmarish bed, my greatest wish was that our border crossing the next day would be seamless. We needed to get back on the right foot, enjoying the riding experience, meeting new people, and discovering what was waiting for us.

AND THE LAST LEG BEGINS

The morning we were to officially cross into Guatemala started with putting yet another tube in my tire. Thank goodness that one worked. It didn't surprise me that I was having problems with the Specialized accessories though. I've had troubles with things like that often in the past with everything from these tubes to helmets to clothes. *C'est la vie.*

The day improved as we were leaving when a few hotel patrons, a husband and wife with two small girls, approached me and asked, "Could we take a picture? We saw the sign on your bike and on the car yesterday and read about you in the news."

I replied, "Well, what news did you see?" I couldn't believe people were reading about my odyssey all the way down at the Guatemalan border.

So, the wife pulled it up on her phone and it was a piece from July in a Prince George newspaper. I figured she must have Googled my sign and that article popped up. We chatted for a while after that and took some photos. One of the girls was rather impressed because she'd studied Alaska in school and had learned how far away it was. I took that as a sign that day would be a good day because it had started with meeting new people and hearing that they'd heard about me and my odyssey.

We still had a lot to achieve that day though, so we said our goodbyes—good riddance to that hotel—before long and headed for the border and Guatemalan customs. Though that day was Remembrance Day in Canada and Veterans Day in the US, no one in Mexico celebrated that, so it was business as usual. We'd wisely checked out of Mexico the night before, but then we'd waited about two hours for motorcyclists to check into Mexico, so we'd decided to head to a hamburger stand and the hotel then. As a result, crossing into Guatemala that morning was quick. We were greeted by a nice agent who concluded all the ordinary official business in about a half hour while Kyle took the opportunity to fly his drone around the border and get shots of both sides with the whole Wild West feeling. Though a border official wanted me to drive the car across, Johana pleaded with them and told them I couldn't drive while I was trying to break the world record. So, the guard relented and told her just to make sure she didn't tell anyone she'd driven it across. As fast as we got through the passport business, however, we did get hung up for a few minutes while they attempted a sort of inspection of the trailer, opening the door, pulling out a bag, putting it back in, shutting the door, and checking the VIN numbers. At the Mexico/Guatemala border, it seemed officials were more concerned with what vehicles were coming and going than what people were coming and going. I found that a little odd. I also had to get back the $400 deposit I'd paid at the Mexican border to bring the car into the country, but at least the place wasn't busy then. Only a group of backpackers were hanging around, waiting to cross the border, so I wrapped that up quickly too.

Fifty meters from the Guatemala border

Once across the border, we stopped for coffee at an outdoor café on a cliff edge whose seating was a strange mix of wood and plastic chairs and leather booths, sofas, and lounge chairs. They even had a cozy spherical swing made of vines hanging right from the tree, so it looked out over the edge of the cliff. As we enjoyed both the view and the Guatemalan coffee, we discussed the problem of buying car insurance. While it's required that you have car insurance here, you're not forced to buy it at the border the way you are in Mexico, so we had to find out where to buy it as soon as possible before we were stopped. Johana called around to see if she could figure it out, and in the end, we had to visit a few different banks to get that done before we left town. It took most of the morning and cost $47 for nine days, but it was worth it. I didn't want my team driving around without insurance in a foreign country.

It was easy to hear the surprise in Wayne's voice and to see it in his face as we chatted over coffee though. His expectations for Guatemala had been rather low, and I think he thought it would be awfully dangerous or full of migrants. But between the vistas even right there at the border and the friendly families we met, it seemed he was pleasantly surprised. Again, we took a lot of photos with the folks we met, all of whom were so short, Wayne and I looked like giants standing next to them. And I loved that all the women we'd encountered there wore the traditional colorfully patterned dresses. I just appreciated the culture of it all.

Finally, rather late in the day, we rode out of that border town following a river into the unknown world beyond. We rode through incredible canyons with far steeper walls than any mountain range we'd seen before, even in the Rockies. Wayne thought it looked like we were in Nepal or something, except the snow had been replaced by jungle. However, despite the cities and towns being quite modern, the highways, jungles, and towns were full of garbage: garbage on the sides of the road, garbage covering a soccer field, and garbage in the jungle. There was so much more of it than there had been in Mexico. I had no idea how they would ever get that cleaned up. That's the difference between first world and third-world governments: they could build modern cities, but they lacked the necessary infrastructure for things like maintenance and sanitation.

We climbed and descended, climbed and descended the rest of the day, following the same river upstream and passing jungles and mountains and farms in the sunshine as we rode down the ever-winding highway. It was a shorter day given our late start and the hurdles we'd had to overcome before leaving for the day, but we made it to a not-small but not-large town called Huehuetenango before dark and found a hotel that really was nice this time. It was clean and well-maintained, and I appreciated the stone floors in the halls, the metal latticework on the windows, and the hardwood furniture lining the halls. The atmosphere shouted colonial and the tropical plants filling every available nook and cranny gave it a cozy, relaxing feel. Rather than go searching for a restaurant that night, we took advantage of the hotel restaurant before turning in for the night. We needed to get a much earlier start the next day. All in all, I'd been right for once. It had been a long, hard, but good day.

***

And we did get an earlier start in the morning. We dove back into the heart of the jungle and the mountains, discovering more novel foliage that looked much like a cabbage palm, though they're native to New Zealand, braving descents steeper than we'd faced the rest of the journey, and encountering more new folks. Even this far south, people still honked at us as they drove by, sometimes shouting, "Hey, Mister! How are you?" in English. In English! I love how more people in Latin America speak English than North Americans speak Spanish. It's pretty telling of the people, I think anyway. But we even met another long-distance cyclist that day, this one from Argentina! It always makes for a great conversation when we meet up with a fellow biker.

Suddenly, with only fifty kilometers and an hour of climbing to go, Wayne and I were stopped in our tracks. Our batteries were dead. We were faced with no choice but to hang out on the side of the road and wait a likely hour for the support team to come back with new batteries. So, we took the opportunity to relax and have a late-ish lunch of some sort of doughnut and apple juice while we waited there, 2,000 meters up with another 1,000 meters left to climb.

When the support team finally found us and we switched out the batteries, we tackled the rest of that climb before stopping to take a photo of the breathtaking view of the city we were stopping in that night: Quetzaltenango. The clouds wreathed the mountains on the opposite side of the city and looked parallel to our position we were so high up.

As we headed for our Airbnb, we were met with another unique sight: a volcano. Despite being in a country located on the Pacific Ring of Fire, it still caught me by surprise to be riding through a city and looking at a volcano nearby. Though most of Guatemala's volcanoes are ancient and no longer active, most of them are situated right where we were riding in southwestern Guatemala.

***

The sky was gloomy and threatening the next morning as we rode out of town on rocky dirt roads full of more garbage. Up into the mountains we went yet again, higher than 2,700 meters this time, until we were right in the middle of those threatening clouds as though we were gods at the top of the world. We had to maneuver around landslides, a parade of trucks full of Indigenous folk, and more garbage before we emerged into sunshine and softer slopes. Then we were forced to stop and fix my e-bike battery rack, but we got some protection from the local police while we finished that up. They too were just as friendly and inquisitive as the Mexican police despite being armed with AK-47s.

When we moved on, we encountered a classic Guatemalan palapa fronting a nursery. There, an intriguing Mayan monument was carved into a cliff, upon which steps led up to a doorway flanked by animal carvings. Shortly after that, we reached the beginning of the terrifyingly steep descents and hairpin turns we had to fly down to reach Lake Atitlan, said to be the world's most beautiful lake. But our first view of the sky-blue water was reward enough with the cottony clouds ringing the mountains on the far side, an odd mix of pine and palm tree on our side, and tiny white boats dotting the surface of the lake. Here, we were going to have to ride around a jungle-covered volcano once we'd reached lake level.

Our first view of Lake Atitlan.

Lake Atitlan itself is actually a volcanic crater surrounded by three volcanoes, I was surprised to learn. Kyle lived there for a time. Surrounded as it is by mountains and Mayan villages, it's hard to imagine that enormous lake once being a volcano. My quiet contemplation disappeared as we continued that descent. And what a descent that was. It had to be the world's best and worst downhill, with around a 25 percent decline in places. I wasn't entirely sure my brakes would last all the way down as we descended into to the crater, tackling switchback after switchback as we went.

Finally, we reached the bottom and thought we were done, that we'd follow a nice, easy road around the lake. Oh no, that was certainly not the case. We had to climb back out of that crater on some inclines that reached as much as 28 percent. Thank goodness Wayne and I were both riding e-bikes and could take advantage of some assist. Then just as we reached the summit and were about to descend again, though not as steeply this time, BAM!

We were thwarted by construction blocking the entire road. At least we caught up to the support van there, so we pulled out all the chairs and got comfortable. Kyle amused himself with filming the scene and climbing the cliffs, entertaining us all in the process, and we took some photos with the project engineer at his request. A convoy built up behind us as we waited: a truck filled with workers, a motorbike, a school bus, and one of those chicken buses. Then a half hour or so later, it started to get dark and the grader blocking the road turned on its lights. We had no idea how much longer we'd be stuck there, and we were hoping like hell we wouldn't have to ride out of there on the dirt road in the dark. Most of all though, I just wanted to get to our Airbnb and find a nearby restaurant because I was starving.

Luck was on our side. We got past the construction and descended to the other side of Lake Atitlan just as the sun was sinking behind the mountains. Santiago Atitlan and our Airbnb were enchanting. We were fortunate enough to have booked a rental right on the lakeshore, and watching the sky slide into shades of orange, yellow, and red over the water was magical. Our luck continued with dinner. We found a beautiful place with a patio also on the water and devoured a most wonderful meal. It was exactly the fuel I needed after the stress of the day, both physical and mental.

***

I awoke the next morning anticipating the two-day break we'd get in Antigua once we'd finished that day's ride but dreading the additional climbing required to get to our destination. We only had around ninety kilometers to go, but it would include more climbing than we'd done on the journey thus far, excluding the previous day. Our route that day would take us around the lakeshore to San Lucas Toliman, north then east to Patzun, down to Patzicia, east in a winding manner to Chimaltenango, then finally due south to Antigua. It would be a challenge to say the least, so we'd be earning our rest days.

We started that day by fortifying ourselves with a hearty breakfast at the restaurant just next door to our Airbnb. There, Johana surprised me with a lovely breakfast pastry with whipped cream and blueberries and *Feliz Anniversario* written on the plate, plus a small bottle of wine, from Gloria because it was our seventh anniversary that day. I thought perhaps I should go off on long trips more often with treatment like that. I had, however, sent Gloria roses back home in Costa Rica and called her before breakfast.

Then it was back on our bikes to master the challenge ahead. At least the weather was on our side, and we were treated to landscapes of coffee plants and convents, mountain views and volcanoes as we climbed and climbed. So many of those inclines I never would have gotten up if it hadn't been for the e-bike, and with all the resulting steep descents, I knew I was going to have to get my brake pads replaced when we got to Antigua. We were also going through batteries a lot faster with all the extra assist we were using. Thank goodness for the support van and cell phone coverage.

As if climbing and descending weren't enough of a challenge, fate decided to throw another wrench into things. Not only did we hit more construction a couple times, but sometimes we'd be riding on a lovely, smooth, paved highway with painted lines, when suddenly we'd have only dirt roads. Once, we even went around a corner and found no more road at all. It had gotten washed away, so Wayne and I had to ford a wide, muddy creek on foot. I wasn't even sure if the van and trailer could make it. The creek wasn't all that deep, but the opposite bank was steep and wet and muddy so I was unsure if the van would find the traction it needed to get up the slope. Fortunately, as I held my breath, the van made it across and up to the other side. Then just down the dirt road a bit was another paved highway. It was crazy.

Before we knew it, we arrived in Antigua, a beautiful old city with some buildings dating back to 1650. We had a gorgeous Airbnb to stay in for three nights and two days. It was two levels and immaculately maintained, and the interior was as stunningly decorated as the outside was landscaped. Furniture of native hardwood tastefully paired with traditional Mayan designs and all the modern amenities completed that spectacular rental, so we relaxed the moment we walked in.

***

I had an interview scheduled with the family of one of my daughter's work friends at lunch the next day, so Wayne and I headed for the old part of town early to wander around and admire all the little stores and restaurants tucked away down narrow alleys and behind garden walls. Yiota, Kyle, and Johana went off to climb the volcano and weren't due back until late the next day.

After strolling through the central square and marveling at how all the structures had been built so ingeniously that they'd held up against the level-six earthquake Antigua had experienced just four days before our arrival, we sought out the restaurant we were supposed to meet my interviewer at for lunch. As we walked, I found I was at odds with how I felt about seeing a volcano looming over the city at every turn. It felt both otherworldly and threatening at the same time.

Our host had chosen a lovely outdoor Italian restaurant to meet at, with a stone floor, metal pergolas, and clay tiles on the main building and forming the floor of the outdoor restaurant. My daughter's friend knew the owner, Claudia, and once she heard of our odyssey, she was happy to have us. She even wanted a few photos with us, so as usual, after lunch, we took quite a few photos with her and a few other folks we got to talking with at the restaurant.

After lunch and the interview, our hosts took us on a walking tour, and we stopped in at a rum bar at happy hour. I tried a few different kinds, but the best by far was the twenty-three-year-old Zacapa, the most famous rum in the area. It was a good thing we didn't have to drive back to our Airbnb!

But when we did get back, there was a knock at the door. A fellow named Fernando had come to say hello. Janet, my daughter, works with a lady from Guatemala, and she had told her cousin about us and asked him to please stop by and say hello. We ended up having a wonderful chat about the government and how it works in Guatemala and the quality of life there. I certainly hadn't seen any migrants walking along the highway since Mexico, so I was curious. According to Fernando, most of the Latin American migrants are from Honduras. Few are from Guatemala because the government and its systems were quite functional, and the people were happy enough. El Salvador had apparently solved many of their problems too, bringing the crime rate down, according to Fernando, and their economy was booming. That meant the bulk of migrants heading for the US were, as we'd discovered, from Honduras, Venezuela, Africa, and China.

That conversation reminded me that I wanted to give a big shout out to the NGOs and the volunteers I'd met along the way—and the hundreds or thousands more that I didn't meet—when I finally got this book together, so here it is. Back in Lake Atitlan, I'd met two young family medicine doctors from Balboa, Spain, volunteering to work for three months in a remote area near Lake Atitlan, and I'd thought those folks were extraordinary as they'd only graduated a couple years ago and looked to be in their early thirties.

Then on my rest day in Antigua, a volunteer surgeon gave me a tour of a small well equipped, and volunteer-run hospital in the center of town. The hospital was actually an old, converted convent that now has eight operating rooms for day patients and such. They just aren't equipped for major surgeries. The recovery room even had a few recovering patients still there when I walked by. Coincidentally, for that two-week span when I'd visited, all the doctors were Canadian, and I spoke to one from Vancouver and another from Saskatoon. The latter had been volunteering there for two weeks every November for the last thirteen years. It turns out the hospital uses a rotation system that rotates among Canadians, Europeans, and Australians for a good portion of the year.

When they told me they'd performed about 195 surgeries in the time they'd been there, I was truly impressed and thanked them for what they do. Like Indigenous people everywhere, the Mayan people seem to have been screwed out of everything. In this case, they'd lost their land and received no services from the government, hence the need for those volunteers who are doing a heck of a job. Plus, I was proud to see the Canadians doing their part. So, here's my plug for this extraordinary partnership. Should anyone have either skills or money, please consider donating to one of these splendid organizations, depending on where you're located: Heineman-Robicsek Foundation, Hermano Pedro Social Works Foundation, Partners for World Health, Health for Humanity, Surgicorps International, Operation Walk, Fundarveja Guatemala, or ONG Quesada Solidaria.

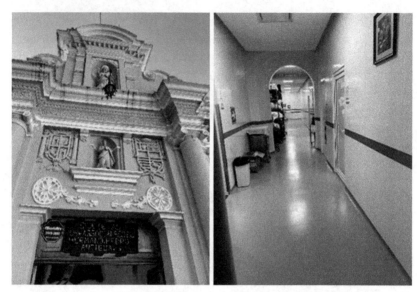

The old convent-turned hospital

Round about the same time, I'd met a lady from Vancouver with an organization that raises money to feed about twenty families in Guatemala. She told me they always need more money and that they're trying to buy laundry basins so the Indigenous women would have a place to do the laundry. The folks in the Mayan villages only have a single tap used for cooking, washing, laundry, and everything else, and she wanted to make their lives a little easier, a little more efficient.

And that wasn't all. The woman from Vancouver was also trying to raise money for efficient wood-burning stoves because the Mayan's main fuel is the wood they collect in the forests. However, they don't have stoves. They simply burn the wood in the middle of the floor in their homes. So not only would a wood-burning stove be safer, but it would also result in the women having to put out less effort collecting the wood and toting it home in bundles on their backs. A stove would burn the wood more efficiently.

As our conversation had neared an end, I mentioned my supporters had raised money—for what had once been toys but had then switched to bicycles—for children in Panama.

She exclaimed, "Oh, what a good idea!" as it made her think that if she could get some bicycles for the women of the villages, then they wouldn't have to carry all that wood over the long distance that they do. I'd promised her I'd get in touch with her later to see if we could find a way to work together to buy some bicycles in the future. I sincerely hoped we could help make a difference.

After my thought-provoking conversation with Fernando and dinner, I went to bed that night with a million thoughts swirling in my head and a tremendous desire to work harder to raise more money to get those kids in Panama as many bikes as I could. Eventually, I fell asleep though and spent the next day just meandering through the old town again, poking my head into the shops and sampling some of the food. Though I'd planned to take Kyle, Yiota, and Johana to Claudia's restaurant to get some great drone footage, both for the Octogenarian Odyssey Instagram account and for Claudia's restaurant, they were exhausted from their trek, so I just went out for a quiet solo dinner.

***

And then we were off the next day in the direction of El Salvador. We got a serious adrenaline boost to start our day when the volcano decided to belch a few times. I'd never experienced that before. And it made absolutely no never mind to the locals. Me, I was at least a little relieved to be moving on. Then we came upon a house-sized rock fall blocking half the road, on our side of course, before leaving those volcanoes behind us.

After that, it was a mostly pleasant ride past sugar-cane plantations in more sunshine, though Wayne did get a flat tire from a little wire. That hiccup cost us a good hour as we tried to repair it. We didn't think much of it at first; we just pulled the tube and wire out and put a patch on the hole. Then we put the tube back in and pumped it up, standard procedure. But as soon as we got ready to ride again, it went flat again. So, we thought, hey, maybe the patch didn't hold. We pulled it all apart again, but no, the patch looked good. Then when we pumped the tube back up, we discovered another hole. So, we put a patch on that hole too, put the tube back in the tire, and started pumping it up. And the tube exploded. After restarting our hearts, then cursing, we realized we had no choice but to wait for the support vehicle to come along. Wayne needed a new tube.

We took a hydration break while we waited for the team, then we put the new tube in and were on our way again. It was unfortunate that we'd been thrown that obstacle because not only had it been one of those wonderful riding days until then, but we also had a long way to go that day. It was a good 145 km to the El Salvador border, and we had no intention of stopping until we got there. We would, however, spend the night and cross over the next morning, allowing us to hit the border early in the morning and hopefully before everybody else, so maybe we could get through with as little difficulty as possible.

As we neared the El Salvador border, we began to see semi after semi lined up in one lane. We rode past truck after truck for about sixteen kilometers and didn't determine the reason for it until we got to the border that afternoon. The backlog was due to protests and ongoing strikes over inflation and the price of gas. In the end, despite what the long truck line-up had possibly portended, we were fortunate. Many other border crossings around the country were closed because of the protests, but the one we were headed for was still open. However, though they were letting travelers and personal vehicles through, they were stopping the semis, so when we got there, there was a three-day wait for a semi to get across, in either direction!

***

Thankfully, we didn't have too many problems at the border after having stayed the night on the Guatemala side before crossing. That doesn't mean, however, that the experience wasn't time-consuming or smooth.

When we pulled up to the border bright and early, the entire place was already in chaos. Semis were parked everywhere with no particular order to anything, and no one was moving, not semis, not vehicles, not people. There was hardly room for a bike to get through, let alone our van and tent trailer, so we squeezed by in some places, jockeyed for position in others, and made a new lane when we had to.

Feeling like stunt drivers at the Guatemala El Salvador border

We pushed through as far as we could until we could go no further. Then Kyle blew me away. He just got off his bike and started playing the part of traffic cop. He started waving his arms and whistling and guiding the vehicles out of the way in an orderly fashion yelling, "Come on, get going!" or "Move over here!" or "Clear the way!" I thought he'd missed his calling! We got to customs awfully quickly after that.

Things moved along a little faster once we got through. We pulled into customs, parked the car ... and waited. Of the hour and a half, we were there, we spent at least forty-five minutes of that waiting. Though there were only three groups trying to cross the border and nine or ten officials working, those officials always seemed too busy doing something or other to help the folks in line. Ah well, patience is always the name of the game.

Once it was our turn, it took less than an hour to check out of Guatemala, stamp our passports, remove the stickers from the van, and make copies of all the required documents for those who would drive the van. Of course, I'm sure much of that speediness was due to Johana's friendly, flirtatious demeanor as she entertained the officials with her smile and tales of our travels. Then we went through no-man's land and into El Salvador. And wouldn't you know it, everything was quiet and orderly on that side. Plenty of trucks were still lined up for what turned out to be another fifteen or so kilometers, but they were lined up in one lane, keeping the rest of the border area clear.

As we rode further into El Salvador, the beauty of it exceeded my expectations. It seemed Wayne hadn't been the only one with low expectations for the Central American countries. I apparently had a bias too despite living in Costa Rica. Just as Guatemala had been breathtaking with its mountain ranges and volcanoes and Lake Atitlan, El Salvador too was marvelous with its clear blue sky, tropical foliage, and sugar cane. And though we started with a fantastic, paved highway in great shape with wide shoulders to ride in, we found we had to scoot into traffic at times because corn kernels and cobs littered the shoulder as they dried out in the sun. Then of course, there was Google Maps. It chose a route to our destination for the night that included a dirt road full of loose gravel that descended at 30 percent. Though we could see the beach tempting us at the end of it, there was no way we were riding down that, so we backtracked once again and found a safer route.

We'd planned to ride further that day, but because the border crossing had taken a big chunk out of our day and we'd had to reroute, we decided to stop after about 76 km when we found an available Airbnb in Mizata. It was a unique structure in a picturesque location where a river met the ocean. The house had only two bedrooms and a bathroom inside and the living and dining areas outside. It also came complete with a big yard and a gorgeous, heated swimming pool.

Our first order of business was to jump in the pool and then head down to the beach. It had been calling to us since we'd seen a glimpse of it at the end of the dirt road. So, without delay, off we went. And what did we see when we got there? Oh, just two extravagant resorts with outdoor pools and dining, so tons of people were on the beach watching the sunset with us. We relaxed and took in the awe-inspiring sunset over the ocean while we ate a glorious dinner at one of the resort restaurants. After the sky had gone from intense blue to brilliant orange and red and yellow to finally fading to a soft purple and indigo, we built a big bonfire on the beach and enjoyed letting loose for a while. It was an evening of pure enjoyment before we retired for the night. I'd had no idea we would find such luxury and modernity in El Salvador after we'd always heard of it in the press.

***

After our pretty much perfect night, I awoke the next morning energized and optimistic, hoping that day would be as pleasurable as the previous night. And we did start off rather well, following the black, sandy beaches of the coast as we once again climbed up to the heavens and back down again into river valleys. We did that most of the morning until we came to a modern city with a Disneyland sort of complex. Later, I heard some beachgoers call it Surf City. But it all looked incredibly North American with a ton of new strip malls and hotels. It really looked like a great place for a vacation. For us, it meant a great place to stop for lunch.

Surf City, El Salvador

As we ate and chatted about the next few days of our journey, we discovered our first complication. We were due to hit Honduras in a day's time, and we'd only spend one day there before getting to Nicaragua. Nicaragua posed a huge problem for us. That country does not permit drones in, so Kyle with his drones and cameras had a decision to make. The first was to have a friend take the drones back to Guatemala then ship them to my place in Costa Rica. Another option was to smuggle them in, or at least one in, but I wasn't having any of that. I told him flat out that we were absolutely not hiding drones in the tent trailer, van, or bikes, so if we went with that plan, he'd have to hide them in his backpack and go through on his own. You can imagine how that went over.

So, with that option out, another option was to ship them via DHL from El Salvador to Costa Rica. I didn't mind that option as it was the easiest, even if it was a bit expensive. But in the end, we came up with a whole new plan. Kyle would stay in El Salvador, then take a bus to the airport where he would fly to Costa Rica, pick up Johana's car, and drive to my place in Liberia. There, he'd stay with Gloria and wait for our arrival. I could only hope the plan worked well because Kyle ended up quite upset that he was in that situation. Granted, it was on me that I'd procrastinated making that decision after they *had* told me we couldn't bring the drones into Nicaragua. It was certainly a lesson on studying *all* entry requirements on my future tours.

That problem finally ironed out, I went to pay for lunch only to discover our debit cards and visas don't work in El Salvador. The manager explained that Canadian credit card companies have blocked El Salvador, so in my incredulity, I paid in cash and called Visa right away. They confirmed what the manager had said, so I explained my situation, after which they made a note in my file and said my card should work now. Just to make sure, I popped over to a nearby beach club and took out a dollar at an ATM to make sure.

Relieved, Wayne, Johana, and I got back on our bikes to finish the day while Yiota took Kyle to a hostel and gave him $20. I was guessing he didn't have a lot of money after paying for his plane ticket. At the same time, I fervently prayed Yiota would make it to the hostel and back to us without incident because though we had tried to get car insurance in El Salvador, we'd discovered it would take three days to receive it. By then, we would have been out of El Salvador and into Honduras, so it just didn't make any sense to pay for it. Besides, we'd be traveling through some wild, frontier country so there wouldn't be anywhere to get it, and we'd be unlikely to be involved in anything.

Despite having to hash out the drone problem, lunch hadn't been all bad. I'd enjoyed some conversation with more folks curious about my Octogenarian Odyssey, including two Texans I'd taken photos with and a local guy who, when he'd found out I was eighty, said, "Oh, you're just like Joshua in the Bible leading Moses and the Israelites to the Promised Land!"

To that, I'd said, "Well, I don't know if Panama is the Promised Land, but that's where we're going anyway," before thanking him and heading out to go try my Visa.

We tackled more mountains, and some tunnels, again after lunch, and I noticed most of us were getting pretty cranky. Wayne was cranky about having to do all that climbing in the heat on his road bike, Yiota was cranky at the Kyle situation—not to mention not being able to access any funds—and I was cranky at the banks and at everyone else's crankiness. Sure, we were all stressed that day for one reason or another, but I'm the kind of person that prefers to face and find a solution to a problem and move past it, but others prefer to bitch, which they did that day. I guess it helps them get their emotions out.

Well, the day just kept getting better and better after that. After Yiota had dropped Kyle off at the hostel, she'd continued on to the rinky-dink town in the middle of nowhere we were to stop in for that night only to find that she couldn't find a hotel. Then she went to the bank and tried to pull some funds out and got nothing but a message saying she'd exceeded the allowable number of tries and she'd have to try again tomorrow. I'd thought I'd solved the problem, but apparently not.

So, when Johana, Wayne, and I pulled into town, we met up with Yiota, who had by then stopped outside one of those love hotels, or auto hotels, again. I looked at her in surprise for a minute until she explained this was the only place available. *Ah well*, I thought. *You gotta do what you gotta do, right?* So, I went in and booked three rooms for the night. Though they cost $20 a night, or $13 for three hours, we needed three rooms because, for obvious reasons, there was only one bed in each room. That meant Wayne and I would each have our own room and the girls would share.

The Love Hotel

Then we went through the hidden gate in the wall that hid the parking lot from passersby to our rooms, where I got the batteries charging and got freshened up a little. I didn't stay long though because I had the bank issue to deal with. We unhooked the tent trailer, and Johana and I went to find a bank in town. Well, wouldn't you know, I found one that was more of a credit union, went in, and discovered I couldn't access any of my bank accounts. I tried my Visa again then, and at least it worked, so I had no choice but to pull $100 off it so we had something to work with until we crossed into Nicaragua, despite the high interest rate on cash advances on a credit card.

When I got back to the love hotel, I gave Yiota $85 out of the $100, keeping the rest just in case, though I ended up pulling out another $300 later. And I have to say that just because it was a love hotel didn't mean it was a bad hotel. It was clean and modern, though there were mirrors on the ceiling. The stress had thankfully lessened by the time I got back as Wayne had gotten a shower and gone to buy some beer. So, though Yiota stayed behind that night as she often did, the rest of us went in search of dinner then.

When we happened upon an El Salvador version of a Swiss Chalet or KFC, we decided that's where we would eat because it was full of customers. I've always found that the busier a place is, the better the food is. And I wasn't wrong. We had a tasty chicken dinner, and I paid the bill with my Visa with no issue before heading back to the love hotel. When we got there, we discovered they had weird hours. They closed at 7 p.m., so we had to call security and tell them who we were, so they'd let us in. I was little confused as to why people there didn't seem to visit auto hotels at night after the bars closed when I thought the most sexual activity occurred, but that just didn't seem to be how it worked in that country.

***

As with all mornings, we all woke with a fresh perspective and brighter attitudes the next morning despite the van that has trouble starting. We had a long ride that day, 140 to 150 km, so Johana and Yiota drove while Wayne and I both rode the e-bikes. The plan was to stop in La Union for the night so we could again cross the border into Honduras in the morning. I assumed it would take a long time to go through the whole checkout/check-in process again, but it meant we were getting close to the end of the odyssey. After crossing the Honduran border, we'd spend just one day there and cross into Nicaragua. And I was looking forward to reaching Panama, but only because I'd received word that day that my contact in Panama had purchased and hand-delivered ten bikes to a school—with more to come—and was in the process of creating a draw for those children the school deemed most in need of a bike given their long distance to school and their economic situation. The teachers would choose fifty children, put their names in a hat, and draw names to equal our final bike total. We were going to fundraise through the entire odyssey, so we didn't know then how many we'd be able to buy in the end. I was to be the lucky one to draw the names, and then I would say a few words about exercise, adventure, following your dreams, and planning how to do that. Though how I would do that since I didn't speak Spanish I did not know. But later that day, I got more good news: we'd raised another $300, so I was hoping we could buy at least another two bikes!

Besides the banking issue though, I was impressed with El Salvador. From what I'd seen in my short time there, it was by far cleaner—with no big piles of garbage on the roadside or loads of plastic floating down the rivers as in Guatemala—which indicated a more stable government and better infrastructure. All the strip malls and amusement parks and restaurants and such illustrated the same thing, especially the fact that they were all new, clean, and modern. The highways were well-maintained, and the people were friendly and happy.

In more fantastic weather, to me the perfect temperature. I thoroughly enjoyed riding on their great highways that day, past verdant foliage, bright flowering trees, and the odd cow. We flew over bridges with brightly painted murals on the barriers and by fruit stands and another volcano, and the van continued to run well, easing my worries in that regard. About sixty kilometers into that day's ride, we stopped at a modern roadside fast-food restaurant I'd guarantee was cleaner than any in North America. On our second break, the girls caught up to us as we watched an enormous extended family pile into an open-backed truck, taking with them coolers and chairs that they also managed to fit in. It was a Sunday, and in many Latin American countries, Sunday is their only day off, so they call it Sunday Funday and have as much fun with their friends and families as they can fit in. We saw evidence of this again much later in the day as we passed a soccer game that we sadly didn't stop to watch.

And it was about then that things turned to crap. Because it wasn't enough that Wayne and I had ridden 145 km and climbed 1,500 meters while still staying positive and appreciating what was around us, with just 2.5 km to go until we reached La Union, I got another flat tire. And that just happened to be a day when I didn't have any patches, plus

Wayne had gone ahead already, and it was already 5:30 p.m. and the sun was disappearing quickly. I was on a four-lane highway too, so I called the support team to come and get me only to learn they would have to unpack the trailer so we could fit my bike in it. Yes, I should have known that, but I was tired, stressed, and starting to feel a little unsafe.

So, after waiting about a half hour, I decided I wasn't going to just sit and wait anymore. I started walking. A few minutes into my trek, the team called and told me they were having trouble unhooking the trailer, but they were still trying. I hung up, feeling rather disgruntled, and realized it just wasn't safe to walk on the side of that highway in the pitch black anymore with all the traffic flashing by with their brights on, even if I did have my headlights and taillights on. I found a rock safely off the road I could sit on and waited it out, wondering if I'd be there all night.

Finally, after nearly falling asleep on my rock, a car pulled over and stopped right in front of me. Johana hopped out of the passenger seat, grabbed my bike, and threw it in the car. On the way to the hotel, I learned that they still hadn't gotten the trailer unhitched from the van, but the hotel owner had been kind enough to lend them his car to come and rescue me, and his wife had been generous enough to drive.

Did I mention the hotel the team found was another love hotel? Yes, we had another night in one of those. Not that they're unpleasant or unsafe, but they do vary in their standards, and while the previous one had been clean and modern and maybe a 3.5-star hotel, this one was no more than 2.5 stars. It was unfortunate, but it was a place to rest our heads for the night and led to one of the most amusing memories of our journey.

So, after I'd eaten and flopped down on the bed in my room, I looked over and saw a little cupboard in the wall. I dismissed it, thinking it was just a place for storing your wallet or something, or maybe they'd had a phone in there in the past. Anyway, I didn't think anything of it. Not much later, I was lying in bed watching Netflix on my phone when I heard a little knocking/scraping noise. It was so soft; I didn't really register the sound. Then it went away, and I thought no more of it.

A minute later, I heard the sound again. *What?* I thought, *Do we have a rat in here or something?* So, I made an effort to look for the noise that time, but I didn't find anything so I quit. Then it resumed again. That time, I went over and sort of looked over by that little cupboard, but I didn't hear anything more and I didn't see a rat or anything running around, so I went back to watching Netflix.

Suddenly, there was a knock at my door and Yiota yelled, "Bob! Bob! Are you awake?!"

I yelled back, "Yeah, I'm awake! Come on in!"

She came in and asked, "Why didn't you answer?"

I was terribly confused. "Answer who?" I asked.

Yiota sighed and said, "Well, the ladies were knocking on the little door over there." She pointed to exactly the little cupboard I'd been curious about earlier.

"What?" I asked, a little discombobulated.

"Yes," Yiota said. "They say that little door over there is for passing in food or deliveries and passing out money and stuff. That way, no one can see you and you don't have to get dressed or anything. It's basically a secret little passageway behind the hotel, so they can serve the clients without interrupting them or using the front door."

"Oh! Ha, I thought it was a mouse or rat scraping away," I said.

"No no, they want you to pay for the room," Yiota explained. "And I don't have the cash, so you have to put the money in there."

I chuckled, shook my head, and replied, "Ok, I will go pay 'em."

And that was the end of both one of the most stressful days and the most amusing days.

***

Because the plan was to get an early start for the Honduran border just thirty kilometers away, we wasted no time that morning. We gulped down some coffee, got the bikes ready, and packed the van. Then we were on our bikes and in the van about to be on our way, when not five minutes before leaving, the van stopped running, never to start again. And I'd said the day before was the most stressful?

Well, we tried to start it again a couple times, but no luck. So, Johana called a security guard and told him of our problem. The guard fortuitously had a mechanic friend, who rode out to us on his motorcycle with all his tools and things. That was just another example, like the hotel owner and his wife rescuing me the night before, of the never-ending generosity and kindness of the Central American people. So, the young fellow checked everything, and in my mind, he did a really thorough job. In the end though, he determined the issue was the fuel pump or float or both and it needed to be taken to the shop. We needed to have the gas tank dropped out to change the fuel pump and the float.

Taking the poor, tired van away to get some work done on it.

That was not what I'd wanted to hear. With a groan, I listened to him call a tow truck, who wanted $75. Our mechanic thought that was too much, so he called a friend who was going to come tow it with a tow line or belt with his car, but I couldn't let Johana deal with trying to control the van as it was being towed. Without the motor running, the van would be just too difficult to handle, so I got the $75 tow truck instead. It took an hour and a half to arrive, but he was a good guy. He towed us all in, dropped the car off at the shop, left it there, drove the tow truck home, got his car, and came back for us. He even took us to a restaurant so we could have that breakfast we hadn't had yet and to a bank so I could pull out some more funds to pay for the unexpected costs I'd just been hit with. It cost me $30 to use the tow-truck driver as a taxi, but even though I thought I got ripped off, we did get to see a little bit of the town along the way, however unplanned it had been. We even got to see the islands in the Bahia de La Union and had a buffet lunch that doubled as dinner at about 4:30 p.m.

As it turned out after all that *and* after they'd put in the new fuel pump and float, they discovered that wasn't the problem after all. The real problem was that it wasn't getting an electrical signal, which was required for it to turn on, so they rewired and put in another fuse and a wire to bypass whatever was causing the problem. Lo and behold, they hooked it up, and it finally worked. I wanted to argue that they'd taken advantage of me by saying it was one problem when in fact it was something else entirely then only discovering that after they'd done all the other work, but when the bill only came to $47 for all their labor and the parts, I had to admit that was more than fair. They even gave us a couple new fuses, showed us how to install them if we needed to, and suggested we take the van to a shop with knowledge of the electrical system at the first opportunity, likely in Liberia.

Fortunately, there wasn't much griping and complaining that day. Everyone just accepted the work was something that needed to get done, and Johana was a great help. On the other hand, however, our one-night stay at the auto hotel turned into a two-night stay. Because it was a love hotel not a regular hotel, we'd had to negotiate when we'd gone to see if we could stay an extra night for another $25 per room per night. While the owner had said yes, we could stay another night, he'd had one condition: we would need to vacate during the day if the hotel got busy while we were out fixing the car. Well, at that price, which I'd thought was good value for my money, I'd agreed because I'd been sure it wouldn't get busy anyway. The first love hotel had been busy with at least four couples popping in within minutes of each other, but here, we'd only seen three couples pull in the whole time we'd been trying to get the car started. Besides, we'd needed to store our luggage and gear in the rooms while we were busy. Oh, you learn so many new things on a long-distance tour. I could only wonder by then what Honduras would have in store for us. Would it be snags or smooth sailing?

ANTICIPATION and PARANOIA

What a relief it was to get back on the road. I'd had to adjust the itinerary and bypass one of the cities I like to visit—León, Nicaragua—and create a little shortcut to accommodate our unexpected rest day, but at least we'd started the van on at least a couple occasions with no problems. It worked just like new.

For all the relief I felt at riding again, I was feeling dark and dreary that day. Maybe it was all the obstacles we'd faced on this tour, or maybe it was that I'd had to start the day by backtracking to where I'd gotten my flat tire to satisfy the Guinness Book of World Records requirements, but I was disappointed at all our late starts every day, upset with all the drama we'd had, and worried about what we'd face in Nicaragua with the government as paranoid as they are ... and we hadn't even crossed the Honduran border yet.

And then there we were, at the Honduran border. I decided then to look at it as a new opportunity while Wayne and I sat there, waiting for the support team to arrive before we crossed over. We were spending just one day in that country, so it felt we were speeding through the last leg. Then I got an update on the fundraising for the children in Panama, and received another $750, thanks to Wayne and his friends and family and my last Facebook post. Maybe we could buy another five bikes. That helped improve my mood. Knowing I could help a few kids made me feel incredibly fulfilled.

Anyway, Wayne and I had no choice but to sit on the side of the road just outside the border waiting to check out of El Salvador and into Honduras because Yiota and Johana had discovered that morning that one of the van's tires had gotten damaged yesterday when it was in the shop. So, while Wayne and I rode for Honduras, they'd had to take it back to the shop and catch up to us. So, that left us stranded. There was no sense crossing without them, so all we could do was watch the time tick by as we waited for them so we could all cross together. It was just another setback that meant we wouldn't get as far as we'd planned—again.

But as Wayne and I sat there, snacking on pastries and cakes and coffee, so we weren't exactly hard done by, I looked around and noticed once again the lack of any real rubbish. As I'd ridden through Mexico, and especially Guatemala, the litter had been everywhere: on the side of the road, in the medians, in the rivers and creeks. The amount of litter on the road that most tourists don't see going to the resorts, but cyclists do see as they travel through the country is staggering and disgusting. I've never been an environmentalist, but as I get older, I find myself turning into one. I can't help but wonder what it's doing to the planet, to flora and fauna alike, and what kind of future my grandchildren will have as a result. It would be world-altering if someone could figure out how to cure that, but I don't hold out much hope with world politics as it is these days. *El Salvador is much, much better, but even here they can't completely eliminate it*, I thought as I at the border looking across the street at a bunch of plastic bags and stuff piled under a lamppost and plastic bottles piled against the curb. And Costa Rica isn't much better.

And I'm no better, truly. Every time I ride down the highway and watch as someone throws a bottle out the window of a car or bus or whatever reminds me of the amount of plastic the five of us had consumed along the way with our water bottles, Gatorade, and Coke and such. I think it's disgusting, so when I do my Octogenarian Odyssey Part Two in South America, I'll have to do something so we're not buying single-serve bottles like we had been.

The support team finally showed up a couple hours later, which surprised me given they'd only been about 35 km away. I heard something about the tire being stuck on or something when I asked them what was up, but I admittedly wasn't paying close attention to their reply because I was focused on getting over the border by then. I wasn't exactly sure how crossing into a country like Honduras would go. Hopefully the government wouldn't be as sticky and paranoid as I was expecting Nicaragua to be.

But we hit our first stroke of luck in some time that day. The border crossing was small, and no one bothered us. We just showed our papers, got our passports stamped, waited a while for officials to clear the van and trailer, and off we went across the bridge that marks the actual border of Honduras and Nicaragua. I have to say though, that the contrast between the tall wall of razor wire contrasted loudly with the Merry Christmas decorations, and all the souped-up Tuk-Tuks with their spoilers and spiked tires and skulls and gas mask decals made for a rather dystopian-movie feel.

Souped-up Tuk-Tuk

As I took in the landscape on the Honduran side of the border, I thought it interesting to discover that there, they use small plastic bags rather than bottles for drinking water. It seemed like something North America should also be using, then we'd lessen the enormous amount of waste from all those plastic bottles that we all use. Perhaps someone should petition the government?

We again rode past a long, long line of parked semis waiting to cross the border. It was no wonder we were having supply-chain issues back home in North America! As we rode down our side of the highway on the shoulder as usual, thinking it was the safest place for us, we continued to come face-to-face with vehicles coming straight us—on the shoulder! Talk about no-rules driving. Not only were they driving in the wrong direction, but they were also driving in the wrong direction on the shoulder. I had no words for what I was seeing. We weren't feeling tremendously safe riding in Honduras at that point.

We did, however, pass more lovely churches and learn a little bit of history. For example, I did not know that Honduras assisted the Allies in World War II, mostly with antisubmarine efforts in the Atlantic and in the air. And as the sun was setting, we passed a good old kids' soccer game, and despite the rampant poverty in that country, those kids had some spiffy uniforms and topnotch gear.

And then we were back beside the ocean again, or more specifically the Gulf of Fonseca, as we pulled into San Lorenzo for the night after a 92-km day. The sun was almost on the horizon by then, and the orange glow gave the city an otherworldly feel, and interestingly, I didn't see the same piles of garbage I'd thought I would. *Perhaps San Lorenzo focused on its city center for the sake of tourists*, I thought. We cycled past the shore and the little fishing boats and pleasure boats on our way to our hotel, where a seahorse as tall as me greeted us.

Dinner that night was enjoyed with a few cold ones on a deck under a palapa overlooking the water, where we watched the last of the sun sink behind the mountains. Also at dinner, we reached another milestone: Yiota finally had a lobster. She'd refused the entire journey, but I think when she saw this one under all the melted cheese, she figured it would be a good time to try. And she must have liked it because she didn't complain.

***

The weather was once again beautiful as we left San Lorenzo the next morning. That was the one thing that had been on our side in the last few weeks as we'd worked our way through all our other obstacles. Wayne still found it a bit hot for him, but for me it was just right. The sky was cloudless and such a bright blue, almost a sapphire blue, that it lightened everything below it, and the water mirrored it, making you feel as though you had no worries.

So, I decided to not worry that day, not about what time we got started or where we'd end up or what would happen at the Nicaraguan border. Depending on how the day went, we'd cross it that night or the next morning. Instead, I just rode my bike and enjoyed feeling the wind on my face and between the straps of my sandals, where I now had deeply tanned zebra stripes on my feet.

But then the riding got hairy again. We were riding on the shoulder again when we came upon another long line of semis, and some were parked partly on our shoulder. I was starting to think riding through Honduras wasn't the best idea. Then a few kilometers later, we finally discovered why the semis had been lined up, unmoving. It wasn't the border this time, but it was a protest. Dissatisfied workers had completely blocked the highway.

Worker protest blocking the highway

Wayne and I got through the blockade with no issues, but the van got held up for a few hours. It was fortunate we didn't have any issues that required the team. We actually just enjoyed a nice ride in the sunshine. We saw a few displays of Honduras's military might with a cannon monument and mural of a soldier pointing a gun directly at us, but then that was juxtaposed with a line of straw Christmas deer on display on the side of the road. Eventually, we stopped for lunch in a larger, surprisingly modern city, Choluteca—at a Wendy's! There's nothing like a little reminder of home.

Again, we came across more corn, red this time, drying on the shoulder of the road once we got back on our bikes. We rode past numerous oxen-drawn carts and riders on horseback, illustrating the disparity between the El Salvador economy and the Honduran, over a steel bridge like those we love so much, and through the tropical forests.

Suddenly, the Nicaraguan border loomed. The border there too was a bridge over a river, in which it appeared a horse was migrating to Honduras. I wondered if he'd get stopped. I could only hope it would be as easy for us.

And it did start out that way. Once the support team caught up with Wayne and I, checking out of Honduras was easy, so easy in fact, that the customs agents wanted to take pictures with me. They seemed to think it was a big deal that I broke the world record, and I wasn't going to complain. Good attention was far better than bad attention.

Then things went downhill. Talk about frustration. Though nobody stopped me as I started riding across the border, suddenly someone hollered at me to come back, so I did and asked, "Okay, what do you need?"

"We need your passport and COVID documents."

"They're in the van, a little way behind us," I replied.

So, he asks, "Where's the van?"

"Just on the bridge," I said. "I'll go get them." Back I went, got all the documents, and gave them to the official. They took a photo of them and gave me a form to fill out—that I never did fill out.

Anyway, Wayne and I moved further into the customs area back in the direction of the Nicaraguan side, and none of the roads led anywhere. We had to ride against the traffic to get to some other building where we were supposed to get in line only to find out there were papers, we should have completed seven days in advance. But of course, we hadn't known about that, so we had to get in a different line. It wasn't very long, but it just didn't move. Half an hour later, we finally got to the front and explained our situation. Fortunately, they said that was okay, but we had to wait, and they disappeared into an office of sorts. So, we waited another hour before they came back out and said, "Your documents are ready. That's $13." I sighed, but then thought $13 was a small price to pay to get through that.

But we weren't done yet. We still had to clear the van and tent trailer. That meant another line. When we got to the front of *that* line, the official looked over our documents, told us they were good, then told us to go stand in yet *another* line for a van and trailer inspection. Line after line after line, we were starting to feel like cattle, and by then, our hunger wasn't helping our patience any.

Five hours later, we made it out of there. And it was fully dark out. There was no way we were getting any further, so after a quick Google search, we found a tiny, rundown hotel just five kilometers away. It was rather treacherous riding on an unfamiliar road in the dark, in Nicaragua at that, but our headlights kept us out of potholes and away from other unforeseen dangers, and we weren't accosted on our way to the hotel. By then, it didn't matter how much it cost or what it had or didn't have; we just wanted to eat and sleep.

***

Though I'd originally allocated a rest day in León because I love its old town, we now had to ride around it, take a shortcut, and ride as far as we could to try and stay close to the schedule. So that day, I was hoping to get to Managua instead. It would certainly be a long, long day.

After another later start than I would have liked, we got out of that hotel and onto the highway. But again, it was sunny, and the highway wasn't terrible. We had to be wary of the traffic, but at least we didn't come across washed-out roads or rocky dirt roads or cobblestone roads. Instead, we came upon cowboys driving cattle across a river and down the highway, locals crushing mountain rocks to extract the iota of gold in the resulting rock flour, and more volcanoes, one of whom gave us a burp again.

Grinding rocks to find gold

The clouds started rolling in as we reached Puerto Momtombo, and its world-famous stratovolcano then rode past spectacular columnar rocks formed from cooled magma and past sugar-cane plantations and banana farms. That's the one thing about long-distance cycling: it doesn't matter how many obstacles you face or hurdles you must overcome, there's always something new to experience and learn and see. It all balances out for me.

By the time we rolled into Nagarote that night after a 140-km ride, I was thrilled we'd only had two issues that day. The first was the car not starting again, and the second was a flat tire, both giving us a late start of course. We'd solved the flat with the new hand pump, but the no-starting issue had taken more work. But again, we'd been on the receiving end of more kindness. The hotel manager had phoned a mechanic friend, who'd determined we needed an electrician. The electrician had put us in touch with one, who'd come out and found that the shaking of the van had caused wiring to separate, causing the car to not start. I'd have to prioritize fixing that on our rest days in Costa Rica.

Until then, we checked into a hotel that night that charged $40/room, where we discovered we had little to no hot water, depending on when we tried, much the way it had been for about the previous ten days. Wayne and I were developing some scratchy beards by then. And the hotel wouldn't even let us in until we had paid in full. At least we were only about fifty kilometers out of Managua, which meant only one more night in Nicaragua, and then I'd be home in my own bed.

So, we went out that night and had a tasty, satisfying dinner at another outdoor restaurant, more like a cafeteria really, then got to experience a rickshaw ride. It wasn't a true rickshaw, more of a motorbike on the back with a covered bench seat up front, but it was close enough for me. And it was fun!

***

Everyone had a delightful time trying to get ready the next morning. The power had gone out sometime in the night, but I eventually rolled one of the e-bikes into the room and turned the headlights on. That gave us plenty of light then, and packing back up went a little more smoothly. I guess I discovered another good use for an e-bike.

We may have been facing a long day ahead the next day, but we started things off right with a stop for Nicaraguan coffee. If it weren't for the Spanish words, you would have thought you were in a Starbucks where we stopped. It had the same modern furniture, the same decor, and the same fancy drink options. The only difference was that coffee was better than anything in North America. To top it off, we got cheesecake and mini cinnamon rolls for breakfast. We had to get those cycling calories in you know!

Then it was off to try and near the Costa Rica border. The closer we could get, the better so we could cross early in the morning. We soon discovered the power was out in the whole city, perhaps even the state. Ordinarily that wouldn't have mattered much, but the van had another flat tire, so the girls had a tough time finding a place to inflate the tire again. In the end, they bought a pump that plugs into the cigarette lighter so they could keep pumping up the tire until we could find a place to service it.

It was a little cloudier that day, so it kept the heat at bay. I enjoyed coming upon all the Nicaraguan culture, their architecture, and monuments, as much as in any other country, but in this case, it almost made me feel uneasy. Much of what I saw referred in one way or another to the president, reminding me of the dictatorship the Nicaraguan people live under and its human rights abuses. On the other hand, I also came across murals depicting "The War of Colonization" and sculptures evincing its ancient Mayan culture. Plus, as we neared Masaya, we got to stop and chat and take photos with a local cyclist again. That always brightens my day.

Yes, I was going to end up needing that motivational boost. That one, and the one I got from the view of top of a mountain of Apoyo Lagoon, a giant water-filled crater surrounded by trees. As close as we were to Granada then, we could even see Lake Nicaragua in the distance. From there, we got a gentle downhill the rest of the day.

Apoyo Lagoon with Lake Nicaragua in the distance

And here's where I needed those motivational boosts. First, we ended up with no accommodation because the owner of the Airbnb we thought we'd booked failed to respond or confirm the reservation. We were left with nothing but a town to head for after about 140 km of riding, 1,300 meters of that climbing.

But we kept going, hoping Johana and Yiota would find us a place to stay. But as the day progressed and it started getting later and later, we still had no destination, and we didn't even know where the support van was. Wayne was running out of power by then, so we stopped and waited for the support team to catch up so he could change the battery. Catch up they finally did, but not until dark. We still had no hotel either, so I told the girls to just pick the closest hotel they could find, which was six kilometers away.

Well, we rode on in the dark with our head and taillights on and navigating in pitch black on a busy highway. Now that's scary. You have to pay attention and watch for potholes, pedestrians, rocks, oncoming traffic, and traffic passing you, all while still watching for anything that might come at you out of nowhere and surprise you. And in Nicaragua, you had to add dogs, horses, cows, iguanas, and crazy-buses—a kind of party bus—to the list.

Anyway, we made it the six kilometers only to find there was no hotel there. I stopped and found a message on my phone saying the girls had gone on and found a hotel, Hotel Victoria, in Rivas. That was yet another seven kilometers away, so the day's ride had become a 153-km day, we were riding in the dark, and it had started to rain. Wayne and I were soaked as we made our way into town, first on the highway, then on some side streets that didn't look like they'd go very far or were in very good districts.

But then we turned a corner and saw some lights ahead. We rode in that direction and came to a beautiful church, its courtyard adorned with Christmas lights and decorated trees. Vendors and restaurants surrounded a square filled with people, and music floated through the air. Beside that was a spectacular four-star hotel, and all my thoughts of arriving at another crummy hotel soaking wet and cold and scared and tired disappeared. When we checked in, we discovered it not only had a fantastic swimming pool, but also wonderful rooms—and hot water! So that day started and ended on a good note, making it easier to put the difficulties behind me. The extra pushing had also put us within forty kilometers of the Costa Rican border, so we would cross early the next day, and with luck, I'd get to sleep in my own bed that night.

***

Well, after shaking off my rough day, enjoying a fantastic dinner, some drinks, and taking in the sights, sounds, and smells of that festive main square, I woke the next morning refreshed and ready to tackle the Costa Rican border. Though

I partially regretted leaving the luxury of Hotel Victoria, I was anxiously anticipating reaching my home in Liberia. As much as I love excitement, adventure, and discovery, there's still something about the allure of home.

While we did get a nice comfortable ride on a clean, well-maintained highway on the way to the border as we rode through a now almost familiar cacophony of birds, truck engines, and clopping hooves, it was awful trying to get out of the country. Strange, I know. Why make it hard for people to leave instead of making it hard to get in? After three hours trying to get out of Nicaragua and another hour working to get into Costa Rica, I empathized for the folks who were just driving through on their way to some other country.

When we finally got across, we met back up with Kyle, who had driven Johana's car there from Liberia. I surprised him then and said I'd cover half the expenses he'd incurred by having to skip Nicaragua given we couldn't take the drones into the country. I think that went a long way to repairing the bad feelings we'd parted with. I hoped it did anyway.

It had also been decided that with two rest days in Liberia, everyone would stay at my place for that night since it was just too late to do anything else. Then the next day, Johana and Kyle would take the tent trailer, pick up her daughter, and go camping on the beach, Johana at one beach and Yiota at another. They would take Yiota with them and drop her off at a beach resort on the way. And Wayne had found a decent hotel for only $28/night, so he'd get some quiet time, and I'd get some family time.

*Back home with my family, Julie on the left
and Gloria on the right*

After the chaos and bureaucracy of the border, I was past ready to be out on the open highway, with nothing but sun and sky and nature. And this was scenery I knew well. Unfortunately, the long delay at the border prevented us from getting home before it got dark and rainy, so I decided to stop early and beg Gloria to come pick me up. I would just have to go back the next day and redo the piddly thirty-five I chose not to do that day. I didn't much care though. I was looking forward to seeing my wife again and sleeping in my own bed, and I wasn't disappointed. Gloria and her daughter Julie came to grab me, and I reveled in the reception I got. It was wonderful to hold my wife again.

We spent some quiet time in the car catching up as we drove home, and when we arrived, I was touched to see the welcome-home decorations Gloria and Julie had put up. Once things had settled a little, we all cleaned out the van before I was surprised with a short visit from a couple friends, Monica, and Emilio, who had thoughtfully brought over a tasty apple pie for me. My favorite!

Well, that day had been so full of highs and lows, bedtime came early for us all, and I think I was asleep before my head hit the pillow of my own bed.

***

I'd been calling our non-riding days rest days to that point, but by the next day, I'd decided to stop calling them that. They're never rest days, at least not for me. They're more like catch-up days. While the others often get to rest instead of taking care of necessary tasks, I find there's always something that needs doing before we move on.

On that day, I had to start my day by going back to where I'd quit the night before, so I could ride into Liberia and satisfy the Guinness Book of World Records requirements. But I got my daily ride in, and it didn't rain, so I enjoyed it anyway. From there though, my focus was mostly on that stupid van tire that the guys in La Union had screwed up somehow.

I spent most of that day running around from place to place trying to get the tire off. The first place tried to get it off with power wrenches and bars, and they did get four out of five bolts off with an air gun, but the fifth one wouldn't budge. So, then they tried hammering at it with a smaller socket, but that didn't work, so they moved to a chisel and hammer. That didn't work either. They sent me to a welding shop then, and those folks tried to heat up the metal so they could mold it into a shape that would fit in a wrench. Of course, that didn't work either. So those guys sent me to a machine shop. Strike three. The machine-shop guy just came right out and said there was nothing he could do and sent me to an auto shop, who also said it was a no-go. Of course, he also sent me to someone else, in this case, a guy who restores cars. He, believe it or not, said he could do it, but he didn't have time to. In desperation, I took the van to a Firestone dealership.

Wonder of wonders, the guy at Firestone said he'd worked on the same situation just the week before. Why hadn't I started there? Anyway, he said if I came back at three that afternoon, he'd have it fixed for me. Unfortunately, when Gloria and I went back at 2:50 after a short siesta, it wasn't done yet. Welcome to Costa Rican time. By the time 4:45 p.m. rolled around and it was closing time, he was still drilling away and coming at it with chisels before taking a welding torch to it. That finally got the wheel off. I was afraid that much work was going to cost me a pretty penny, but I had no choice but to get that tire off so I could put a new one on. Somehow, those guys in La Union had managed to destroy one of the bolts, and now that the tire was constantly going flat, it was obvious I needed a new one. The only other options were to keep inflating the tire, usually twice a day, or using my Costa Rican car, but it didn't have papers, a roof rack, so neither option was feasible.

I felt bad for making the guy stay late, so I told him we'd catch a cab home and come back in the morning so they could close the shop up and deal with it tomorrow. Once we got home, I gave Wayne a call and we went out to a great Indian restaurant I knew of. It had been a long, frustrating day though, so after a wonderful meal, I headed home early to hit the hay. I seemed to be more tired than usual.

I did, however, get some good news that brightened my day through all that. I learned that our fundraising had allowed my contact in Panama to purchase sixteen bikes for the kids in Panama. Word was getting out, so I not only hoped that we could still raise more money and buy more bikes, but also that my message was spreading. The whole reason I'd started this odyssey in the first place was to motivate seniors to move, get out, get off the couch. I wanted to remove the stereotypes and stigmas around seniors and retirement and wanted to inspire them to at least try something new, anything. And if I reached younger people with that message too, so much the better.

***

Neither was my second rest day an actual rest day. When I got up in the morning, Gloria called the Firestone dealership to see where they were at, and we discovered that they couldn't fix the tire. I would need a new one. I had expected that, so I told the guy that was fine, to go ahead and do that. Then after a nice home-cooked breakfast, it was off to my dermatologist so she could scan me for skin cancer. Given all the time I spend outside in the sun, that's something I do often.

Anyway, she didn't find anything needing a biopsy, and while I was relieved about that, I did walk out of there with much of my body frozen from all the little spots she'd taken off. C'est la vie. It was better than the alternative.

Afterward, Gloria and I walked down to Firestone and picked up the van. That was another $300. This trip was sure getting expensive. But there was nothing I could do about that. So, I turned my attention to the fun evening we had planned and headed to Walmart to pick up all the snacks we needed for the shindig we were throwing that night. We were expecting around twenty people to come, but in the end only fourteen came. It was a great night though. I enjoyed chatting with everyone I hadn't seen in a long time. My friend, Doug, who owns the local brew pub, brought over five gallons of beer. So, though we only drank about half of that and a couple bottles of wine, the good food and pleasant company with all my friends from Liberia and Gloria's presence made for a wonderful, relaxing evening it seemed I really needed.

***

I'd had what I thought was an epiphany the night before, but when I woke up with a clearer head in the morning, I realized it hadn't been such a smart idea. I'd thought originally that I would take the hitch off the van and put it on my Costa Rican car, but I'd first have to take the van to a locksmith to get the lock off because it too had been damaged on our journey. Then I'd put the bike rack on and leave the tent trailer behind in Panama.

But then that morning, it dawned on me that perhaps that idea was not a good one. There was the possibility that we'd get to the border, and when the official checked the car out of the country, they might ask where the tent trailer is. And if I explained I was leaving it behind, they could very well come back and say I can't do that, that I'd brought it in, so I'd have to take it out. It just wasn't a chance worth taking. Besides, I only had a thirty-day temporary import permit on the van and tent trailer, and by the time I got back to Costa Rica, it would likely be December 15, leaving me only about ten days to get them out again.

I didn't want to have to do that so when the team came back from the beaches, we packed up the van and tent trailer again. Packing it back up reminded me of my irritation when we'd cleaned it out because we'd had so much food that needed to be thrown away, plus there was so much we'd duplicated, like ten packages of spaghetti and three containers of black pepper. Beyond that, we even had all kinds of spices so that it looked like a gourmet kitchen even though we'd done little cooking since way up north.

Anyway, though they were somewhat disgruntled that they'd cleaned out the van and tent trailer with the idea we wouldn't be taking it any further, we got everything packed back up again. I tried to take up as little space as possible by switching to a smaller suitcase since I wouldn't need much in the last nine or ten days, we had left of the Octogenarian Odyssey Part One. Of course, it was then I learned the roof of the tent trailer was leaking around the skylight, not earlier when I may have had time to fix it, but I supposed I had led them to believe we weren't going to need it anymore. I relished one last night with my wife before turning in early again in the hopes we could get away fairly early with everyone rested and refreshed and our stuff packed up already.

***

I took Gloria to work that morning, picked Wayne up, and brought him to the house where everyone was preparing to leave. I was still hopeful we could leave by 8:30 a.m., but there was so much stuff happening, I quickly started to lose hope. Before I knew it, it was 9 a.m. and we were almost ready. *Well, okay, good,* I thought, *that's still an early departure time.* We'd decided Yiota would ride the other e-bike with me while Wayne rode his road bike, and Johana and Kyle would drive the support van. So, I went to leave them to hook up the tent trailer and straighten up as Yiota, Wayne and I hit the road. But once again, Yiota had a flat tire. Wayne chose to go on ahead anyway, and we'd catch up to him somewhere down the road.

Well, I repaired the flat tire and of course found a little piece of wire once again. Those things had caused us so many problems on this journey. I realized then I should have put some liners in that e-bike when I'd put in the liners on mine, but it was too late by then. Again, hindsight is blinding.

Finally, Yiota and I set off to tackle 130 km. I'd originally thought it would be mostly flat, but I later discovered it actually included 1,300 m of climbing in the last section. At least when you're riding an e-bike, you don't really notice it if you use some of the higher power settings. It wasn't so great for Wayne of course, whom we'd caught up to about fifty kilometers after we'd started. He'd been waiting for us in a service-station restaurant. Because he'd been waiting awhile though, Wayne set off before us again as Yiota and I hung around a few extra minutes to finish off a few snacks and some water.

However, once we picked up the ride again, the rain clouds started threatening, and it started to drizzle.   .

Thankfully though, we didn't have to worry about the road because they'd built a new four-lane highway with a median separating the two directions. That meant we only had to worry about the traffic passing us, and there was little of that. We usually had the road to ourselves. So, we made pretty good time between that and the state of the new road, and I pointed out some of the sights to Yiota, like our Ponderosa amusement park, the terraced fields, the irrigation canals, and hand-built stone walls. Wouldn't you know it though, Yiota's battery started to run out of juice, and that slowed us down quite a bit, so we never did catch up to Wayne after our snack break. Eventually, her battery completely died, and she rode with no battery because the support crew was nowhere to be seen. We kept trying to contact them to let them know about the battery, but they never answered. For some reason, communication was somehow breaking down.

A couple hours later, the team finally showed up. It turned out they'd left the house quite late and stopped to pick up a bit of food and more tubes for the tires. I didn't say anything then, but I wasn't happy. We just changed the battery and started riding again. Then it started drizzling again and then it got heavier and heavier, so we decided to stop eighty-one kilometers out and wait out the rain in a restaurant across the highway. We were soaked by the time we got there, so we downed some coffee and a ham sandwich, and once we'd dried off, some ice cream.

When the rain eased, we hit the highway again, but our problems weren't over. We still had more than fifty kilometers to go, and it was 3:30 p.m., which meant we only had about two hours of daylight left. Plus, Wayne had taken shelter about two or three kilometers further up from Yiota and I, but because I'd been riding so fast in my haste to make our stop for the night, I'd forgotten to look for him. I went right past him! Boy did that upset him. So, when I got his message, Yiota and I stopped at the ninety-kilometer mark and waited for him. But then when he rode up, he said, "You guys better get going on those e-bikes, so you have a chance to get in before dark. I'll ride in the van." Wayne was really good about knowing when he needed to let me go because of Guinness World Record I needed to ride fast to make it to the Airbnb so I would not have to back track the following day.

Yiota and I took off and booted it as fast as we could to get in. It was getting steadily darker, but I was starting to think we just might make it. But then came yet another kink in a series of many. The directions I'd been using to get to the Airbnb outside and a bit north of Puntarenas were erroneous. They led to nowhere. Not knowing that, I rode on, and within eight kilometers of what should have been my destination, it got quite dark. So, I took the Alaska to Panama sign off the back of my bike so the taillight would show and tried riding on the bike path, but it became too dangerous because other bikes had no lights, so I went back to the road only to find no Airbnb.

The darkness we had to contend with while trying to find our rental.

When I told Yiota about the problem, she Googled it again and sent me some new directions that indicated I had another fourteen kilometers to ride in the dark. I had no other choice though, so I set off. About six kilometers later though, I noticed a message on my phone. Yiota was already there. So, I stopped and found I'd already pasted the location about three kilometers earlier. I turned back, followed the directions to get to Yiota, and finally found the house.

The darkness we had to contend with while trying to find our rental.

What a welcome sight it was that day! We had a gorgeous house on the beach, and from what I could see in the dark, it came complete with a beautiful pool. Boy was I happy to be there. I vowed then that if I had time in the morning, I would get a good look at the beach and take a dip in the pool.

Strangely though, the van had not arrived, and I discovered that Wayne had been sending them texts asking them where they were because he was still standing on the side of the highway in the dark waiting for them. It was a good fifteen minutes before the van, and Wayne, finally pulled up, so I had a chat with Kyle. "What's with the breakdown here? Our communication doesn't seem to be working. We send off messages and nobody answers them and there was Wayne, stranded on the side of the road."

Kyle said, "Ah, it wasn't all that long."

To which I replied, "It's pretty dark now. What was going on?"

"Oh, I was doing my computer editing and all that for social media, so I didn't see the messages."

"Well, the safety of the riders comes first," I said. "And by 4:30 p.m., we need to have the vehicle ready to pick up whoever deems themselves needing a ride, so they don't ride in the dark. If we're close, we will try to motor in in the dark though," I added.

Kyle got a little irritated and asked, "Do you want social media, or do you want us to be with the riders?

"The riders come first," I said. "The social media can wait. We need to know where you guys are always, and when it's rainy and dark, we need a pickup."

Well, he wasn't too happy with that because he said, "Well, you told us the other day our social media wasn't working, and we needed to work on that."

My reply was, "Yes, but that's the secondary thing, plus two things can be true at the same time."

So, he didn't come to dinner that night. The rest of us went to dinner though and had a decent dinner in a club on the beach right next door to our Airbnb. It was one of those clubs where people can just pay to use the pool and eat at the restaurant, but we were the only ones there. I figured it was the rain earlier that kept them away, but while I would usually have missed the atmosphere, it gave me an opportunity to have a chat with Johana and Yiota about being supportive and getting to the riders quickly if needed.

***

The rain was nothing but a memory as we rode out in the sunshine beside the ocean the next morning. We had a mountain to summit ahead of us, but after that was a nice flat ride past more beaches. Believe it or not, despite having lived in Costa Rica for seven years by then, I hadn't ridden a good one-third of that stretch, so I was looking forward to it. My spirits were buoyed by that and the fact that we'd raised yet more money to buy bikes for Panamanian children, so we were up to seventeen or eighteen bikes.

That day became one of those rare gifts to long-distance cyclists. We got to ride along in perfect weather on stretches flat enough to appreciate the scenery and feel of riding and the sounds of the ocean. Steep, green-carpeted cliffs dropped off into the ocean beside us, and the tanker ships lurked on the water as we pedaled along.

Then we had to go over the famous Crocodile Bridge, so we absolutely had to stop and take it in. That bridge is directly over a river favored by fourteen-foot crocodiles, so it provides the perfect safe place to get close to that many crocodiles that big. Kyle had a great time zooming the drone down and getting some fantastic footage.

Four-meter crocs at Crododile Bridge. Photo courtesy of D. Hunt.

Not long after that though, we did have one hard climb to conquer though, and it was almost too much for Wayne. With a 19 percent grade, he almost overheated tackling it, so we stopped and had a refreshing lunch in Jaco. After we got back underway though, we had zero issues all the way to our Airbnb in Quepos. Wayne rebounded after lunch and finished strong, and I just couldn't believe that we'd ridden in the neighborhood of 130 km that day and had had nothing go wrong, no flat tires, no dead batteries, no bad directions. There wasn't even any wind to contend with. We rode through a seemingly never-ending palm-oil plantation, and I learned along the way that Costa Rica is now the home of one of the C-7 planes used in the clandestine Iran-Contra operation because the secret airstrip the Americans built for them is on a ranch in Costa Rica. I only learned that because we rode right past one on display that day. Even curiouser is that the surviving C-123 used in that same operation is now a bar in the area.

To top our lovely day off, Airbnb was lovely and had rooms enough for us all. And it had hot water! Funny how things those of us in first-world countries take for granted are luxuries in much of the rest of the world. The rental was close to the number one tourist area in Costa Rica, Manuel Antonio, whose many long stretches of beach, huge resorts, and fantastic restaurants draw people from around the world. There was to be none of that for us though. We were happy to simply relax that night and let the wonderful day sink in.

***

This might be hard to believe, but we got just as wonderful a day the next day. The ride was nice and easy with just some rolling hills, blissful weather, and a well-maintained highway with wide shoulders as we again glided past more palm-oil plantations. We enjoyed a relaxed stop for coffee in Dominical, found some treehouses you can rent, and were reminded Christmas was nearing thanks to the Christmas keg tree at a microbrewery we stopped at. Then came more beaches, some waterfalls, and Indigenous sculptures, likely for sale from what we could tell.

Unfortunately, that's where our luck ran out. The Airbnb we'd rented for the night in Palmar Norte was just about the worst ever. In fact, I'd say it equaled the hotel where the power went out. Here, there wasn't even enough room for all five of us, so Johana and Yiota went and stayed in a nearby hotel for $30/night. Kyle, Wayne, and I stayed in the Airbnb that had only a bunk bed that Kyle and I used and a double bed for Wayne. I was so disappointed; I couldn't even bother to take the time to give them a bad review. At least we managed to all meet up and find a clean outdoor restaurant where we had dinner.

***

The next day, I woke up early, full of optimism after the incredible two days we'd just had—besides the Airbnb of course. There was only ninety-three kilometers left before we hit our last border crossing, and I was just as full of anticipation as optimism.

And then I was thwarted. We had to stop and take shelter from heavy downpours. Not that it was all bad as it led to meeting some great people. During the first rainstorm, I ended up talking to a local who was waiting for a bus to take him wherever he wanted to go, which is a thing in Costa Rica. The next time we stopped, we shared a shelter with motorcycle riders who were changing into their rain gear. I privately agreed with Wayne: they were wimps. We just ride in the rain and get wet. The last time we had to take shelter, a local saw us standing there under the overhang, soaking wet, and invited us in. So, we started off standing in his garage, but when Kyle and Johana showed up and she got to talking with him, he ended up inviting us to sit on his porch. He even kindly made us coffee in his humble abode. He was a friendly fellow I was happy I met and rather typical of the people we'd happened upon on our travels.

Once all the rain stopped, we found ourselves just thirty kilometers from the border when Yiota told us that the hotels in the border town we'd been going to stay in were completely booked, probably thanks to Costa Rican tourists going to shop, I thought, that and the many migrants. So, we had a decision: go on another ten kilometers plus the thirty we already had to do and look for a hotel there, or stop where we were at that moment.

I wasn't sure of the best decision, so I left it up to the group, who decided we'd push on. That was a good decision too because we covered that distance far quicker than I'd thought we would. Johana and Kyle went ahead and found a hotel— for $100/night. Though that was probably the most I'd paid for a hotel the entire last leg, it did have four beds, so I only had to pay for one room. Yiota and Johana shared one bed and the rest of us had our own bed. But the rest of my hundred dollars was certainly wasted. It had one toilet, the bathroom door swung off the hinges, the cabinet door under the sink was missing—as was the shower faucet, which was only a spigot—and of course, the water was always cold.

Anyway, we went in search of a restaurant so we could relax, and maybe even celebrate that we'd arrived at our last border. We had a few beers, and then a few more. The owners were from the Dominican Republic, and their joyous demeanor was infectious. They brought out some homemade liqueurs and we ended up staying there for dinner, where we again ran into some migrants.

From left, restaurant owner, Wayne, Kyle, Yiota, Johana, restaurant owner, and me enjoying beer and shots at the Costa Rica/ Panama border.

We'd seen a few walking up the road the previous day too, but that night we got another chance to talk with them and hear their stories. In that case, we met even more Somalians; they were definitely in the majority at this border. They all spoke English, were rather well-dressed, and had enough money to eat and such. There were plenty of migrants from Venezuela too, though they didn't seem to be as well off as the Somalians. One Venezuelan fellow we spoke to was trying to sell candies, which of course we bought to help him out. His sales must have been poor though because he swiped a bunch of leftover food off our plates. I'm not sure if he asked anyone if he could do that because I wasn't always looking, but he must have been starving if he felt he had to go to those lengths to eat.

But we had an eye-opening conversation with a few of the Somalian migrants. They'd flown to Ecuador, then walked across it and Colombia until they'd come upon the Darién Gap. On their perilous journey, they'd witnessed many people die. Those folks had incredible perseverance and determination though. They knew they had no choice but to keep pushing on, so negative talk was not permitted among their group. There were no saying things like, "Oh, I'm so tired. I'm just going to sit here and wait awhile." Nope, with those folks, it was always, "You have to keep going."

As with the migrants we'd met in Mexico, these folks too spoke of the treacherous mountains they'd had to climb, which were the worst part of their trek with their sharp, rocky slopes and the deep, swift rivers in between. I don't know that I would have been able to cross one of those rivers with the water whooshing around me up to my throat, threatening to pull me down, even in my youngest, strongest days. And when it wasn't the mountains, they were braving, it was the crocodile-infested swamplands, although a few people we spoke to had said there are markers, blue flags, for people to follow as they try to make the crossing. Still, numerous people—no one knows how many—die undertaking that journey. Their journeys sure contrasted loudly with my comfortable odyssey.

They also told us of how often they threw their belongings away as they walked when the weight of carrying it outweighed the need for it. Most migrants ended up with nearly nothing to their names by the time their crossing was complete. With each person I spoke to, I found I was unable to figure out why they didn't just walk along the highways. When I decided to ask, they indicated that the police were not to be trusted, that they all wanted money and some pointed guns at them. I later learned that part of the stretch doesn't even have a road, so not only was the mountain pass the safest route, but the only route. My heart broke a little when one fellow said if he'd known how hard the Darién Gap was to cross, he never would have made the journey from Ethiopia.

After talking with migrants from a few different countries, I discovered that all but the Venezuelans went on to the US, who journeyed to Honduras because that was as far as they could legally go. Unsponsored Venezuelans just aren't allowed in the US. One young Venezuelan fellow, exceptionally fit and looking like he could hold his own in any situation, told us he was a deserter from the Venezuelan Special Forces, so if he went back, he'd be arrested for desertion and likely jailed for life or executed. Speaking in fantastic English, he said he'd had no choice but to run. He didn't want anything to do with that government and the resulting poverty, so he'd had to get out.

In that moment, my previous assertion that anybody who undertakes a risky, death-defying journey like those people do to make a better life for themselves and their families should be welcomed into Canada came rising to the forefront again. I just don't understand why politicians can't see something as clear as this. Those migrants have such strong wills, stamina, endurance, and determination, such a desire to work hard and make a better life their families that they deserve a place in our country. It's people like that who should be able to proudly call themselves Canadian, not just natural-born citizens who oftentimes just rest on their laurels and do nothing but complain about our country. It would only make our country stronger, and that goes for the US too. That kind of effort, that drive, should immediately qualify them for entry rather than just those who have money or connections or education and just buy their way in because they can set up a business or invest or have sponsors.

Boy, I have a lot to say sometimes. So anyway, it was another interesting day and night. Kyle got a long interview with one of the Somalian fellows on camera, so I'm hopeful we can get some of these migrant stories in a sort of documentary. Maybe we could improve a few more lives if we could get those stories out into the world. So, I guess by then I'd discovered that I not only wanted to erase the stigma surrounding seniors and get them up off the couch, to get people moving and living and trying new things, but I had a tremendous desire to shine a light on the stories of migrants and their ordeals. I want the world to know the truth, not the falsehoods the politicians and media would have you believe.

JOURNEY'S END —SORT OF

Dozens of tour buses carrying hundreds of Costa Rican duty-free shoppers pulled in and jockeyed for position at the Costa Rica border as I sat savoring my coffee early the next morning. Cars were lined up in no real order, and people were already milling around like disconnected ants as they waited to cross. *A good night's sleep would have been optimal to get us through the chaos we had to brave that day*, I thought, but I'd known that was never going to happen in that tiny hovel with five of us packed in. But *c'est la vie*. Panama was our last border crossing, so we'd just make the best of it.

Wayne had escaped the hotel room that morning too, freshening up for the morning in the restaurant's bathroom before we tackled the hodgepodge of lines, we'd have to both find and wait in. Hopefully, by the time all was said and done, we'd get the van and tent trailer checked out of Costa Rica and into Panama and still retain our sanity. You just never know. Every border has its own issues, and at this one, I had to worry about convincing the officials that our return ticket was bringing the van back to Costa Rica given we didn't exactly have plane or bus tickets or anything.

Eventually, I put my empty coffee cup down with a sigh and went back to the hotel to meet up with the crew and get the process started. Getting it over with would mean getting across to Panama and ushering the Octogenarian Odyssey to the finish line.

Our first obstacle was trying to determine where to go and where to start. After asking a bunch of people already waiting in line, we found our first line and went to go stand in it. Since most everything is outside, we were lucky to have a partially cloudy sky to shield us from the worst of the day's heat, yet no rain to make our lives miserable. Still, we remembered to stay away from long grasses and those nasty no-see-ums.

Finally, we got to the front of our first line only to be told, "No, you have to go pay your exit tax first." So, we hiked across the street to pay the tax, which we'd been told was $8.

You can't leave Costa Rica without paying the shady exit tax

But of course, the tax guy says, "Oh no, it's not $8. Today is Sunday, so it's $15." I was flabbergasted but not surprised. Being ripped off or paying bribes is just the way of things. What do you do?

So, I paid the Sunday price and went back to the first line we'd stood in. After enduring that once again, we reached the front only to have the official not even look at the tax receipt. He just stamped our passports and told us to get in the next line to check the van out of the country. Go figure.

Eventually, that official told me I was okay to check the van out but getting it back in would be a problem. By the time I got back to Costa Rica, I'd only have a week or two left to keep the van in the country before I'd have to take it back out again. By that time though, after all the borders I'd crossed, I really didn't care. There was nothing I could do about it in that moment anyway besides make a mental note to talk to my lawyer about it and see what my options were.

Suddenly, we were on the Panamanian side. Our last country, the last leg, the last few days of our odyssey. We lined up yet again to get some car insurance, lined up again to show our documents, lined up again to get our passports stamped, then lined up yet again to get the van checked into Panama. There it turned out they had to do some work on our papers to give us more time with the van in Panama—but we'd have to pay the guy $10 to speed up the process of course.

Fast forward three hours, and we were finally out of that labyrinth. The chaos thankfully behind us, we rode down a well-constructed highway, with much less litter than Honduras and wide shoulders. We only had thirty-five kilometers to go before we'd meet up with my friend, Nina, who'd been helping me raise the money to buy the bikes for Panamanian children. She and her friend, Elizabeth, were going to ride with us and guide us down some country roads to their beach condos they'd offered to let my team and I stay in for two nights. The next day, I'd be heading to the school to present the children with their bikes, and the day after that, I was looking forward to a turtle release. Plus, I was going to get to enjoy the company of some expats like me while we were there.

During my ride that day, I made sure to appreciate every tiny thing around me, from the sign marker proclaiming it was 486 km to Panama City, to the forest bursting with green on both sides of the highway, to the sun warring with the clouds as they began to build, and to the sky darkening as the storm clouds gathered in the sky above the sugar-cane fields. It was to be one of my last days on the road, so I savored every moment. We even took a moment to stop along the way to look at a small church in Alanje that's famous for its wooden carving of Jesus inside. Unfortunately, I didn't end up seeing the carving just because I don't usually go inside the churches, but I did learn that a miracle was supposed to have happened there, hence the carving of Jesus. It is, however, quite elaborate I'm told.

After our detour and some lunch, where we met up with my friends, we were on our way again. Those clouds that had been threatening the sugar cane fulfilled their promise. They opened up and let loose a torrent of rain that fell down on us in buckets. We took shelter under a grocery-store overhang until it seemed to stop, and then we continued. That day, we had no choice but to make it to our destination rather than adapting and stopping wherever we had to.

So, off we went again, and wouldn't you know it, we only got a few blocks further down the road before the rain came down again, harder even than before. Elizabeth and I chose to keep riding anyway, and it seemed we'd won the battle for a bit by outriding it when suddenly the storm found us again. We were completely soaked. And of course, I have this nasty habit of forgetting to zip the pockets of my raincoat closed, so they fill up with water given they're waterproof. Thank goodness I never carry my phone in those pockets, or I'd really have a problem.

But we did prevail in the end and arrived at a beautiful condominium on an even more gorgeous beach. What a wonderful reward for our perseverance that day. As the rain cleared, a rainbow appeared over the building, making it feel like a good omen or a blessing on our journey. After waiting around for a bit for Nina and my team to show up, we wandered around and came across Richard, Nina's husband. He kindly let us in, and the van, Wayne, and Nina arrived shortly thereafter.

Our rainbow over Nina and Roger's condo in Panama

After the last few days of crummy accommodations, the team and I had endured staying in a modern condo with space and amenities felt like a little slice of heaven. It even had a garage for the bikes! Throw the refreshing pool and breathtaking beach in there, and you had a recipe for inner peace. It was all thanks to Nina and Roger's generosity. They'd offered us the use of their whole condo, facing the beach even, while they moved upstairs to stay with Elizabeth. Kyle, however, stayed upstairs with Nina and Roger rather than downstairs with us just for space considerations. There were, after all, only three bedrooms and there were five of us.

Well, we dried off, unpacked the van, charged the bike batteries, then hopped just next door to a fabulous four-star restaurant. I relaxed and enjoyed not only the meal but meeting a group of sixteen condo owners who all ate Sunday dinner in that restaurant. We had a bit of a chat, and I discovered that they all help organize and run a Christmas party in the area where they try to feed two hundred families and give the children gifts. So, though the service was slow at every phase of the meal, the food and the company were excellent and exactly what I needed that night.

***

The next day was a momentous day. I'd been looking forward to it ever since our departure in North Pole, Alaska. What a great idea it had been to hand out bicycles rather than having to decide what presents to buy for the kids. I am eternally grateful to Nina for the idea and for the assistance arranging it all.

Bright and early that morning, some folks came in four pickup trucks and loaded up the bikes. The team, Nina, Roger, and I followed them to the charming, brightly painted little school in the country. We got a quick tour of the classrooms, which were all clean and painted, before heading to the open but covered courtyard where rows of chairs were set up for their Mother's Day celebration. Mother's Day in Panama is apparently on December 8, so the school was celebrating both Mother's Day and Christmas with our special presentation.

Then it was time for my presentation. Along with the fifty children the school staff had chosen as those eligible for the bicycle draw, the team and the staff and I assembled in a large, enclosed room. Anticipation and curiosity filled both the air and the children's eyes. The only downside was the ever-present masking on most of the children, yet another reminder of the COVID-19 pandemic that hadn't yet been declared over. It would have been nice to see the smiles too.

Those fifty children were among the poorest and/or had the longest distances to walk to school and ranged in age from grades three to seven, and I couldn't wait to make a difference in the lives of a few of them. Before I got to do that though, we were treated to a student poetry recitation and a violin performance. Then the principal introduced Wayne, me, and the team and described our odyssey to the children, with the English teacher translating. While that part didn't take all that long, what did take a long time was my speaking to the children and answering all the questions they had about Santa Claus and other North American things like that.

Finally, we got to the draw. The looks of wonder and happiness in their eyes, even as some tried to contain their excitement, meant the world to me. As did getting to step into my old principal self again for a little while, standing before a room full of children, talking with them and hopefully both entertaining and inspiring them. I hope our appearance, our journey, and the bikes mean something in their life and make some sort of difference in their futures.

Joy like this is the best gift in the world

The best part of that moment for me wasn't even the joy on the recipients' faces but knowing that just seventeen days later, eleven more children would get bikes at the Christmas party the condo owners were throwing. In the end, our family and friends and supporters, and the wonderful condo owners, raised enough funds to give out thirty-one bicycles.

We celebrated later over breakfast at another local restaurant where I reveled in a tasty but typical Panamanian breakfast of eggs and beef and *hojaldra*, Panama's deep-fried bread. Yiota took a pass on that breakfast, but I know at least Wayne and I really enjoyed it and talking with some of the locals.

The only thing bringing things down that day was the tingling throat that had set in the day before, likely from riding in the rain. By the time I'd gone to bed, it was obvious I had a full-fledged cold, so I hadn't gotten much sleep and had suffered through it for the duration of the presentation and breakfast. So, after breakfast, I went back to the condo and lay down, trying to get some rest. It didn't work very well.

On that note, I spent the rest of the day with a stuffy, dripping nose and breathing through my mouth. I was hoping it would disappear faster than Wayne's had because he'd been complaining of a raspy voice and stuffy nose for three days, so we spent the rest of that day resting when we could.

But we couldn't miss the turtle release. Right at sunset, we strolled down to the beach and watched a crew release 328 turtles. A large crowd had gathered to watch the little guy's scamper to the ocean and head out into the big wide world. Hopefully some of them survive.

Nina's husband, Richard, is a member of a program that finds turtle nests and takes the eggs back to a safe area they've created on the beach. There, they care for them and keep them safe from both animals and locals who like to eat the eggs. What a crazy sight it was to watch 328 turtles make a run for the water, tiny flippers flailing and shells scooting across the sand until the tide picks them up and pulls them out.

Once that excitement was over though, I wasted no time in finding my bed. The end of the odyssey was calling, and to enjoy it, I needed to be healthy.

***

And then it was Sunday. The last Sunday we would spend on part one of this journey. That day's target was Santiago, but to get there, we'd have to go through the metropolis of David, not far from the beach we were currently staying at. The city was jam-packed with yellow taxis going this way and that, leaving not much room for other vehicles, let alone bicycles. Fortunately, we safely maneuvered our way through it on a great highway—the Pan-American Highway—with decent shoulders at that.

Also fortunately, we managed to make it all the way to Santiago with only one incident. Yiota's back brake failed again. It needed to be replaced, so we had to put her bike in the car, though she wasn't happy about it. But I wasn't going to have her riding with only a front brake. If it failed and she was on a steep downhill, that would result in only disaster. The team drove ahead then to find a bike store in Santiago that could fix it by the next day, which they did. And it only cost me $20 for new brake pads and fluid.

So Wayne and I rode the rest of the day in brilliant sunshine, passing fascinating mortarless stone walls and living walls alike. I'm not sure why we don't have living walls on farms in Canada and the US, at least that I know of. They're brilliant! Instead of digging postholes and burying posts, here they just dig a little hole, plant a piece of a tree, and let it grow. Then as we do up north, they connect the trees with, like the ones we saw, barbed wire.

In David, besides the taxis, we rode past ornately detailed churches, an odd modern-art fountain in a 3D pyramid shape surrounded by giant candy canes for the holidays, and nutcrackers standing guard. Back on the highway again, we glided past more lush jungle and stopped to get some drone footage of a towering though skinny waterfall. Perhaps it was because I was nearing the end of my journey, but somehow it felt as if every tiny thing I passed was just a little more beautiful, a little more wonderous, than usual. I finally got another opportunity to meet another road warrior too. That had been happening less and less the further we went, so I was thrilled to chat with this guy from Saskatoon of all places. He was riding down to Argentina from San Jose, Costa Rica, as he'd already ridden from Canada to Costa Rica the previous year. That was only the fourth long-distance cyclist we'd encountered since Mexico. I'd thought we'd meet more, but perhaps it had something to do with pandemic restrictions still being a little restrictive. I did know, however, that there was a tour group about twelve days behind us, and there were probably twenty cyclists in that group.

Well, we reached the hotel in fine time, with the sun still shining higher up in the sky than usual. Though it had a lovely pool and hot tub, that of course we availed ourselves of, the interior was rather dated, too brightly painted, and rather small for all of us.

***

Our second last day on the road gave us more wonderous scenery and even better weather. Tropical flowers, jungle vegetation, and more mountains off in the distance with clouds rolling their way over them became our backdrop. Seeing those mountains reminded me of the volcanoes in Guatemala, of how majestic each one was, with each turn offering me a silhouette that was grander than the one before. The Panamanian landscape was no less breathtaking, just a little less imposing.

That day's ride was nothing difficult or troublesome either. It was a long ride, yes, a good 135 km, but we didn't get soaked, we didn't have to battle terrific climbs or scary descents, and no one got a flat tire. As we approached Aguadulce, we started to smell the ocean air once again as we'd ridden east since David. Our goal that day was Rio Hato, right on the coast of the Gulf of Parita. As I rode, I started to feel a little anxious and a little excited. We were so, so close to the end of the odyssey, which was exciting. We had broken the world record and we had almost ridden across an entire continent. That was exciting. But it meant the end of my journey. It meant the end of discovering and overcoming. It meant the end of my time with my team.

But we arrived nonetheless at a superb Airbnb in Rio Hato, just as some dark clouds were gathering. We were on the fifth floor of a high rise overlooking the ocean, and it had the largest pool in all Central America. It was created to look like an artificial lake complete with a white sandy beach and palm trees. Because that wasn't enough though, the enormous complex of five or six high-rise condos also offered an individual pool for each building.

After wandering down to the beach and taking some photos of the water, the beach, and the buildings, we went in search of somewhere to eat dinner. We found an attractive, modern place with an outdoor patio adorned with patio lights that called to me. It was yet another good find as a group of women expats recognized us and said, "Oh wow! We saw you on the highway!"

Of course, that led to lots of picture taking and some energizing conversation. Better yet, that night happened to be Mother's Day, so the restaurant was offering a free bottle of wine for each table. So, one thing led to another and with us being just one day away from the end of our journey, we all had a little too much to drink and stayed up a little too late. Even Yiota joined us that night. What a fantastic evening.

***

As fate always has it, what should have been an easy, relaxed ride on our last day turned into a race.

We awoke early, anticipating the last day of the Octogenarian Odyssey. The original plan had been to enjoy the last 119 km of our ride and enter Panama City. However, to get to our destination in the center of town, we had to cross the Bridge of the Americas. We discovered shortly after waking though, that we were going to have to hit turbo. Johana's friend sent her a text saying that the Bridge of America closes from 3 p.m. to 8 p.m. every day. If you miss that window, you get routed to another bridge 20 km away. That was not good news.

In panic mode rather than adventure mode then, we hurried to get ready and on the road. We had no choice but to put our heads down and push to reach that bridge in time. There was every chance that being detoured another 20 km would mean we would not complete the journey that day.

Well, the ride started smoothly again on the well-maintained Pan-American Highway as we rode on those wonderful shoulders. Then as we neared the city, we started picking up lots of traffic, high-speed traffic at that, and the shoulder began to deteriorate. Potholes of all sizes started appearing. And at every bridge, the shoulder disappeared. We had to ride in the traffic then, and they didn't want to give us any room. It had been a while since we'd had to ride in heavy traffic.

Just as I thought we were making progress, we hit some hills that slowed us down. But we managed to stay on schedule and arrived at the bridge at 2:15 p.m. I was hoping that buffer would leave us enough time to get on to the bridge and across before it closed. But we got lucky. Even with six lanes of highway, the road was mostly clear. In the end, we zipped over incredibly quickly. And we didn't even have to worry about wind on that bridge because there were enormous wire screens taller than a vehicle in place to prevent people from jumping to their deaths.

The only complaint I had about crossing that bridge was the potholes. I'd never before seen a bridge with potholes, but that one had them. At least we could safely avoid them with the light traffic. Because it was so close to 3:00 p.m. I figured much of the traffic behind us had been stopped and diverted to the other bridge. It turned out I was right because even Johana and Yiota had gotten rerouted.

And then we were on the other side—in one piece. We only had 2.5 km left before reaching the finish line in the park in the historic old center of Panama City called Casco Viejo, which means "the old man's helmet." We—Wayne, Kyle, and I—rode into the park and ....

...Crickets. No one was there to greet us yet. So, the three of us pulled some high-fives and relaxed at an outdoor restaurant with a couple cold beers. Eventually, after those couple beers, Yiota and Johana showed up in the van, and shortly after that, Wayne's wife, Jutta, arrived. Last, Gloria and her mother came, and we hugged and celebrated and took so many team photos and photos of us lifting our bikes over our heads that the police wanted to know what was happening. When we told them, they wanted their photos taken with us too!

Our incredible team celebrating the successful completion of the Octogenarian Odyssey, Part One.

***

And that was the end of it. Five months and five days. 14,274 km.

After taking some time to wander the square and appreciate all the old architecture, the shops and churches, we dragged our tired selves to our accommodations for the night. In my case—with Gloria, Johana, and their mother—it was another beautiful Airbnb a few blocks away. I'd chosen to stay in the historic center of town for not only the same reason as usual, that being I love the history and architecture and culture, but also because I'd visited three times before, the first time in 2015. It has a certain allure for me, as with many other historic cultural centers, and this one only improves every time I come back.

Many, many years ago, the old town had consisted of only wooden buildings until a few fires swept through it, razing it to the ground and forcing the people to rebuild time and again. Then the French came and built a canal. They ended up settling in the area then, so now it's reminiscent of the French Quarter in New Orleans and other places with a European French influence. Nowadays though, it's packed with tourists, especially at night given all the bars, rooftop patios, and restaurants around. Many people still choose to stay in Panama City's modern skyscrapers or one of the beachfronts or Malecon hotels, but I'm always happier in the old town. Whether on a long-distance tour or not, I'll be back.

But by the time we got to the hotel, we were so tired, we just went out for a quiet rooftop dinner before retiring for the night. I wasn't sure quite why I was more tired than usual after a day of riding when that day especially I should have been energized, but it was what it was.

***

The next day was all about paperwork for the Guinness Book of World Records. There were a million things to do to get my odyssey approved, but we had all kinds of proof, so I was sure it was just a matter of tedious work and time.

But that didn't mean we didn't celebrate. We all met one last time for our final dinner at a fancy Italian restaurant. Drinks flowed and laughter bubbled, and I got up and thanked my spectacular team for their hard work and for sticking by me through desert heat and tropical rains, mountain cold and wilderness hardships, mosquitos and horse flies and no-see-ums. Even love hotels. We'd waited out a hurricane, ridden beside belching volcanoes, detoured around rockslides and washed-out roads, and forded rivers together. As with any team, we might have had some conflict and tension here and there, but there was no way I ever could have achieved that major life milestone without them.

An interesting fellow named Sergio we'd met earlier on the side of the road even came and joined us later. That guy had experienced quite an adventure too on his travels from Quebec to the Arctic Ocean on his way down to Argentina. He'd sat out four hurricanes and had to pay a $500 fine in Nicaragua for a missing document or some such thing.

It just went to show what kind of camaraderie you find out on the highway. Whether you're riding a road bike, an e-bike, or a motorbike, there's a bond that exists born of a curiosity, a thirst for adventure, and a desire to explore. If I've achieved nothing else with the story of my odyssey, I hope it's that I've inspired at least one person to try something they've always wanted to do but have been either too afraid to do or thought they'd wait for "someday" to arrive to do.

***

On my third day in Panama, my last day before I turned around to head back home to Costa Rica, it was time to pack up and take stock of both my supplies and my thoughts. I took things slowly that day. There was no rush because I was alone just waiting for Gloria and Johana to get back from taking their mother to the airport, and I was still feeling drained. Yet as I puttered, getting things together, making sure I had everything I needed, I realized that it was more a mental exhaustion rather than a physical exhaustion. All I had the energy for was going to dinner at night.

But on further reflection, I also realized that this odyssey had been full of both stressors and excitement. Rarely were the days ever quiet and ordinary, and they were certainly never routine. I'd spent every day with other people, and there had always been at least one problem to solve and plenty of decisions to make. That all takes energy. Some would say those were good reasons to not embark on these sorts of adventures, but I disagree. Sure, I was tired, but it was a good sort of tired. Fear of the unknown isn't a good reason to not do something or try something new. Fear of failure is an even worse reason. You don't know what you can do until you try, and the only failure is not doing something or giving up.

And part one of the odyssey was complete. The next day, Wayne and his wife would fly home to Canada, Yiota would fly home to Greece, and Johana, Gloria, Kyle, and I were going to drive a hundred kilometers back in the direction of Costa Rica. There were some loose ends to tie up, and we were going to start back at Nina and Richard's condo on the beach. Not a bad ending really, some relaxing time on the beach.

That day though, I met with a local named Mark Vargas. He was a tour guide who showed folks around all the historic sights and beaches and such Panama has to offer. We chatted for a while, sort of like an interview, about my Octogenarian Odyssey, and he said he would publish a story about it. Where I didn't quite catch though. I was hoping he had a website advertising his tours because then it would serve as another vessel with which to get my message out. Funny how I'd started with one, maybe two messages and ended up with five, all equally important to me. The first was getting seniors off the couch and living life, the second was to eliminate the stigma attached to seniors, the third was to inspire everyone to live life fully without fear and self-doubt, the fourth was bringing the truth of the migrants' travails to the world, and the fifth was the environmental impact of the litter we all leave behind. Wow. Until I wrote it out like that, I didn't fully realize how big my soapbox had become, but those issues are just so important.

At that moment though, I was glad this part of the journey was over and that we had all arrived safely and not far off schedule. We'd lost some time to the hurricane in Puerto Vallarta, Mexico, we'd had to adjust for some Google Bike Maps mess-ups, and we'd altered the itinerary to split up some harsh climbing days, but we'd still made it to Panama City just six days later than planned.

As I sat alone in my Airbnb scrolling through the Octogenarian Odyssey's social-media accounts, I came across a Facebook post from my sister-in-law, Johana. I think her words bring the most fitting closure to part one of the odyssey and encompass many of our shared feelings after a journey of this size.

Life is short, some say. I say that life is a path of growth, and it is everyone who makes it outstanding. Every storm or every sunrise will be the best story of our long or short life—for everyone who sees it with their own eyes and inner knowledge.

I loved every sunrise of this odyssey, and I am proud of me and my colleagues—Wayne D. Grover of Canada, Kyle Walker of the US, Yiota Georgakopoulou of Greece—because every day we grew as people, four cultures living together 24/7,

in hot and cold,

with dreams and revelations,

in big houses and hotels,

in tiny homes and hotels hidden in the middle of those forgotten villages of Central America.

A bicycle 🚲 that with each pedal left our story.

A van 🚐 and a trailer 😊, which was our home, our kitchen, our bed, our protective roof from rains, hurricanes, and the strong desert heat.

We of course learned how to put aside our food—helping each one to understand the difficult gastronomic Spanish 😭😵😲—oh God! If I could tell you what we ate hahaha.

But my biggest thank you is to "the boss" ha-ha, the reason why we all came together: my dear friend, Robert Fletcher, who had a dream and worked to fulfill it. We admire you for your great effort. Octoodyssey was magical.

I appreciate every person who crossed our path:

Canada 🇨🇦
United States 🇺🇸
Mexico 🇲🇽
Guatemala 🇬🇹
El Salvador 🇸🇻
Honduras 🇭🇳
Nicaragua 🇳🇮
Costa Rica 🇨🇷
Panama 🇵🇦

You will always be the greatest participants in this odyssey.

Alaska to Panama

Octogenarian Odyssey, Part One complete

EPILOGUE

So, here's the long and short of it. I did it. The bike trip that had been on my bucket list for a while now finally came to pass this past December, in 2022. My team and I spent over five months riding over 14,000 kilometers, from July 4 to December 9, through nine countries and eighteen border check-ins and checkouts. While the trip was full of fun and became a great learning experience, it also tested my patience, challenged me in new ways, and forced me to grow as a person. And to think it almost didn't happen because of one little unplanned hiccup at the beginning: I shorted out the electrical system on my e-bike. But like all the hurdles I encountered on the journey, I persevered and overcame. And it was worth it.

More than a month after finishing part one of my Octogenarian Odyssey, I sit here doing double duty after another morning ride in the paradise that is Costa Rica. On the one hand, I've had plenty of "i's" to dot and "t's" to cross after completing part one, and on the other hand, I'm well into planning part two of my Octogenarian Odyssey.

My first, and most immediate, problem from part one that required attention was the van issue. I'd made a big mistake when we'd crossed the border into Costa Rica when they'd asked how long I was going to keep the van in the country. Of course, then I hadn't given it much thought, so I'd just showed them my itinerary. It showed that I'd have it in the country for only seven days, so they'd given me twenty-eight days. What I should have done was ask for the ninety-day visa that I usually get because then I would have had three months to figure out what I was going to do with the van. And by then, I'd likely have Costa Rican permanent residency so I could

358 | ROBERT D. FLETCHER

have imported it without paying as much tax. Instead, I'd been faced with possibly paying $8,000 in taxes to keep it in Costa Rica.

Fortunately, I found another solution. I parked the van in a government customs lot for ninety days so when I can pull it out, I'll receive a ninety-day importation permit. That'll solve both a part one problem and a part two problem because then I can drive it to Panama and hopefully ship it down to Colombia.

While I love being at home, spending time with my wife and my friends, and sleeping in my own bed, I already miss not being on the road. I still ride for a couple hours every morning to stay in shape after I take Gloria to work, and I'm planning a short, week-long solo ride soon on mostly dirt roads I haven't explored, but the rest of my time is taken with tying up problems from part one and planning part two. That leaves little time for adventuring.

And I'm no planner as I've discovered. Going places, I've never been to before and doing things I've never done before has become my comfort zone in recent years, but planning a tour as long as the Octogenarian Odyssey required such planning that it forced me out of my comfort zone. And that's good! No one should stay stagnant. That's how you end up getting old and apathetic. Life is full of opportunities and experiences every day we're on this planet, so it's our responsibility to discover and live them, regardless of age or means. Along the way, experiencing teaches us lessons, keeping us learning every day of our lives.

And boy, did I learn some lessons on the first part of the odyssey. A few smaller ones include not using Google Bike Maps in Central American, and likely not South American, countries; not leaving more time for border crossings and long climbs; and spending a small fortune on my Don Quixote, tilting-windmill kind of trip. Despite a few efforts at times, I spent much of the journey handing the financial reigns to Yiota and Kim and then Yiota and Johana and Kyle. I paid for all our meals in both dives and fancy restaurants and shelled out for Airbnb's, hotels, and campgrounds. I even paid each crew member $25/day, so those costs didn't take long to add up. On my Octogenarian Part Two, I'm working to attract more sponsors and asking people to pay for slots to ride with me on preselected sections. I'll of course pay for accommodations and food, but any extras like snacks, treats, and alcohol will this time be up to the individual. At the same time, rather than having a team of strangers support me on the journey, I'll have a team of family. My wife, Gloria, will come with us—and we'll rent the house to family while we're gone—and her sister, Johana, will again be part of the team. My stepdaughter, Julie, will even join us after a month. A family team will be a new kind of interesting, so stay tuned!

But before I can launch a new adventure, there are all the Guinness Book of World Records requirements to deal with. That was the second most critical issue demanding my attention. For starters, when we reached the finish line in Panama City, it had been so long since we'd thought of the world record that we'd completely forgotten to get signed witness statements from those in attendance that day, such as the waitress who'd served our drinks and the police officers, we'd taken photos with. We'd also forgotten to get signed witness statements on every day of the journey as Guinness required.

But while I couldn't track down everyone from every day in every country to get signed statements, I did at least connect with the waitress and the police officers. I came across the waitress on Facebook, and she both signed a statement and found the officers outside her café again and got them to sign statements. At least I have that now, signed statements from the beginning and the end of the journey. Otherwise, I have all the data from my odometer and photos and reels from each day of our journey, plus a good hundred other documents and five hundred or so receipts proving where I was when, how far I went, and that I did not cheat. I even had my crew sign a page for each day they traveled with me, testifying that they witnessed me riding. I'm still hopeful that will all be enough since it's too late to go back and do things over again or track strangers down. Either way, I know in my heart I did it, and every memory is in my head. I know, and my team knows, I rode every inch of the way, just like I did on my Anchorage to Mexico City tour when I won the EFI award, which means, "Every effing inch of the way."

As it stands, my application has been approved, but it could be some time before I hear if they officially designate me the world-record holder for longest e-bike ride. That's something that while it felt fulfilling to achieve, I wouldn't do again. Having to be places on time and jump through hoops was a millstone around my neck, even if it did keep me motivated and from giving up on the hard days when I just wanted to get in the van. I won't have that problem on the second part of the odyssey. If I'm tired or the bike breaks down or we can't find a hotel, I'll just hop in the van, and we'll drive until we get to where we need to go.

The tent trailer is another problem affecting both parts of the odyssey. It's in rough shape. So not only does it need a major overhaul to make it sellable, but I also have to take it out of the country for ninety days as I did the van. As I write this, my plan is to take it to Nicaragua and park it there for cheaper, then bring it back up to Costa Rica and get it fixed before we head out on part two.

The one downside to this lifestyle I live at is having to be checked for skin cancer as often as I do. The doctor cut a bunch of skin out of me just before I left on part one of the odyssey, and just today I had more cut out. Half of those needed biopsies, so now I have to go back and let them cut out more flesh to ensure they got all the cancer. I know I should wear more sunscreen, but I try to wear long sleeves sometimes and always wear a helmet. I know, I know, that's not quite enough, but admit I just don't like putting it on.

Anyway, now that I've mostly wrapped up all the issues from part one, I find that planning part two has me reflecting on the first part of the journey. At the oddest moments, memories jump to the forefront of my mind, and I lose valuable planning time as I recollect. The most vivid memory is of experiencing the Day of the Dead in Oaxaca. Meeting so many people, feeling both the solemn-ness and the excitement in the air, and discovering the decorated graves was such a highlight.

Johana, Wayne, and me ready to celebrate the Day of the Dead!

Meeting new people was an integral part of my journey. It always is. Then I'd post something about my journey on Facebook, and the comments I received from family and strangers alike motivated me to keep going. Those comments showed me I was inspiring people, I was encouraging other seniors to live life, and I was giving young people a reason to create their own goals and see the world in a more all-encompassing light. It warmed my heart to know that people were receiving those messages, and at the same time learning how wonderful and kind the people of these Latin American countries are. They're not the criminals and monsters the media would have you believe they are.

The scenery was fantastic everywhere, and at once both so contrasting and similar. I loved the wildness of the north, the redwoods and atmosphere of the American Pacific coast, the challenge of the Sonoran Desert, and the charm of the colonial cities in Central America. I hope I've convinced at least a few people to toss aside the all-inclusive resorts and stop, or at least take a side trip on their vacations, to see what these cities and towns and cultures are all about, to experience life there.

Guatemala and the volcanoes around Lake Atitlan were a breathtaking experience, figuratively and literally, as we descended those steep hills and climb backed up them. There was something almost otherworldly about riding through that part of the world. And El Salvador too was a pleasant surprise. The landscape was lush, the people were friendly, the roads were well-maintained, it was cleaner than other Central American countries, and the beaches was beautiful. The only downside to our time in that country was having such problems with the van's tire.

The time spent in Honduras was too brief for me to have really experienced anything other than to be reminded of how much garbage humanity creates and the infrastructure necessary to take care of it well. And surprisingly, Nicaragua had the best roads, though the Pan-American Highway was in good shape too for most of the way.

There wasn't anything that caught my attention in Costa Rica, but that's only because it's already my home and we only made a few brief stops. The foliage and flowers and history are just as delightful as in the other Central American countries, and I suppose there was the Crocodile Bridge and all those enormous crocs.

But while I was out riding the other day, I did remember that as we were riding through Alaska with all the forest fires burning there, people were worried when they hadn't heard from us. They were afraid perhaps we'd gotten caught in the fires. But no, we just had no cellphone reception or Wi-Fi. However, all that smoke and haze made the sun turn incredibly orange, a sort of pink-orange, and you could even look at it because the smoke was so thick. While I appreciated the sight, I didn't think any more of it until we reached Panama. I was standing on the balcony with the team and my friends and looking at the moon as it rose in the east one night. It was a breathtaking bright orange ball in the sky, and I couldn't help but make the comparison between Panama and Alaska. We started the journey with a big orange sun, and we ended the journey with a big orange moon.

I remember each and every person we met on the road, and I remember all the colors of the trip, sometimes as clearly as if I was still there. There was the turquoise blue green of Boya Lake, the deep green of the Guatemalan jungle high in the mountains, and the brightly colored traditional clothing of the women in El Salvador, Guatemala, and Nicaragua. Most of all, I remember the feelings, the sun on my face as it shone through the pines after days of rain and cold, the chill of the marine layer on the Pacific coast, and the withering heat of the Sonoran Desert. Or perhaps I enjoy most the memory of the smells of the northern pines and the cedar on the logging trucks; the decaying-seaweed, fishy aroma riding down the coast of Oregon and California; and the Mexican taco stands. Or maybe still it's the sounds I remember most: the festive music on the Day of the Dead, the utter stillness on the remote Alaskan highway where the only sounds were the wind whipping through my helmet strap and the whine of my bike, or the elephant seals barking at each other as they fought for the attention of the females on the Pacific coast. Or maybe they all hold equal places in my heart.

My hope is that the documentary and this book convey my experiences and thoughts, that people can live vicariously through me if they're not in a position to undertake such a thing but are still intrigued. You might ask what made me

364 | ROBERT D. FLETCHER

think I could or should write a book or put a documentary together. No, I don't think that much of myself. But after touring the world since Beth's death in 2013 and experiencing adventure after adventure, I realized from all the comments I received on social media that people wanted to know about my experiences. They wanted to either live them through me or be motivated to create their own experiences. So perhaps my head did get a little big, but I wrote this book because I want to share everything with as many people as I can. Human connection is a wonderous thing, and it doesn't have to be live and in person to have the same effect on people, on me.

And that leads me to part two of my Octogenarian Odyssey. I've had to fast forward all my planning because I only have about six months this time to do that. It's a good thing I learned those lessons from part one because it took a good year to plan, and let's not forget that planning is a little outside my comfort zone. On that note, I've put my team in place thus far, I've found some sponsors—namely EVELO again plus Aggressor Adventures, Cyclemeter, Redshift, and Rapha though I hope to get more—and I have some folks interested in riding with me. I'm still working on the route now, but I know I really want to ride through the Bolivian salt flats if I can, even though I've heard it can be terribly difficult. I'll have to research whether the bike will stand up to all that salt.

I have decided though, that my starting point will be Cartagena, Colombia, and I'll head down south somehow to Ecuador and Peru and Patagonia before finishing in Argentina. The Colombian stretch will be the most arduous however, with around 40 percent of the total amount of climbing occurring there. The whole trip should end up being about the same distance as part one was and take about five months to complete. Having learned not to use Google Bike Maps though, I've spoken with a friend of mine, Joan, who did the same tour about a year ago. She's generously giving me all her GPS files showing the route she followed, so I think that's going to end up being my lifeline, that and the route I know a touring group out of Toronto took.

And then there's the problem of getting the bikes and all their accessories down to Colombia. That will create both financial and logistic issues, so I'm still working on that one as I also have to ship the car in a container and drive down there to pick up Johana and sort out all the official documents with the government. My most fervent hope is that EVELO will help with the bikes at least as part of their sponsorship given all the social-media and press coverage I try and drum up for them on my travels. With luck, they'll even cover spare parts as they did on part one.

Despite the issues attached to ending one journey and beginning another, the excitement of being on the road, having something new to do every day, and anticipating finding new accommodations in different towns and enjoying rest days in foreign places still thrums in my blood, still impels me to keep going. Knowing I'll meet more kindred spirits, be an ambassador for my country, discover more incredible landscapes, learn about new cultures, try more new foods, and unearth unexpected finds urges me to keep going, to keep riding around the world. It's that very compulsion that pushes me onward even when I want to give up, when I want to quit as I'm riding up a mountain or planning a journey or learning something new. I'll even admit that as I sit quietly at home, a feel a little sad, not at the end of part one of the journey, but at the loss of the attention I've come to learn I love so much and conversations with new people.

I suppose that's rather why I've felt less excitement and achievement since we completed the journey than I'd thought I would. I feel the loss of discovery and adventure and attention, and at the same time, I suppose I see the journey as incomplete. It's almost as though I'm just on hiatus with the second season to come in just a few months. Perhaps I'm a little crazy for always riding around the world, for pushing myself to try new things and go new places, even to ask complete strangers to sponsor my crazy plans and dreams. But my motto has always been, "All they can do is say no." It's gotten me through all the hardest moments of my life, from asking a girl to dance to asking Bill Gates and Sir Richard Branson to sponsor my Octogenarian Odyssey. And most of the time, it has worked for me. So why let fear and self-doubt get in your way? Why wait for retirement to do something you've always wanted to do? Why quit before you've even begun?

So, I urge you, go out into the world and take a chance. Fill your small slice of time in this world with experiences. Don't wait, don't hesitate, and don't fear. If an ordinary guy can see the world and bike among volcanoes and outrun horse flies, you can try something new. You may or may not live longer, but you'll live better. And while you're living life to the fullest, stay tuned for Octogenarian Odyssey Part Two, Never Stop Pedaling.

Just this morning in my inbox I received the following email from Guinness World Records. It is now official; my team and I accomplished one of my goals and I am now the world record holder.

Dear Robert Fletcher,

We are thrilled to inform you that your application for Longest journey made by a motorized bicycle has been successful and you are now the Guinness World Records Title Holder!

You are now eligible for one complimentary Guinness World Records certificate.

You can order your complimentary certificate and purchase further certificates for your new record by visiting the Guinness World Records store.

For more information on certificates please visit our certificate FAQs.

Access your Online Application Summary here.

Please log into the store using your Guinness World Records account login and password and your free certificate will be added to your basket automatically.

Congratulations, you are Officially Amazing!

Kind regards,

Records Management Team
Guinness World Records

A SMALL REQUEST

If you enjoyed this book, please take a few moments to write a review on Amazon—or wherever you bought the book—for me. As you've learned, I'm just an ordinary guy, not a marketing expert, so I can use all the help I can get to try and hopefully motivate as many people as possible. So to keep sharing my message with seniors and others and to continue sharing my adventures with the world, I need your assistance. Just a short review will have a powerful impact and help my mission succeed.

I guarantee I will personally read and respond to every review. Your help and your thoughts matter to me.

Thank you! From my family to yours.

From left, Annika, me, Janet

From left, Julie, me, Gloria

A WORD ON BIKE SAFETY

Riding a road bike or an e-bike offers exhilaration, excitement, and adventure whether you ride long distances or short, but it also comes with responsibility. It's up to you to stay safe, for you, your family, your friends, and even motor vehicle drivers. So while cycling may not be for everyone, if it's something you're interested in trying, always keep these rules in mind when you head out on the road—and before you even leave.

Before You Ride

Prepare Your Bike:

1. Always keep your brakes and chain in good shape.
2. Ensure your tires are correctly inflated and the treads are still acceptable.
3. Adjust your seat height so your leg is nearly straight when your foot is flat on the lower pedal.
4. Adjust your handlebars so they're comfortable and the stem is tightly fastened.
5. Equip your bike with both a bell and a horn. A bell is to warn pedestrians; a horn is to warn vehicles.
6. Add a headlight and a taillight—night AND day. A reflector just isn't enough most times. And both out of respect and driver/rider safety, don't use a flashing light as it can blind on-coming drivers and riders. If you must use a flashing light, en-sure it's on the pulse setting, not the strobe setting as strobes can precipitate seizures.
7. Install a mirror, whether on your bike, glasses, or helmet. It's easier to handle a situation if you can see it coming.
8. Most importantly, make sure you have the right size bike for you. Riding a bike that's too big for you can cause you to fall and have difficulties dismounting, both of which will likely re-sult in injury.
9. And if you're riding an e-bike, add these steps to your checklist:

10. Make sure your battery is charged—and if you're cycling a long distance, have a backup battery.
11. Ensure your lights are working properly—front and back.
12. Check the quick release levers or nuts on your axles to make sure they're tight.

Prepare Yourself:

1. WEAR A HELMET. You will inevitably fall, whether it's due to loose gravel, a pothole, a loose rock, a broken spoke, or even not unclipping your foot in time. Worse yet, you may collide with something: another rider, an obstacle on the road, or a vehicle. Whether you're young or old, whether it's hot or cold, whether you're on a busy highway or quiet side road, WEAR A HELMET.
2. Be visible and streamlined. Wear reflective clothing, including on your sides, and tuck in or strap down any loose clothing so nothing can get stuck in your chain or get in your way at the worst possible moment.
3. Protect your hands and skin. Wear gloves to improve your grip and protect your hands from the elements. It's hotter and brighter on the road than you think because the sun reflects off the surface. Also wear gloves for that inevitable moment when you will fall to protect them from road rash. From personal experience, use sunscreen before you go out, even if it's cloudy. You do not want a doctor to cut pieces of skin out of you every few months.
4. Ensure you have supplies for your ride. Carry water to avoid dehydration. It sets in faster than you think. Also carry a high-protein, high-calorie snack in case you're out too long or you exert more effort than you expect.
5. Pack supplies for your bike. Carry tire tubes and the necessary tools to fix a flat or a broken chain.
6. Always have a phone with you, especially if you're biking offroad.
7. Ask your family or friends to track your phone if you're biking offroad, in the backcountry, or long distance.
8. Plan your route in advance, especially when riding long distance, cycling to a new destination, or riding on a new route. Always use an updated cycling map and keep in mind your ability and experience.

If you're riding an e-bike, all the same rules apply to you.

While You Ride

1. Ride with care. Ride in a straight line and do your best to be predictable.

2. Ride distraction free. Don't use mobile devices or headphones so you can always be aware of your surroundings. If you ride with music, use just one earbud and refrain from skipping forward or backward on your playlist.

3. Communicate with other riders and drivers. Always use hand signals when turning, slowing down, and stopping. Before passing, warn riders with your bell and your voice. Use your horn to warn drivers of your presence or a situation.

4. Respect road rules. While bicycles are allowed on most of the same roads as vehicles in most places, that means you have the same responsibilities as drivers. Know the rules of the road and obey traffic signals, signs, and right-of-way rules, such as passing only on the left.

5. Pay special attention at stoplights. Wait a few extras seconds before going at a green light to ensure no drivers are running a yellow or red light.

6. Be aware, follow the law, shoulder check, and use hand signals and your mirror when changing lanes.

7. Avoid high-traffic roads wherever possible.

8. Ride with traffic, not against it. It may sound obvious, but some people believe it's safer to see the traffic coming. However, the opposite is true. More

bicycle-car collisions occur because drivers don't look for traffic coming in the wrong direction.

9. Make eye contact with other riders and drivers, especially at intersections and stoplights.

10. Yield to pedestrians. Go slower in pedestrian areas, yield to those on foot on sidewalks, and be aware that in many places, the law prohibits riding a bike on sidewalks.

11. Share paths respectfully. Keep your speed to 15 km/hour or less when you ride on a mixed-use path, be aware of your surroundings, slow down before crossings and junctions, and respect pedestrians.

12. Use the buddy system. Ride with a friend when riding long distance and/or when riding in the backcountry. Also carry a phone and have family or friends track it.

If you're riding an e-bike, also follow these safety rules:

13. Ride in the lane in urban areas unless there are designated bike lanes. It's much safer than hugging the curb, gives you more room to maneuver in an unexpected situation, and makes you more visible to drivers. It also eliminates any chance of being "doored" by a parked car or even traffic.

14. Ride at the posted speed limit in town. Most urban areas have low speed limits in the first place, and when it is higher, traffic is often moving slower simply due to the stop-and-go nature of traffic.

15. Ride defensively as you would when you're driving. See situations before they occur. For example, many drivers think "slow" when they see a bicycle or even an e-bike. They'll underestimate your speed

and assume they can take a turn or cut in front of you when in truth, you're going as fast as they are, so they cannot. ALWAYS assume drivers will exercise bad judgment and you'll be that much safer.

16. Be aware of drunk drivers. They are out there at any time of the day or night, but especially on Friday and Saturday nights. And though it may not bear saying, don't drink and ride.

NOTE: *Most importantly, control your road rage. Even cycling, it will pop up. Accept that you will be cut off, vehicles will come at you in your lane, and you will get squeezed by buses and trucks. Just pull over and let a line of traffic go by instead. Getting angry will only get you hurt—or worse.*

The bottom line here is don't be like me. Don't learn bike safety the hard way. I've endured terrific road rash, broken bones, broken helmets, and broken bikes from all my incidents on the road. The only thing I haven't experienced is a broken skull, and that's thanks to me always, always wearing a helmet.

Biking can be both fun and safe. It's an incredible way to see the world, learn new things, meet new people, gain some freedom, and stay healthy. You just have to stay safe as you do it. And over time, much of it will become automatic as with any other skill. But never become complacent. Tragedy can come out of nowhere and when you least expect it. Have fun, be happy, and be safe.

OCTOGENARIAN ODYSSEY SPONSORS

Corporate Sponsors

Aggressor Adventures: the adventurer's choice for world-class, intimate, and artful adventures on ocean, river, or land.

Airbnb: Find the perfect place to stay at an amazing price in 191 countries.

Classic Vacations: Specializing in long-term rentals in Mexico.

EVELO Bicycles: EVELO makes elegant yet powerful electric bikes for recreation, commuting, and exercise. Every bike comes with a 4-year/20,000-mile warranty.

Grove Enterprise: Tela Communication

iFlyCameras: Aerial and Ground Video/Photo-Video Production

Ironsimith Hard Helmets: Smart helmets with Bluetooth and camera

McGrady Rourke Investments: Managing investments to ensure growth, preservation, and income flow is the heart of what we do.

Rapha: Wherever and whenever you ride because it's never just a ride. Discover a range of new colors and styles across this season's collections.

Redshift: Redshift Sports' innovative cycling components allow riders of all abilities to get the most out of the bikes they already own.

Swagman Bike Racks: All our racks are backed with a limited lifetime warranty.

Individual Donors

- June McGregor

- George and Marilyn Clarke

- Val and Dave Olson

- Bernice Aebly

- Joan Donohue

- Tim Bellaart

- Jen Berkly Jackson

- John Hulford

- Rachel Champagne

- Ben Johnson, Mountain Madness

- John Adomonis

- Nina and Richard Tartakoff

- Corrine Leistikow

- Barb and Marc Tougas

- Marija Slavnic